George W Strettell

The Ficus Elastica in Burma Proper

George W Strettell

The Ficus Elastica in Burma Proper

ISBN/EAN: 9783744761062

Printed in Europe, USA, Canada, Australia, Japan

Cover: Foto ©Thomas Meinert / pixelio.de

More available books at **www.hansebooks.com**

THE
FICUS ELASTICA IN BURMA PROPE

OR

A NARRATIVE OF MY JOURNEY IN SEARCH OF IT:

BY

G. W. STRETTELL.

Rangoon:
PRINTED AT THE GOVERNMENT PRESS.

THE
FICUS ELASTICA IN BURMA PROPER

OR

A NARRATIVE OF MY JOURNEY IN SEARCH OF IT;

A DESCRIPTIVE ACCOUNT OF ITS HABITS OF GROWTH AND THE PROCESS FOLLOWED BY THE KAKHYENS IN THE PREPARATION OF CAOUTCHOUC.

Accompanied by a Map

SHEWING THE GEOGRAPHICAL DISTRIBUTION OF THE TREE IN ASSAM AND BURMA PROPER.

BY

G. W. STRETTELL.

Rangoon:
PRINTED AT THE GOVERNMENT PRESS.

1876.

CONTENTS.

PREFACE.

	Page
Chapter I.—Introduction	1
Chapter II.—Stay at Mandalay from 14th to 18th December 1873	26
Chapter III.—Journey between Mandalay and Bhamo, including return voyage	55
Chapter IV.—Bhamo, including a trip to the Kachyen hills viâ the Taping river	73
Chapter V.—From Bhamo to Mun-tsoung (latitude 26°) and back viâ Mogoung	121
Chapter VI.—General recapitulation of all facts associated with the *Ficus elastica*	208
General Index	I—V
Table of Errata	I—II

MAP

shewing the Geographical distribution of the tree in Assam and Burma Proper.

PREFACE.

THE INTRODUCTORY chapter sufficiently accounts for the delay in the submission of my MSS. to the press in the first instance, it therefore now only remains for me to explain the reason for so many months having elapsed before the completion of the work.

The nature of my official duties demanding my presence in the districts for protracted periods, it was not until my return to headquarters, after gaps of two or three months, that I was in a position to revise proofs and sanction their being finally struck off. Unfortunately, at such intervals, it often so happened that the Government Press was over-crowded with other work, or that there was a deficiency of the type in which this report is printed : thus, when I was in a position to push on the work, the press was not available ; or *vice versâ*, and so on this see-saw game was maintained, until more than one " reminder" from Government brought forth an order from the Secretariat, that my report was to keep pace with other official publications, which resulted in the completion of the last four chapters within the last six months.

My inability to do justice to the valuable materials at my disposal, has ever been a source of deep regret to me, and when it is found I am the first European who has trodden portions of the country described, and that many other parts referred to still remain involved in a mystery equally attractive to the traveller and naturalist ; the most striking feature in this report will unquestionably be the absence of interest it affords, and to no one can this fact be more obvious than it is to myself; indeed, the scant manner in which I have alluded to the affinities, languages, customs, and faiths of the different tribes met with, makes me wish I had confined myself to the details set forth in the concluding chapter until circumstances permitted of my turning to better account the information I am in possession of; but it is now too late for alterations, or even for a final polish to the rough and sometimes incoherent simplicity of the work, it must therefore go from me in its present unvarnished condition, with the one redeeming clause, that, if there is an absence of interest in the narrative, accuracy has been strictly maintained, for I have carefully endeavoured to overcome all approach to exaggeration.

Compilation, it will be admitted, is at all times an arduous undertaking, but in the present case the task has become more laborious by my having had to conduct it in the midst of other business which more than absorbed the time ordinarily allotted to Office duty; thus the few hours I could borrow from night was the only available time for this work—leisure hours, that after the business of the day, were alike ill-adapted for calm reminiscences of past impressions or the unravelling of voluminous notes. Apart from this drawback, the collation had to be carried on in the districts, where I was both debarred the use of a scientific library—which materially detracts, from the value of deductions drawn—and the assistance and advice of scientific men—a *sine qua non* to one so absolutely unscientific as myself. This will amply account for the very superficial manner in which I have treated on the *fauna* and *flora* of the country traversed; but I hope during my furlough in England, with the aid of my extensive collections and the assistance of competent authorities, to re-produce an illustrated edition of this work, that will prove of equal interest to the general reader and naturalist.

Chapters I. to IV. will doubtless hang heavily on those familiar with the physical geography of the country between Rangoon and Bhamo, such parts having already been frequently written about by literary architects; but as I was accurate in my observations, and regardless of the experience of those who had gone before me, I yet hope the subject has not been entirely exhausted, and that the reader may find something new or attractive in my narrative.

I owe my best thanks to Mr. Buchanan for the trouble he has taken in preparing proofs for me—no easy task, when dealing with the manuscript of one whose caligraphy has often been compared to the trails of a spider after an ink bath.

I would here also beg respectfully to draw attention to the very commendable manner in which my Interpreter, Moung Yan Sing, behaved throughout the journey, boldly facing every difficulty and standing by me in the thick of danger; and I trust the local Government will see fit to recognize his good services in such manner as may be deemed adequate for work faithfully performed, even at the jeopardy of his own life. He is not only a remarkably well-educated man, but is strikingly intelligent, and I can without hesitation strongly recommend him for promotion to the rank of Sub-Assistant Conservator—an office he is peculiarly adapted for, having a good constitution, and already acquainted with the local (and in many instances botanical) names of most of the forest trees, and their various economic uses.

It now only remains for me to add that, although my mission was attended with privation and danger, yet I shall ever have reason to look back on this tour as a bright and merry holiday; the work deputed me, is a life I revel in, and the fact that I have succeeded in bringing my errand to a successful end, is of itself ample compensation for the hardships encountered.

Although my connection with this province is about to be severed, and it is questionable whether I shall ever see the fruits of my labour, yet I shall always feel a deep interest in this branch of forest industry—a new and important source of economic wealth, that must redound to the credit of the Chief Commissioner (the Hon'ble Ashley Eden), whose great administrative powers has rendered his name a household word in the province.

G. W. STRETTELL,
RANGOON; *Deputy Conservator of Forests,*
The 11th April 1876. *British Burma.*

THE
FICUS ELASTICA
IN
BURMA PROPER.

CHAPTER I.
INTRODUCTION.

SOME delay having occurred in the publication of this report, it is necessary that I should briefly explain the reason. It was on the 13th May 1874, I returned to Rangoon from my mission in Upper Burma, after an absence from British territory of nearly six months. During this time such of my divisional duties as demanded immediate attention were either disposed of by the Conservator, or the Sub-Assistant Conservator in charge of the Government Timber Depôt; while other matters that could lie over till my return—which was, however, uncertain—were allowed to do so. All who have had work fall into arrears must well know how difficult it is to make up lost time; and in the present instance the ordinary difficulty was materially increased from the fact that numerous references had to be made to timber contractors, and other officials in the districts, before the questions pending decision could be disposed of. All this took time, for postal communication in Burma is confined to the more important towns, and Forest Officers have to communicate with their subordinates and others as best they can. Thus it was the 15th of July 1874 before I found my work reduced to the ordinary daily routine of a divisional officer's duty: just then, I had to leave for the districts, to select a suitable area for a lac preserve—a duty allotted me by the Chief Commissioner. By the 1st of August, I had completed this work, selected a suitable site for the "preserve," and prepared a system for introducing lac culture as a branch of forest industry. I now received a demi-official from the Conservator, informing me that the publication of my report—which I had already intimated was sufficiently advanced to pass through the press—would be postponed until my return to Rangoon, as the Chief Commissioner had

Delay in publication of report explained.

ruled it should be curtailed, and open from date of my arrival at Mandalay. This rather upset my original arrangements, and the hours I had spent at night, compiling my notes from Rangoon northwards, were wasted as concerns the present report.

2. It had at first been my intention, before dealing with the geographical and physical character-istics of the country and river north of Mandalay, to have recorded all items of interest that came under observation from the day of embarkation at Rangoon, thus rendering my journal more complete and of greater service to future explorers of the country over which I had travelled. The present account of my tour in Upper Burma I would, however, now wish accepted merely in the light of jottings on all subjects other than those affecting the main object of my mission, to which I intend devoting a separate chapter, wherein I shall recapitulate, *seriatim*, all matters of interest associated with the *Ficus elastica*; finally treating briefly on the system I propose should be adopted for the introduction of the tree into the forests of British Burma, together with instructions, which may prove useful, for propagating the species, should it hereafter be found expedient to replenish our stock from Upper Burma. Mr. Nepean, the Assistant Conservator, under whose management I had placed the propagation of lac, being new to the work, it was necessary I remained in his sub-division for a time, to start the project; and, while instructing him in the system, I also completed the necessary arrangements for the supply of sleepers in my division for the Rangoon and Irrawaddy Valley (State) Railway, and inspected the Kyatsoo Creek, with a view to establishing an unimpeded through traffic during the cold season. It was the 10th September ere I returned to Rangoon. The Government Press was now overstocked with work, and unable to take up my report; and as the map that accompanies it had not been received from Calcutta, where it was lithographed, there was no immediate hurry for the work being taken in hand. I again left for the district, where my services were urgently required, on the 6th October, and did not return to Rangoon for two months. On the 10th of December 1874, I solicited permission to print my report, and on the 3rd of January 1875, sanction was accorded.

Present narrative to be received as jottings on subjects foreign to object of mission—a separate chapter being devoted to this latter object.

3. Having explained the cause of delay in the publication of my travels, and accounted for the incomplete form in which my journal is now presented, it is only left for me to say a few words as to the origin of my mission to Upper Burma, concluding this introductory chapter with a brief notice of Prome and

Origin and object of mission to Upper Burma explained.

Thayetmyo,—both places being in a measure associated with the duty deputed to me. I shall also notice a few of the more interesting places passed *en route*, and describe the process of box-making at Nyoun-goo, the general impression being at present that the articles are lacquer-ware, which is erroneous.

4. It was in July 1873 I first heard through the Conservator that the Chief Commissioner had conferred on me the honour of carrying out the wishes of the Government of India, regarding the formation of *Ficus elastica* plantations, and ascertaining the best method for working them in British territory. To facilitate this object, Mr. Eden directed that I should at once proceed to Upper Burma, and examine the forests there, making myself familiar with the general habits of the tree, the soil and locality best suited to it, the different methods of tapping, and the various systems pursued, in order to bring about the coalescence of the *caoutchouc*. The unhealthiness of the forests and difficulty of travelling during the rainy season, however, proved a barrier to my starting at once, and it was considered expedient to postpone my visit till November. Accordingly, I started on my mission from Rangoon, on the 22nd of that month, in the steamer *Ashley Eden*, this being her maiden voyage. The strength of my party consisted of one Burman interpreter and seven Burman peons, three of whom were armed each with an old *Brown Bess* and half a dozen rounds of ammunition.

5. The voyage between Rangoon and Mandalay occupied a fortnight, which I believe is a little over the average run at this season; the delay was partly brought about by accidents that occurred at different times, and partly by the low state of the river and shifting nature of its channels, which more than once necessitated the anchor being cast and soundings taken before the navigable channel could be decided on. Each day, as we progressed onwards, fresh charms presented themselves—scenes of interest, not only to the pleasure-seeking excursionist, but equally so to one in search of wealth and knowledge. The scenery becomes bolder and more diversified the further we recede from British territory, until, a few miles south of the Golden City, we unexpectedly find ourselves entering what nearer resembles the Bay of Naples than any other place still fresh in my memory. Just here the river takes an almost right-angular bend, and it is not until the elbow is rounded that the beauty of the scenery is fully apparent. Now we find ourselves steaming beneath the picturesque range of the Sagain hills, studded with Buddhistic buildings, of all forms and sizes. The pagodas, but lately white-washed, and capped with *htees* recently gilded, and the dark tripled-

Time occupied in voyage from Rangoon to Mandalay.

roofed monasteries,* set in clumps of palms and other arborescent vegetation—all illuminated by the glorious lights of an eastern sunset—serve, with Mandalay hill as a back-ground, to complete a picture that cannot fail to impress itself on the memories of all who have been fortunate enough to view it.

6. After leaving Rangoon, the first place we remained at sufficiently long to admit of a ramble on shore, was the neat little village of Donabyoo, which is celebrated for the manufacture of mats made from the *Morantha dichotoma*. The pagoda here is also celebrated, I believe, and at certain seasons attracts thousands of people from great distances to witness the peculiar light sometimes to be seen encircling the *htee*. Like many other phenomena, various fanatic traditions are attached to this light; it is supposed to have something ominous in its nature, and that success will attend all who have the good fortune to witness it. It is not improbable that the halo is nothing more than what is to be seen round mast-heads in northern and southern latitudes, or, perhaps, proceeds from a decomposition of animal or vegetable matter, or it may be brought about by the evolution of gases, which spontaneously ignite in the atmosphere. But I must not give more time to a description of this station: our stock of fuel has been replenished, and we are off, so I proceed with my *jottings* further north.

Particulars of visit to Donabyoo.

7. Between Rangoon and Zaloon the scenery is uninteresting in the extreme, though not so, perhaps, historically. The features of the country are in general paludosal, and the banks lined with tall *Saccharum* and *Arundo* grasses; but arborescent vegetation is markedly sparse. Zaloon is the northern limit of tidal influence, and also that of the *Pandanus odoratis*.

Description of scenery and observations made between Rangoon and Zaloon.

---

* The origin of these tripled-roofed monasteries will be readily understood by the following quotation from the *Mahawanso*, on the dedication by the Rajah Dutthaganimni, of the Maha Thapo, in Ceylon, and which words manifest the deep signification of the umbrella as a symbol of Buddha. He said:—Thrice over do I dedicate my kingdom to the Redeemer of the World, the Divine Teacher, the Bearer of the Triple Canopy—the canopy of the heavenly host, the canopy of mortals, and the canopy of eternal emancipation."

Yule, in his *Ava*, seems to coincide with Burney as to the origin of the peculiar class of architecture one of the pagodas at Mengoon presents; and the interpretation of the seven-roofed *khyoungs* may be traced to the same source I have no doubt. Referring to the pagoda at Mengoon, Burney writes:—" Perhaps this structure is symbolical of the great conical mountain Myen-mo (Maha-mera), surrounded by its seven concentric and graduated ranges, in the centre of this *sakwala* or mundane system, which again is encompassed by a circular wall of rock, called the *sakwala-gala*—(see Hardy's *Manual of Buddhism*, chapter I.). One of the Burmese feasts at the termination of their *Wa*, or lent, is called *T'sec-me-myen-mo*, or *Myenmo* lamp-lights. The streets are illuminated, and in them are exhibited high, round structures: to represent Mount Myen-mo covered with little figures of its spiritual inhabitants."

simus, though this tree is met with occasionally the whole way up the river, the natives cultivating it for its fragrant flowers, with which the young women adorn their hair; and also for its fruit, which is used for hackling thread. A Burman's love for flowers is remarkable: where circumstances admit, each house is fronted with a few roses, *hibiscus*, or a gorgeous creeper; and few dwellings will be found without their flower-pots filled with some favourite plant; boatmen even delight in decorating their craft with these embellishments of nature, while the gentle sex do not consider their toilets complete unless a tastefully-arranged wreath of flowers entwines their hair; and yet, perhaps, there is no country in which its gardens serve as a worse guide—chronologically, politically, or geographically—than those of Burma.

8. The *Rhizophora mangle* is, of course, the staple shrub of the delta, where also varieties of the *Acanthaceæ* are observed. The fruit of *Rhizophora mangle* is edible, and attention might be turned with profit to the tanning properties of its bark. Nothing is more desired in England than a substitute for oak-bark; but the bark of this shrub could not be exported with profit, owing to its bulk, though extracts might be made in the country, and shipped with ease. It would be well worth a trial, as an extract of this tree is said to perform its office in half the time of oak-bark. The tannin would have to be made in an earthenware vessel, as iron communicates a principle which causes the leather to become brittle and discoloured.

Properties of Rhizophora mangle briefly discussed.

9. We are now well out of tidal influence, and I was told would bid adieu to our candle-light pests—but not so; for no sooner do we make fast for the night, and the head-wind dies away, than we are tormented by small flies, of innumerable species, mosquitoes, and that most odious of insects, the flying bug,* all of which, attracted by the light, swarm round the lamps in such numbers as often to extinguish them, even at the peril of their own lives. These little pests seem to find a pleasure in worrying all who are within the influence of the light. The bugs insinuate themselves between one's skin and clothes, diffusing a most disagreeable scent, which is only intensified by any attempt to release them; saucy crickets, too, swarm and spring up at one's face, whilst the mosquitoes maintain a constant guerilla warfare, trying no less to the patience than

Visitation of insects by candle-light.

---

* The disagreeable scent at all times exhaled by the bug tribe *(Geo corisæ)* is no doubt the insect's only means of defence and guard against extermination.

to the nerves. None but those who have been assailed by these most insatiable of bloodsuckers can really understand the injury and discomfort they cause to man and beast.

10. Shortly after leaving Myanoung, the river becomes more defined in its course, and, even here and there, the erosion of its high banks is observable, though not, perhaps, to such an extent as marks the characteristic features of the Indus. The surrounding landscape, as we steam onward, becomes more and more engaging—in a word, we are leaving the low, flat country of the delta, and entering the region of mountains and woodlands, with a foreground of richly-cultivated plains. The Arakan range, with its prettily-wooded slopes, here sends out an eccentric spur to the water's edge, whose face is decorated with carvings of a Bhuddhistic type, many of which are of very recent date. This forms the civil boundary of the Thayetmyo and Tharrawaddy Districts, and here the river becomes more tortuous in its course, and the current increases in strength. Proceeding onwards, the hills are sufficiently neared to distinguish the class of arborescent vegetation now fast falling before the ruthless hand of man, to make room for culture yielding a more speedy return.

Description of country from north of Myanoung to Prome.

11. I was not a little surprised to hear from Mr. Hough, late Sub-Assistant Conservator of Forests, that a large proportion of these clearings had been effected within the last three years; and even still may be seen large areas covered with felled trees ready for burning—a process of agriculture familiarly known as *toungya* in Burma, and corresponding with the *dyah* of India. If clearing continues at the same ratio in this vicinity, we may expect to see, at no distant date, the whole of this range denuded of its timber. In this instance less harm is being done, perhaps, than generally results from this barbarous method of culture, for the trees felled are, as a rule, useless timber, and are replaced by fruit trees; nevertheless, in estimating the benefit of forests, it is necessary to consider the value of trees, both individually and collectively—that is, as furnishing the every-day necessaries of life, and influencing surrounding objects; but the evil effect of robbing hill-sides and tops of their trees is too well known to be dilated on here. This system of cultivation is, and I fear always will be, a bone of contention between the Revenue Officials and Forest Officers. The latter, alive to the interests of their own department, point to the calamities brought on other nations by similar wasteful and destructive practices which have been permitted to continue unchecked; while the former support

Extensive toungya clearings observed. Evil effects briefly noticed.

their views, which are opposed to the summary ejectment of these tribes by the undeniable argument that it is always necessary to sacrifice revenue to the suppression of crime.

They very rightly point out that the principal tribes, who are dependent on this rude mode of culture, are a *quasi*-barbarous lot, who shun the civilized world; but that, though rude and ignorant, they are not destitute of spirit, and that to attempt summarily to deprive them of this their only mode of livelihood, would simply drive them to despair, and act as a stimulus to cattle-lifting and other crime, if not to open rebellion;—while, if they fled the country, the last state of the forests would be worse than the first. There is no doubt but the arguments advanced on both sides are sound, and deserving of consideration. The system, then, that suggests itself to me as one most likely to meet the requirements of both departments, is to teach these predatory tribes, by example, to appreciate a higher class of agriculture. This is not, of course, the work of a day, or even a year, but it is to be accomplished by a little perseverance and kindness; and the first move towards working the reform will be to secure the services of these hill tribes, in consideration of free grants of land and other privileges they are known to appreciate. This is the system I have often followed, and found to answer admirably well.

12. We have now reached a part of the Irrawaddy that requires no great stretch of imagination to recall to memory some of the more charming views on the Rhine—near the castle of Drachenfels;—the orchards of carica, papaya, custard-apples, and pomegranates, forming a substitute for the artistically-grown vineyards that yield the well-known "Drachen-blut" or Dragon's-blood wine. It is from here, we are told at page 9 of Yule's *Ava*, that the vegetation begins to lose its tropical character—a conclusion apparently arrived at by the sparse and stunted habits of its growth. I am not prepared, however, to endorse this opinion, but attribute the parched, unhealthy character of the trees to geological causes, rather than to climatic influence. Groves of palms may still be seen growing in luxuriant profusion, while the cocoanut also thrives.

Charming views and extensive orchards.

13. Besides these were noted the following trees:—*Shorea robusta, Urtica fructibus*, teak, tamarind, *Ficus, Bombax, Gardenia floribunda;* and, among the more common species, *Stravadium, Arostichum difforme,* and *Epiphytical orchiden;* while by far the greater portion of the short turf grass, is formed of *Andropogon acicularis, Cynodon Dactyton,* and, in sandy places, *Imperata cylindrica*. Where the soil is wetter,

Trees and grasses noted.

Ameletia Indica is abundant, giving a heath-like colour to the turf with its pale purple flowers. Wherever there is standing water, its surface is reddened by the *Azolla : Salvinia* is also common.

14. At Shoaydoung Myomat, which is on the east bank of the river, eight miles below Prome, rocks were for the first time noticed above water, and a few miles further north may be seen the teak plantation of the Forest Department; but as there was no time for inspecting it, I refrain from passing an opinion.* At a quarter to four P.M. on the 27th, we anchored abreast of Prome, having accomplished this portion of our voyage in 124 hours.

Rocks first observed.

15. There is nothing sufficiently attractive in this town to engage the attention of voyagers, beyond, perhaps, its having a more civilized appearance than any place hitherto passed. To a resident, no doubt, the case is different, though we are not told so—the result of a press of work probably preventing officers devoting their time to anything beyond the usual daily routine of business. Running parallel with the river is a row of European houses, fronted by a strand nicely avenued with trees, valuable both as shelter and ornament. In the background is the town, studded with pagodas and other Buddhistic buildings, set in groves of palms and plantains, all of which combine to make a charming picture as viewed from the river. The population within the municipal town of Prome is 25,631, and in the district, 266,067, the increase within the last five years having been, respectively, 536 and 23,291. This of itself speaks for the growing prosperity of the district and the contentedness of the people. Prome, I am told, is noted principally for silk-weaving; but amongst its other manufactures are the following, which are arranged according to their relative importance :—

The town of Prome; its population and manufactures reviewed.

1st.—Gold-smiths.
2nd.—Silk-weavers.
3rd.—Carvers.
4th.—Workers in lacquer-ware.
5th.—Copper-smiths.
6th.—Gilders.
7th.—Gold-leaf manufacturers.

16. There are 1,651 silk-weavers in the town of Prome, and 6,139 in the district. The raw silk, I believe, is chiefly obtained from the

---

* Please, future excursionists, do not, however, note this plantation as one of the engaging sights on the river; nor be too severe with the "critic's lash;" for, remember, all things must have a beginning, and this plantation, I am told, ranks among the first of arboricultural experiments in Burma.

Shoaylay, Myodoung, and Yunbein Circles of the Prome District: a small amount comparatively is obtained from the Kyoongone, Mahathaman, Poungday, and Padoung Districts, the latter place being on the west bank of the river. There are no factories for the manufacture of raw silk in the town of Prome or its immediate vicinity; but a large proportion of the silk goods exposed for sale in the bazaar are manufactured at Shoaydoung and Mandalay. The Shoay Sandaw Pagoda, which was so shaken by the earthquake of 1858 as to bring down the *htee* and portion of the superstructure, is, of course, one of the sights to be seen, while the nicely-designed market also repays the trouble of a visit. About midday is the time to see this latter place to advantage; then the different stalls, generally kept by women, are tastefully arranged with gaudy Manchester piece-goods, and other foreign and indigenous tawdry, which sell at fabulous prices. The *beau monde* of the place are now to be seen promenading the arcade in crowds, dressed in their gayest attire, which rivals even the colours of the rainbow, and add materially to the gaiety of the scene.

17. I had not much leisure, however, to spend among this gay and happy throng, for the little time there was to spare I devoted to an examination of the few *Ficus elastica* trees that are cultivated by followers of the Buddhist faith; but, as our stay was too limited for me to gain all the necessary information, I was obliged to ask Mr. Hough, the Sub-Assistant Conservator of that division, to assist me in collecting data, which he, in his usual good-natured way, very kindly undertook to do, accomplishing his task in that faultless manner that characterizes his work generally. I cannot do better than quote verbatim Mr. Hough's replies to my questions. " With " regard to the India-rubber trees planted by the Forest Department " in the Prome plantation, they came from Bhamo, were obtained " and brought down by Captain Spearman; twenty-three plants " in number, of which six plants were sent to Rangoon for the " plantations in that division. They were received in May 1872 " and planted in June of the same year; their heights varied from " 9 to 18 inches—two of them were 4 feet in height; they lived " about ten months. It is not known whether or not they were " seedlings or cuttings,—believed to be the former. They were " planted, some in the valleys or *quin* of the plantation, and some " on slopes. The soil in the valleys is alluvium, derived from " sandstone; on the slopes sandstone soil moderately deep. " The soil in which the plants were brought down from Bhamo " was put in round the roots, when they were planted at the planta-

Marginal note: Examination of *Ficus elastica* at Prome.

"tion; they were fenced in. They were surrounded by teak trees,
" which shed their leaves in the dry weather; there being also in-
" sufficient moisture, they were found in May 1873 to have died
" without exception. There was a good deal of undergrowth weeds,
" &c., around them.
 " With regard to the India-rubber trees in the town of Prome
" there were five trees, *viz.*, one at the big pagoda, called Shoay
" Sandaw; two at the temple or " Tasoung'," called Pooteing-koh-
" ka-tasoung (ပုဒိန်ကိုကာသောင်); one at the Shoay Palindaw Pagoda
" (ရွှေပုလ္လင်တော်ဘုရား), Nawing quarter; and one at the Kangyin
" (ကန်ရွင်) *kyoung*, near the Shoay Sandaw Pagoda.
 " 1*st*.—The tree at the Shoay Sandaw Pagoda.
  " It was planted there thirteen years ago, and was brought
   originally from Mandalay.

   " Height approximate ...   ... About 14'
   " Girth of stem about 8' from ground ... 1'   9½"
   " Do. of thickest aërial root ... ... 1'   1⅜"

   " Its roots are smothered in brick, piled round loosely and
    " no soil visible, so that its roots cannot grow close
    " to the surface. This tree is the parent of the other
    " four, all of which are cuttings from it: it has never
    " been tapped.
 " 2*nd*.—The tree at the Kangyin-kyoung, near the Shoay
   " Sandaw Pagoda.
  " It is a cutting from the tree at the big pagoda.

   " Height approximate ...   ... About 12'
   " Girth of stem   ...   ...   6"
   " Thickest aërial root ...   ...   3"

   " Roots do not grow along the surface. Was planted about
    " August four years ago (Burmese year 1232). The
    " outer shell of a cocoanut (the fibre) was split, then
    " tied round a branch of the big tree; this was watered
    " every morning and evening by allowing water to
    " drip slowly on it for about two months, when roots
    " appeared; then it was cut off and planted at the
    " *kyoung*, the cocoanut-shell being put into the
    " ground with it to rot and manure the roots. It was
    " carefully watered during the dry weather.
 " 3*rd*.—The two trees at the Pooteing-koh-ka-tasoung.
   " The information about these trees was obtained from
    " the daughter of the man who planted them. She

"does not remember the exact date, but says they
"were planted about ten years ago; they are cut-
"tings from the tree at the big pagoda, and were
"taken by earth wrapped round the branch instead
"of cocoanut.* These, as well as all the trees here
"were planted in sandy soil. They have never been
"tapped, but a storm broke one of them some years
"ago. They are looked after by worshippers of
"the Buddhist faith.

"No. 1 measures—
    "Girth measured 8' from ground ... 1'
    "Ditto thickest aërial root ... 7¾"
"No. 2—
    "Girth measured about 8' from the ground. 1'½"
    "Ditto thickest aërial root ... 4½"
    "Height of these trees, about 15 feet; ordi-
    "nary roots tend to a surface growth.

"The aërial roots on these trees are very numerous,
"so also are they on the tree at the big pagoda. I
"should have mentioned that the tree at the big
"pagoda (the oldest tree), when first planted, was
"about 8 inches high, has never flowered or given
"seed (nor have any of the others), and, according
"to the Burmese, it foliates and defoliates on alternate
"months throughout the year.

"*4th.*—The tree at the Shoay Palindaw Pagoda was planted,
"in the Burmese year 1233 (1871) in Kasoung (May)
"so that it is three years and one month old. It
"is a cutting from the Shoay Sandaw tree: height
"approximate, about 10 feet; girth of stem, 8¾ inches,
"aërial roots, very small. They say it was simply
"a cutting from a branch which was planted in sandy
"soil and bricked round. It was watered every four
"or five days during the dry weather, and it has
"never been tapped. All these trees are protected
"by brick-work, and there is little shade around
"them. Some of them are protected from the
"evening sun by peepul trees, or pagodas, &c. The
"stem and leaves are some of them slightly covered
"with gold leaf at the present time by the people,
"as a mark of reverence. They do this whenever

---

* This system is known in India as *Gootee* graft.

"they feel inclined; there is no fixed time for the operation. This, I think, completes the information about the India-rubber trees, except, perhaps, I might mention that some Burmans deny that the trees here are real India-rubber trees. They say they are Nyoung-peing trees (a species of creeper), but by courtesy they are called India-rubber trees from their resemblance. The trees planted at the plantation, and those sent to Rangoon, are the same as the India-rubber trees at the pagoda here. I have seen the Nyoung-peing-ngai creeper in the forests in the Prome District, and, though they are very much alike, they are not the same as the trees known as the India-rubber trees."

18. Seven hours' steaming, after leaving Prome, brought us to Thayetmyo, and at about 4 P.M. we were moored below the Irrawaddy Flotilla Company's cargo sheds, which are situated about a mile south of the Cantonment. The temporary nature of these buildings and the absence of a suitable landing-place, pier, or quay, materially detracts from its appearance, and leads passers-by to form a misconceived idea of the prosperity and importance of its trade. Thayetmyo is situated on the right bank of the river, and is the last place of importance in British territory. It is garrisoned by a wing of a European regiment, a native corps, and a battery of artillery. The road from the landing-place to the Deputy Commissioner's house, leads through that portion of the town apparently occupied by the principal shopkeepers: among them I noticed the names of some European firms. There was not much time to reconnoitre; for, after conversing on different subjects with Colonel Horace Browne, and arranging for an inspection of the silk works in the jail, before leaving on the morrow, it was too late to venture far, so we rode to the band, and returned home by a nicely-avenued road that skirted the Cantonment. I may here mention having seen, in Colonel Browne's compound, the largest *Bugainvillea spectabilis* I have ever noticed: it had quite grown out of its natural scandent habit, and assumed the form of a tree. The trunk, at four feet from the ground, measured four feet six inches in circumference.

Station of Thayetmyo noticed.

Visit to Thayetmyo Jail in connection with Sericulture.

19. According to arrangements made the previous evening, Colonel Browne, accompanied by Mr. Parrot, the Assistant Commissioner, very kindly showed me through the jail the next morning, and spared themselves no time or trouble in

explaining the various processes followed in the manufacture of the different articles. After devoting some time to an examination of the system followed in the manufacture of raw silk—the branch of industry to which my particular attention had been directed by the Chief Commissioner*—Colonel Browne had to leave for a Committee; but still I was never at a loss for information on any subject, for Mr. Parrot seemed to have taken a deep interest in all the branches of jail industry, including horticulture.

The process followed in the manufacture of raw silk has already been so carefully described by Colonel Browne, in the *British Burma Gazette*, that on this subject no more need be said. In the rearing of the insect the system is faultless; the three essentials to success—good ventilation, abundance of green food at the right time, and cleanliness—all having been carefully observed. In the process of winding, however, I noticed that the water in which the cocoons were boiled had been allowed to reach too high a temperature, which is apt not only to harden the silk, but also weaken it. There appeared, also, a want of care in reeling, so as to reduce the number of fibres taken up to a minimum. We noticed as many as six picked up and formed into one thread: this causes *goutiness*, which materially decreases the value of the staple. These errors are easily remedied, and no doubt my suggestions have already been acted on. There is no reason, that I can see, why, with a little more careful manipulation, and an abundance of green food, a far superior quality of silk may not be introduced into the market than what we have at present; and, judging from a letter received from Mr. Blechynden, Secretary, Agri-Horticultural Society of India, I am inclined to think the art of sericulture has retrograded of late years. This gentleman writes: "From what I have seen of silk from Burma, I agree with you, and think it might be considerably improved by care and attention. Some samples that came before me (the first I had ever seen from Burma) some twenty years ago, were really very good, and impressed me with the conviction that the country was well suited for the development of silk culture. Regarding the species of worm from which the silk of Burma is obtained, I will not at present hazard an opinion, for I cannot speak with any certainty. I had hoped ere this to have been able to satisfactorily dispose of this question by replies to references made to Europe; but I have been most unfortunate: my first consignment of worms, &c., never

---

* *Vide* No. 2570-94F., dated 16th September 1873, from the Secretary to the Chief Commissioner, British Burma, Public Works Department, to Conservator of Forests, British Burma.

reached their destination, while the second was so imperfect, that identification was impossible, and there has not been time for a report on the last specimens I forwarded."

I believe, among some, a certain amount of importance is attached to the end of the cocoon at which reeling commences; while others, again, hold that the operation should start from the middle. Experiments might be made in this direction, and results noted. The mulberry on which the worm feeds is cultivated in the jail garden, and is beyond doubt the *Morus indica*. It was flowering when I saw it; but the insignificance of its flowers had failed to attract attention; and the fact of its not producing fruit had evidently led to the error that it did not flower. The cause of the tree casting its flowers before the fruit forms, results from the fact of its having been propagated from cuttings—a physiological phenomenon in plant-life, not alone restricted to trees of this or any other variety in particular. The sugar-cane, when multiplied year after year from cuttings, ceases to flower, while the seeds of the *Dalbergia sissoo*, when grown from slips, are also barren. In Rangoon the *Morus indica* grows to the size of a small tree, and produces fruit abundantly. I was also shown the *Broussonetia*,* a scandent shrub, on which the silk-worms are fed when the mulberry fails. It is the same shrub as is used in China for the manufacture of paper, and in Burma for the manufacture of a coarse variety of the same material. Colonel Browne tells me this plant grows in prolific abundance all over the district; and I

---

* Parabeik, which is the Burmese for this description of paper tablets, is made both from the fibrous parts of the "wanet" variety of bamboo, and bark of the *Broussonetia*. When the former is employed, the following is the process adopted : The bamboo is cut into short lengths, and the knots discarded. The pieces are then stripped of their outer bark and soaked in lime-water sufficiently long to separate the fibre into fine, short filaments, when it is removed from the water and reduced to a pulp by pounding. This pulp is now again steeped in a fresh solution of lime and water for a week, when the fibrous matter is transferred to a large vessel of clean water, and is ready for moulding. The mould consists of a square from two inches deep with a cloth bottom, varying in size according to fancy. The manufacturer now dips his frame into the vessel containing the pulp, and, by a backward and forward motion, distributes an equal layer of the pulp on the bottom of the frame, which he lifts up, allowing the water to drain off through the cloth, and places the frame in the sun to dry. When paper is required instead of the Parabeik, the only difference in the process is regulating the thickness of the layer of pulp taken up. The system followed in the preparation of the *Broussonetia* paper is exactly similar to the above, with the exception that the bark is thrown in the lime and water, immediately it is stripped from the tree, and less time is required to reduce the fibre to a pulp. There is both black and white Parabeik. The form is simply coloured by steeping the tablets in a composition made from starch, the juice expressed from the green leaves of the *Dolichos fabæformis* and charcoal powder of teak. After drying, the tablets or paper are pressed and ready for use.

When the paper is required to spread gold leaf, it is cut into three-inch squares and subjected to a process of beating on a brass anvil, a little larger than the paper, with a wooden mallet, which gives it the appearance of good oil-silk—this sells at Rs. 4 per 1,000.

constantly met with it in my travels up to the twenty-sixth degree of north latitude.

20. Among the other works of jail industry, the manufacture of rope and gunny-bags from the roselle fibre seemed of most importance. The plant grows everywhere in Burma, and the idea of utilizing the fibre, I believe, was first started, in September 1873, by Mr. Miller, the Jailer. At present the absence of machinery of any sort renders the work far more expensive than it would otherwise be; but, even under these unfavourable circumstances, it is, I believe, found a profitable occupation.

Jail manufacture of ropes and gunny from roselle fibre.

21. The roselle *(Hibiscus Sabdariffa)* is the Indian sorrel; the people sow it either in the rains or cold weather, and the leaves serve as a very agreeable culinary vegetable. From the calyx, tarts are made, and a deliciousjelly, which serves as a capital substitute for red currants, is also prepared. There are many other fibrous plants, indigenous, which grow all over the province in abundance—such as the *Calotropis, Agave, Urena,* &c., to which attention might be turned with considerable profit. It may be remembered it was from the leaves of the *Agave* that the natives of Mexico, before the Spanish Conquest, prepared their paper; and I have seen most excellent twine made from it.

Suitability of this and other fibrous plants growing in abundance in the province, for this purpose.

22. In Sind, nearly all the fishing nets are made of twine manufactured from the *Calotropis Hamiltonii*, which is proof against the decaying principle of water. Among my notes on the medicinal properties of plants in India, I find the following quotation regarding this plant: " On the banks of the Ganges, the larger white-flowered subarboreous species prevail; in the interior, also, the smaller purple-flowered kind is seen. Dr. Davis states he has been in the habit of using the medicine copiously, and vouches for the cure of eighty cases, chiefly of leprosy, by the white variety, gathered on the Ganges, whilst the purple of Rotas and the neighbourhood was quite inert. A Dr. Irvine, again, used only the purple, and pronounced the white inert. As a rule, I believe, a preference is always given to the white."

Calotropis Hamiltonii—reputed medicinal virtues.

23. My attention was next called to some experiments that had been made in the cultivation of Havannah and Virginia tobaccos: neither variety looked very promising; but evidently great care and attention

Data on experimental cultivation of tobacco, cotton, Carolina rice, and sorghum, obtained from Mr. Parrott.

were being bestowed on the culture. I am indebted to Mr. Parrott, for the following interesting information regarding the culture of the plant from the beginning:— " The seed was sown in July, and germinated freely; but the Havannah, which was evidently old seed, only grew to a height of three or six inches, burst into flower, and died off. The Virginia gave a capital crop, * * * and I have preserved some of the seed for planting later in the season." Experiments were also being made, in growth of Egyptian and New Orleans cotton, both of which, I am informed, yielded a fair crop; but Mr. Parrott has been unable to supply me with the exact yield, as, owing to carelessness, a large proportion of the cotton was lost or destroyed. He speaks of the Egyptian variety having been very much destroyed by a small red insect. This variety has also been found in India more susceptible to the attacks of insects than any other; in some parts, I have observed, it has been attacked by a small black fly that bores a hole in the young *boll*, where it lays its eggs, and the cotton is eventually destroyed by the caterpillars. Various remedies have been tried, but the only one that has been found to succeed is, I believe, the destruction of the fly. The following figures give the results of experiments in Carolina rice culture:—10lbs. of rice were sown, and, when about one foot high, transplanted into an area of 2,660 square feet: the yield was 32lbs. of paddy. Mr. Parrott attributes so small a yield to an insufficiency of rain at the right time—an opinion I am inclined to endorse, as it was only on those portions where the water seemed first to have failed (the ground having a fall towards the middle) that the crop suffered. The success with which the culture of sorgham was attended will be gleaned from the following extract from Mr. Parrott's letter :—" Four lbs. of sorgham were sown in an area of 150 by 75 feet. From 1,678lbs. stalk, 390lbs. of juice was obtained, which yielded 64lbs. of molasses." I much regretted having so to hurry through my visit, for there was much that interested me, and which might have formed a subject for a day's enquiry, instead of a couple of hours; but my time was limited, and I had to be on board again by 8 A.M.

24. We left Thayetmyo at 8.30 A.M. on the 29th, and at 9 A.M. anchored at Allanmyo, on the opposite bank. Here is the frontier custom-house, and extra barrack accommodation for European troops, in case of an epidemic breaking out at Thayetmyo, which, at certain seasons of the year, I am told, is insufferably hot and unhealthy. This might be expected from its position; and, whether regarded from a sanitary or strategical point of view, it almost seems a matter for

Allanmyo briefly noticed.

(17)

surprise why the former town, instead of the latter, had not been chosen as the head-quarters for troops. There are no doubt good and sound reasons for the selection, though not obvious to passers-by, who, as a matter of course, base their ideas on the physical characteristics of the country and hearsay report, which, in this instance, is not in favour of Thayetmyo. Shortly after leaving Allanmyo, the frontier station of Meaday is reached, and here the limits of British territory cease. The boundary is defined by two masonry pillars—one on either side of the river—but whose insignificant appearance suggests to the traveller the idea that they were not intended as permanent landmarks.

25. Meaday presents the first sign of the Burmese appreciation of European intelligence, by the introduction of a neatly-constructed telegraph office—communication by wire now being in a measure, established between this and the capital, Mandalay. Here the precipitous alluvial banks and recently-created intersecting islands mark the fall of the river at this season, and point to the magnificent sheet of water it must present during the floods. We now steam past the prettily-wooded island of Loomgyee, whose beauty Symes would seem to have overrated, though the mountainous scenery on the west, clothed in the most luxuriant growth of arborescent vegetation, and dotted with pagodas, lends so charming a feature to the scene, that one can well understand the pen of an enthusiast being carried away by poetic romance. To the east the country continues low and undulating ; but on both sides the banks of the river are prettily cultivated and intersected by groves of palms, plantains, and clumps of trees, that add to the picturesqueness of the scene. By noon of the 30th, we reached the pretty village of Joungyah, on the left bank, embowered in trees, chiefly tamarind.

Meaday to Joungyah.

26. Here some of the Chinese and Indian firms of Rangoon have established agencies for the purchase of lac, cutch, cotton, and other raw produce brought from the interior. Abreast of this village we passed the Woon of Mergui, in a small native boat on his way from Thayetmyo, where he had been for European medical aid, and it had taken his boat six days to accomplish what we had performed in one. Thoungaum is the next well-wooded island of significance we passed; and from the foliage peep out several pagodas, that have a striking effect. Above this the river narrows, and its banks on either side are well covered with trees—*Murraya paniculata*, perhaps, being among the most common. Rounding the

Agencies of Chinese and Indian firms at Joungyah, and progress to Minhla.

3

elbow is first sighted the charming little village of Maloon, situated on an eminence on the right bank, and crowned with a pagoda. The shelving banks below to the water's edge are fenced off into gardens, which are cultivated with peas, tobacco, beans, Indian-corn, and other indigenous vegetables, while the hill in the background, it may be remembered, was the centre of the stockade taken in 1826.

27. *30th.*—Minhla, the head-quarters of the Governor of Maloon, was made by 8.30 A.M. Here we anchored three hours to admit of sufficient fuel being shipped, to last the better part of our voyage to Mandalay.

Minhla, head-quarters of Governor of Maloon, and fuel station for steamers.

The wood at this station is regarded the best on the river, not that it contains a larger percentage of cutch, but chiefly owing to the billets being thicker and better seasoned. The stacks are neatly built on terraces fronting the village, a work apparently performed by the female portion of the community, who are likewise employed to wood the steamers. The readiness and good nature with which the people perform this latter work, speak for the just treatment they receive at the hands of the steamer officials.

28. Minhla having been burnt down in 1872, the houses were all new, and presented a strikingly-neat appearance. A river frontage of about 80 feet wide has been left as a promenade, which is prettily lined with tamarind, jack, mango, and *zizyphus*, together with ornamental trees, whose wide-spreading branches serve to shelter idlers who throng the bank on the arrival of a steamer, or any other scene of attraction on the river. This strand is kept remarkably clean, it being incumbent on all tenants to sweep up and burn the rubbish that may have accumulated the previous day in front of their houses—a system of sanitation that contrasts favourably with our own. The filth that is thrown below the houses is soon cleared away by pigs and dogs, with which the place swarms, and who make capital scavengers. A Burman regards the under portion of his abode as a legitimate place to throw filth of all sorts. The flooring of every house is perforated with holes, varying in size, to admit of rubbish being thrown away. This peculiarity is not confined to the houses of the poorer classes, for I have observed the same conveniences in the Hall of Audience, at the Palace of Mandalay, and seen the Ministers in their abject, semi-kneeling, prostrated position, with faces nearly touching the ground, utilize the smaller holes as the only means of disgorging their quids of *pán supparee* prior to His Majesty's entrance.

Minhla Town described.

Minhla is estimated to contain 1,500 houses, the larger number being built parallel with the river, but whose continuous line is here and there broken by pagodas and *kyoungs*, embowered in clumps of palmyra, which add considerably to the effect. The buildings in the rear are equally neat, and are reached by cross-paths, likewise avenued, and all having their little plots of garden prettily enclosed with bamboo-fencing, covered with flowering creepers. The architecture is of the usual Burman type. The flooring is either of planking or split bamboo, raised off the ground some two or three feet. The material of the entire framework—*i. e.*, the principal supports, pillars, &c.—depend on the owner's means, the richer having teak or other serviceable junglewood, and the poorer, bamboos: so also with the walls, which are either of plaited split bamboo or planking; but not so with the thatching: which is, without exception, of *Saccharum spontaneum*.

29. The Governor's house, which is situated in the middle of the front row, is uniform in design with the others, but larger, and enclosed by a high bamboo-mat fence. Fronting the entrance-gate, are a few old pieces of ordnance, whose rusted condition and dilapidated state of the carriages show they have long since been out of use. One peculiarity that marks a Burman official's house, is the cross-bar over the gate, and the privilege of having it coloured red. This former mark of distinction would appear to signify submission to the yoke of official sway.

The Governor's house.

30. The south end of the town is allotted to the females of *easy virtue*, whose quarters are enclosed in a high bamboo fence, and known as "the bamboo square." These unfortunates are subject to laws of a most rigid nature, and are not allowed to leave their quarters after the prescribed hours, which extend from sunrise to sunset.

South end of town allotted to certain class.

31. I here noted the finest specimen of a tamarind tree I have ever seen: it measured round the stem, at four feet from the ground, 8·75 feet; beneath it was an English screw cutch-press. The climate of these latitudes seems peculiarly adapted to this tree, for, as we progress northward, it becomes more plentiful, and grows with greater luxuriance.

Tamarind thrives well in this locality.

32. Here also is a market-place, built entirely of wood, with the exception of the roofing, which is thatched. In design it closely resembles a *khyoung*, and each vendor has an apportioned place, the whole presenting a gay and busy scene. Various articles of Eng-

Market and wares described.

lish manufacture were exposed for sale at exorbitant prices, including silk and cotton handkerchiefs, muslins, long-cloth, red turkey, beads, knives, scissors, and even those circular combs, used for keeping children's hair off their foreheads—an article of toilet, that Burman mothers have already learnt to appreciate. The compartment allotted to the sale of vegetables was remarkably well stocked; but what attracted my attention most was the splendid tomatoes and ginger roots, both of which thrive remarkably well here—indeed, the latter grows wild, as also many other varieties of the *Zingibercœea* order.

33. My interpreter, Johnson, *alias* Yansing, when eliciting information for me, got immensely chaffed and worried by the young damsels who keep the stalls, for they are full of fun and *repartee*, and not bad hands at *double entendres* when occasion demands. I was highly amused at the delight he displayed when my questions were at an end; and on our way back to the steamer, he ventured to tell me, with a very solemn face, that the Burmans could not appreciate this thirst for knowledge, but attributed my inquisitiveness to a mild form of madness.

Interpreter chaffed by Burmese maidens.

34. Shortly after anchoring, the "Woon" came on board, accompanied by a retinue of followers carrying a gold umbrella and sword, the insignia of office, and other paraphernalia, consisting of a gold cup and *supparee*-box of the same costly metal, a silver spittoon, and goblet of water carefully covered over with a piece of nice, clean, white muslin, all of which, I am told, adds to dignity in the eyes of a Burman. Among the followers evidently was a secretary, who was provided with the common black tablet of the country, and steatite pencil, to take notes. The former makes a capital substitute for a slate, having all its advantages without being fragile.

Visit of the " Woon," or Governor.

35. The hilt of the sword and scabbard were covered with sheet-gold, and the former handsomely inlaid with precious stones. This weapon, I am told, is not merely a badge of office, but indicates that the bearer has the power of taking life. In this instance the sword was a gift of the King.

Badge of authority.

36. The old Woon seemed a most intelligent and agreeable man,—one evidently who had mixed a good deal in European society. He breakfasted with us, and seemed quite at his ease, though, of course, he made a few *faux pas*, such as re-placing his bones in the dish from which he had been helped, and using his knife where

The " Woon" described.

we would a fork, and so on; but this latter practice is a mere matter of custom, and would hardly be noticed by European foreigners.

Before sitting down to breakfast, the Governor's attendants were ejected, but, eager to see their worthy master feed, persisted in flattening their noses against the panes of glass at the end of the saloon, much to the annoyance of the Quartermaster, who remonstrated, but to no effect. The Governor was evidently aware of my being on board, though he appeared ignorant as to the exact object of my mission, by the various questions put to me. I was frank in my replies, for there was no occasion to be otherwise.

37. During the conversation, the secretary seemed busily engaged taking notes of all that transpired, and I only regretted my ignorance of the language would not admit of my rendering his notes more complete by a description of the sad fate that befell the immortal Mr. Pickwick under similar circumstances.

Secretary taking notes.

38. Before leaving, the Woon expressed his regret that our stay was so limited, as he had hoped to entertain us in the evening with some amusing tricks by a learned pony and a *pooay*. He seemed highly pleased with the politeness shown him by Captain Bacon, and likewise with the bargain he had made in the purchase of a diamond ring from a Burman broker (*en route* to Mandalay to purchase India-rubber for some Rangoon firm) for Rs. 450, the original price asked being Rs. 750. The Burman, whom I knew sufficiently well to congratulate on the small margin of profit he had gained, could no longer control his countenance, and confessed to having cleared Rs. 270 on the transaction; and, laughing, expressed a hope that he would be able to drive a few more such honest bargains with the rest of his diamonds, which it was his intention to exchange, at Mandalay, for rubies.

The Woon purchases a diamond ring. Profit made by broker.

39. At noon the anchor was weighed, and we were once more in motion. After leaving Minhla, our progress was much impeded, not only by a current of greater velocity, but also by a strong head-wind and sand-storm. The left bank, with its red sandstone interspersed with rocks and cliffs, and wooded by clumps of trees, showing here and there little peeps of meadow-land, looked quite pretty. It is here that the large village of Mengoon is situated, numbering some 200 or 300 houses. The river now begins somewhat to change its character, and widens out considerably. The distance from bank to

Further progress up the river to Nyoungoo.

Mengoon.

bank is not less, perhaps, than four to five miles, which feature it preserves to the mouth of the Kyendwen, the whole being cut up at this season into a series of little islands. To the east, the country is more hilly and undulating, but the geological formation still retains the character of red sandstone. The beds of the ravines are at this season deep in sand, showing that they serve to drain the interior, during the heavy rains, when the rush of water must be considerable, though perhaps of no great depth, nor of long duration.

40. My introductory chapter having already become more lengthy than was originally intended, I must take a giant's stride to Nyoungoo, which is celebrated for the manufacture of its boxes, and thence to the capital, leaving a description of the intermediate places of interest, for some future time, when I shall not be limited for space, and can ventilate my ideas with a seeming disregard, perhaps, of the conventional restraints of ordinary official correspondence.

<small>Nyoungoo, and its manufacture of boxes.</small>

There are few people, I imagine, who have not even visited Burma, but have heard of the little boxes for which it is so noted, and which serve for a number of purposes, from a snuff-box to a lady's bonnet-box; but I question whether there are many familiar with the process of their manufacture. I had seen in Yule's *Ava* and other books these useful little articles described as lacquer-ware—an idea still prevalent, I believe; but such is a mistake, as will presently be seen. Fortunately for me, a few miles north of Pagan, something was discovered to have gone wrong with the engines, and at 4 P.M. we were compelled to make fast for the night abreast of Nyoungoo, which is now as celebrated for the manufacture I am about to describe as Pagan originally was. One of my escort, being related to a box-manufacturer was the means, no doubt, of my getting such a capital insight into the whole process; for, until the relationship had been satisfactorily traced and discussed, I found my enquiries accepted with suspicion, and met by evasive replies.

41. The shell of the box, or whatever the article may be, is of the finest bamboo-work, and on the flexibility of the article the value is regulated. This shell is first covered with a wash of cow-dung sufficiently thick to fill up the crevices, and give the whole an even surface; when dry, a second coating of cow-dung mixed with sissel oil is applied, and allowed to dry gradually in a vault below ground, at a temperature of 130° F. When thoroughly dry, which takes about four days, all irregularities or unevenness is removed by an

<small>Box manufacture described.</small>

artificial piece of pumice-stone made of sand and lac. A third coat, consisting of bone-charcoal worked up with *melanorrhœa* oil is now laid on, and forms the ground of the whole pattern. The box is again placed in the vault, where it remains sufficiently long to thoroughly dry. Now commences the designing of the pattern, which is performed entirely with a style. The whole of the black ground is removed, except such portion as is intended to form part of the design. This is either accomplished on the lathe or by the hand alone, according to the figure to be described. The next colour of the pattern, which is composed of a Chinese body colour and *melanorrhœa* oil, is now laid on, and the box replaced in the vault for a fortnight or more, when a similar procses is followed, and the whole of the last coating removed but that next in the design, and so on until the whole pattern is completed, when the box is put on a lathe, and the colours made to blend by a process of pumice-stoning, the final polish being given with a little oil and paddy-husk. Thus it will be seen that, with the exception of the artificial pumice-stone, lac in no form is used in the manufacture of these boxes. The bonâ fide lacquer-ware boxes for which Sind is so celebrated are as different from the ware here described as is possible for two articles to be.

42. The following is a list of plants observed between Zaloon and Thayetmyo : *Lomaria scandents,*

Plants, scandent shrubs, and Epiphytic Orchide between Zaloon and Thayetmyo.

Crinoid giganteum, Soneratia apetala, Areca, Butea, Cynometra acacisides, Sonéralia acida, Stravadium Calamus, Excœcaria, Acrostichum aureum, Acanthus ilicifolius, Bombax, Zizyphus jujuba, Erythrina indica, Lagerstrœmia grandiflora, Ficus, Urticea fructibus, Bignonia suberosa, and *Bignonia crispa, Acacia catechu, Acacia farnesiana, Aroideum Hypercicum, Herpestris, Rumex, Dentella, Bauhinia, Crotalaria, Aristolochia, Dioscorea, Hedyotis,* also a large variety of scandent shrubs, including *Ipomœas, Thunbergias,* and *Clerodendrons,* varieties of grasses, including bamboos, also *Epiphytic Orchideœ.*

43. The trees cultivated for their fruit were mango, plantain, cus-

Fruit trees.

tard-apple (which thrives best in the vicinity of Prome), lime, orange, papaya, pomegranate, bullock's-heart, and tamarind, which last seems to thrive better as we progress north of Thayetmyo and up to

List of trees.

Mandalay. The following trees were also noted : *Dodonœa Burmanniana, Euphorbia, Carissa, Prionitis, Olax mimosa, Ximenia, Capparis pandurata, Gymnema, Calotropis, Mudar, Borassus, Crotalaria, Guilandina, Jasminioides,* and *Tectona ternifolia.*

44. This last tree being considered equal to cutch for steamer fuel purposes, and great dissatisfaction having been expressed by the Flotilla officials, regarding the restriction lately placed by Government on the felling of the latter variety of tree, I shall take this opportunity of expressing my views on the subject. Wood for steamer fuel is stacked on the banks in piles 10′ × 10′ × 3′ 6″, and is said to contain 1,000 billets, which have been roughly estimated to represent 16 cwt. of coals—the hourly consumption of fuel when under steam. The stacks are generally made up of *Cordia, Sibia, Dillenia,* and also *Inga*. The steamer authorities were so averse to the restriction lately placed by Government on the cutting of cutch, that they seemed to think it would shortly be found more economical to burn coal than wood, if the prohibition was not removed, though they had no data to support their views. This led me carefully to note up to Mandalay the pressure of steam and revolutions per minute, when steaming under coal and when under wood-fuel. The difference was comparatively *nil*, which I pointed out to Mr. Nicol, Superintending Engineer of the Company. Experiments made by Marcus Bull in America, and M. Prelet of France, go to prove that the same weight of dry wood of every kind has the same heating power, therefore the main point for consideration is the respective weight of the different woods, and I do not think the difference in the specific gravity of cutch and the other woods in use is sufficient to warrant dissatisfaction being shown to the restriction on using cutch. Again, in drawing a comparison between wood-fuel and coal, it must always be borne in mind that wood dried in the ordinary way—and that, too, in a far less damp climate than Burma—25 per cent. of its moisture remains undissipated, consequently the remaining 75 per cent. of combustible matter is proportionately diminished, for the heat that would be produced by the same quantity of perfectly dry wood is actually wasted in the conversion of latent moisture into vapour. Now, in the case of the fuel we shipped, I noticed the larger proportion of the stacks was made up of unseasoned wood; under these conditions the value of wood-fuel *vs.* coal, or a comparison between jungle-woods and cutch, is simply valueless.

Wood-fuel vs. coal discussed.

45. The following list represents the birds noted from Rangoon to Mandalay, but I have not recorded the exact place where each was observed, as this information has already been supplied by Mr. A. O. Hume, who has kindly identified my collection, and noted their habitat in " Stray Feathers," a periodical that must be in the possession of all interested in birds :—

List of birds.

Polioaetus ichthaetus, Strix indica, Harpactes erythrocephalus, Halcyon Smyrnensis, H. pileata, Alcedo Asiatica, Cymbirhynchus affinis, Hydrocissa albirostris, Chrysocolaptes sultaneus, Megalaima hodgsoni, Xantholæma hæmacephala, Zanclostomus tristis, Upupa longirostris, Grancalus macei, Brachyurus moluccensis, B. cuculatus, Garrulax belangeri, Oriolus melanocephalus, Corvus impudicus, Dendrocitta rufa, Acridotheres tristis, A. fuscus, Lobivanellus atronuchalis, Metopodius indicus, Porphyrio neglectus, Gallicrex cristata, Hypotænedia striata, Ardea purpurea, Nettapus coromandelica, Dendrocygna arcuata, Graculus fuscicollis, Pelicanus onocrotalus, and *Leptoptilos argala.* From under the tail-coverts of these latter are obtained plumes known in England as *marabout* feathers.

CHAPTER II.

My stay at Mandalay from 4th to 18th December 1873.

46. The capital Mandalay was reached on the evening of the 4th December, about sunset. The mails as usual were immediately handed over to an escort party from the Residency, and by which opportunity I reported my arrival; later on in the evening an elderly gentleman joined us, evidently a friend of many on board. I was introduced, and had hoped to have gained some useful information from my new acquaintance, who, I found, was in the King's employ, and an old resident of Mandalay. His conversation, however, was chiefly addressed to his friends, and related to the progress he had made in the construction of certain vessels, and the terms under which he had agreed to serve the Burmese Government; which were, to use his own words, *pay first, and work follows; no pay, no work*. These conditions, he told us, had been scrupulously acted up to on both sides, and, in his opinion, were the only terms under which Europeans should serve the King. Irregularities in payments apparently are not the only cause for complaint on the part of the king's employés. Men fresh from England and ready to do good service, soon have their energies hampered by the dilatory and obstructive tendencies of the Burmese Authorities in power,

47. As illustrative of the type of the official employés Europeans have to deal with, I here give a case in point. A gentleman carrying on some mining operations for the King, which were not progressing as rapidly as he wished, found occasion to represent the matter at the palace; a wrong motive was at once attributed to his complaint, and he was informed that, so long as his pay reached him regularly, complaints of the nature he now preferred would only arouse His Majesty's suspicion and displeasure. This circumstance affords a good illustration of the painfully indolent and apathetic disposition of the Burmese, and explains their natural tendencies as a people. A certain per-centage of the labour, I was informed, is forced, and the rest paid either in grain, or gold coin. By the time the former reaches the workmen, the original quantity has been considerably reduced by the different hands it has had to pass through; and the gold coin, though supposed, when issued from the Mint, to represent

Illustration of the unsatisfactory nature of dealings with Mandalay officials and malpractices of Mint Authorities.

Rs. 5; has only a market currency of Rs. 4-12, and a similar value when received as revenue.

48. My new acquaintance now being about to leave, I thought I would ask a few questions associated with my mission; but unfortunately, these were matters in which he was little interested. He dilated largely on some wonderful turtle exhibition, and the intelligence displayed by these creatures. He also spoke of some extensive gardens on a creek a little north of Mandalay,* where spices of different sorts were grown, including cloves, cardamoms, and nutmeg-trees; but he seemed positive that there were no *ficus elastica* trees grown anywhere near the city, and that all the India-rubber in the market had been brought from Bhamo, and northwards.

Failure to elicit information from a resident of Mandalay.

49. On the departure of my garrulous friend, I turned in for the night. Unfortunately, however, my cabin was that nearest the companion-ladder; and only separated from the deck-passengers by a thin panelling; sleep was quite out of the question, so I lighted my pipe, and listened to the musical entertainment carried on by the Burmese passengers amidst peals of laughter and a clatter of tongues, each endeavouring to obtain a hearing by raising his voice a key higher than his neighbour. The only instrumental music was my inverted copper basin, and a couple of tin-pots, which were made to serve as an accompaniment to the voice. Evidently one of my party was the "Don Juan" of the evening, and notedly more noisy than the rest. He seemed a great favourite among the opposite sex, and long before quitting the vessel, had evidently gained their entire confidence, each deluded creature imagining she was the favoured one, no doubt. The same individual distinguished himself at a public *pooay* at Bhamo, where his services were recognized both by the public and myself—though indifferent ways. Eventually he turned out a most incorrigible blackguard, invariably being found drunk, or having added one more to his numerous wives; in fact, with the exception of two of my escort, my whole party were more or less debauchees, and of a stamp that could not obtain employment in British territory; for so great is the dread of the climate and tribes north of the capital, that men willing to earn an honest livelihood would not accompany me, and I was obliged to content myself with any riff-raff I could enlist,

Incidents of the night, and character of escort.

---

* *Note*—Probably these gardens are those referred to by Yule on the banks of the Madeya-koung: a little exaggerated in respect to the spice groves: areca palms, betel-vines, coconnuts, custard-apples, jacks, and a few other fruit-trees alone being cultivated by the people on this picturesque creek.

hoping to make them more manageable and of some service when beyond the jurisdiction of appeals, laws, Acts, and Regulations. Eight bells had now gone, and the more noisy of the party had fallen asleep, and before the next hour was struck, all was quiet.

50. Day had hardly dawned, however, when all were up again, and busy, preparing for their intended departure. Those whose *lares et penates* could be carried by the owner, were the first to get off, while others, whose baggage was of a more bulky nature, lost no time in engaging carts, which now crowded the bank in such numbers, as to make it absolutely dangerous to thread one's way through them. The bullocks, restless with their close proximity to one another, kept up an incessant kicking-and-butting process, that imperilled the lives of passers-by. The younger portion of the female passengers now lined the ship's rails, and amused themselves by chaffing their male companions, who were politely bargaining for carts for them—an office my minstrel peon seemed far more interested in, than his legitimate duty. After a deal of squabbling and abuse, the bargains were struck and the carts loaded, the fair owners being seated on the top of their property, where they had to remain patiently, until the carts in advance had moved on. The scene, though a very noisy and dusty one, was not altogether uninteresting; crowds of gaily-dressed people, representing all colours of the rainbow, now thronged the bank, either for amusement, or to welcome their friends. The elderly men and women were content with the more sombre colours, and satisfied with the umbrellas of their own country, manufactured from bamboos, and water-proof paper covering of the same material; but the younger portion of the crowd showed a preference for the European sunshade,—yellow, green, and red being the principal colours, the first predominating as productive of that yellow tint of complexion so much admired by both sexes.

Preparations for landing and attendant circumstances described.

51. Nor had our Burmese passengers neglected their toilets; evidently much care had been bestowed on the arrangement of their hair, and improvement of complexion by an application of a cosmetic common to the country.* The fashion of Upper Burma had apparently been carefully observed both by the men and the women. With the former, the difference in costume principally consists in the arrangement of the *goung-*

Costume and toilet of Burmese described, and contrasted with that of British Burma.

---

* There are two descriptions of cosmetics used in Burma,—one manufactured from the starch of rice, and the other *(thanakar)* made by grinding the bark of *murraya paniculata* on a sandstone pallet with a little water; the paste is applied and allowed to dry on the body, when the whole is carefully rubbed into the pores of the skin with a towel.

boung, or head-dress, which with the Lower Burmese is an ordinary coloured silk handkerchief, covering the whole head, while at Mandalay it consists of a piece of white muslin rolled in a neatly-folded band, and tied tightly round the head like a coronet just above the eyebrows, the two ends forming a butterfly-like tail at the back, in the arrangement of which no little trouble is bestowed. This mode of head-dress is adopted no doubt with a view to displaying the hair, which is tied in a knot at the top of the head, and, when neatly arranged, closely resembles what sailors call a *turk's head*. Both men and women are exceedingly proud of thick, long hair, and take every opportunity of displaying their luxuriant dark tresses (sometimes of extraordinary length) when they can.* There is little difference in the manner adopted by either sex in dressing the hair. With the men the knot is worn on the top of the head, and with the women quite at the back, and generally finished off with an artificial wreath or single flower of French or English manufacture. The pith-flowers originally in use, have apparently long since been superseded by foreign imitations, which are now largely imported, and find a ready sale. I have seen artificial Chinese flowers exposed for sale; but they are poor specimens in comparison with the European article, while the difference in price does not compensate for the inferiority of quality in the eye of the fantastic Burman *belle*. A preference is always given to real flowers when obtainable; and among the rural classes, when these are not in season, a delicate tuft of grass, or a few variegated leaves of some plant or shrub, is selected as an ornament for the hair by the country maidens. The costume of the women of the Upper and Lower Provinces differs in respect to the jacket and cloth worn round the loins. At the capital, the *loongyee*† and little white or coloured jacket is never

* Yule in his *Ava* writes: Capillary deficiencies are often supplied artificially. I was surprised, in a list of property made out to be charged against the Burmese Government, as having been carried off from a village near the frontier, to find an entry of twelve sets of false hair." The author was apparently unaware that the females of Burma like our own country-women as a rule, not contended with the gifts of nature, enlarge their back-knots by the addition of *sazoos* (thick pieces of false hair) for which often as much as Rs. 9 is paid. Naturally the Burmese have a most prolific growth of hair, which I am inclined to attribute to the shaving of the head in their early youth, and the excellent hair-wash they use, which is made from the bark of a *grewia* and the seed of the *acacia concinna*. A mucilage is prepared from the bark of the former, and mixed with a decoction of the seeds of the latter, which serve to stimulate growth, and prevent the hair from turning prematurely grey. Judging from the records of the past, it would appear that masks, fans, muffs, and false-hair were of Italian origin, and introduced into France about 1872, but it was some years later before the fashion reached England. In *Love's Labour Lost*, written about 1594, we find mention made of "Don Armado," a fantastical Spaniard, railed for taking upon himself the office of a lady's fan-bearer. In *Romeo and Juliet*, again, allusion is made to fans; while, when Queen Bess died, her wardrobe was said to contain twenty-seven fans, one of which sold for £400.

† The *loongyee* is a petticoat without a string, fastened round the waist by gathering in the black and tucking in the gathers. No jacket is worn, as is often the case, the *loongyee* is srought up under the arm-pit so as to conceal the breasts. The pattern is either in stripes of various colours, or neat plaids.

adopted, excepting by visitors from British territory, where the better educated and more respectable classes have already commenced to show an aversion to the *tamine** and open lawn coats, though they are undoubtedly the natural costume of the country. The *loongyee* evidently has been introduced from Moulmein, where it was, perhaps, borrowed from the Malayan Peninsula.

52. The last of my things had just been carefully packed away, when I received a note from the Resident, Captain Strover, asking me to stay with him, and saying he had sent a pony for me, and the requisite orders to pass my kit through the custom-house. I was fortunate at this time in forming the acquaintance of two gentlemen, residents of Mandalay, who had come on a visit to the Commander of the *Ashley Eden*. They very kindly volunteered to show me the way up to town, and seemed somewhat curious to know the exact nature of my mission. I was only too glad to avail myself of their offer; for though independent of a guide, Captain Strover's *syce* knowing the way, yet this offered a good opportunity of getting the numerous questions answered, that would naturally suggest themselves to a new-comer. It is not improbable that a little fiction was added to truth when the different objects that attracted attention were being described. I think however, I was able to sift the wheat from the chaff without much trouble, for my companions did not seem inclined to *charge* me with those abominable misrepresentations, which often mislead new-comers to a place, and result in the inaccuracies appearing in print which do so much mischief.

<small>Invitation to put up with the Resident.</small>

53. The Residency is about three miles from where the steamers anchor at this season. The line we took led across an open uninteresting country, the bridle-path meandering through paddy-fields, until, just before reaching the suburbs, an unbridged stream delayed us a little, while I had a slight

<small>What transpired during ride from landing-place to the Residency.</small>

---

* The *tamine* differs from the *loongyee* in that it is worn open in front, and consists of three separate pieces. It is worn in a manner to expose the shoulders and arms, but sufficiently long to trail on the ground; the entire width is three cubits: each piece, which goes to make up the whole, varies in price, pattern, colour, and name. The centre portion, however, is what regulates the value, and varies from Rs. 5 to Rs. 200, according to the pattern, which is often most elaborate and brilliant—the gaudy red and serpentine designs being the most costly. The three pieces are the *ah-htasin*, the *tumain-go*, and the *tumain-nah*—each being one cubit wide. The first is generally of some common red or dark cotton stuff, a preference being given to the latter; the second is that already described, while the third generally consists of some cheaper silk in coloured stripes. The whole are sown together and lined with a piece of white long cloth. The *putso* is an article entirely of male attire: it extends from the waist to a little below the knees, and the entire length is about twelve feet; the superfluous material is either worn in a pinch of gathers in front or thrown over the shoulder in a *negligé* manner. The system of fastening is most insecure, and necessitates an everlasting process of tying and re-adjusting.

engagement with my pony, which showed a disinclination to cross. He was a stubborn little brute, and remarkably observant, so much so, that there were few objects he passed without stopping stock-still to examine, no matter at what pace he was going. This peculiarity resulted in my landing on his neck at the start-off, for his huge proportions and sluggish habits deceived me; and although I had broken a stirrup leather on mounting, I was careless in my seat, and paid little attention to anything but the surrounding country. My luggage took the road that was being repaired for the convenience of the *French Embassy,* who were shortly expected, for which privilege a charge of Rs. 1-8 per cart was made. This toll may have been levied to defray the cost of construction, but it is more probable that the neighbouring villages had to contribute their labour gratis, and that the proceeds of the tax were pocketed by the officials in charge, who, it would appear, have been taught to regard such pickings as a prerogative in compensation for their small and irregularly-paid appointments. The noble My-lee-doung range of mountains, which forms the eastern back-ground to the capital, chiefly absorbed my attention; indeed, beyond this scenery there is nothing sufficiently engaging to excite the curiosity even of a new-comer: neither vegetable nor animal life offers an exception. The different villages we rode through were comfortably embowered in clumps of trees, generally mango, jack, tamarind, pomegranate, *papya,* and so on, and principally populated by an agricultural class. Here and there were patches of land under garden culture, the vegetables being those most highly prized by Natives, among which were some magnificent specimens of tomatoes; *Oxalis corniculata, Malpighia occigera, Corchorus capsularis, Triumfetta rhomboidia,* and *Melochia corchorifolia,* were common in the fields, but the arborescent growth was represented by stray trees scattered over the place, consisting of *Petrospermum acrifolium, Bombax malabaricum, Columbia floribunda, Buettneria pilosa, Corchorus capsularis,* and so on.

54. On the right are some extensive sheds within a bamboo mat enclosure, constituting the royal granary, and a little further on is His Majesty's summer residence, surrounded by a similar description of walling. Of the interior nothing could be seen but the tops of some carved-wooden buildings. This country seat, I believe, has never been occupied by His Majesty, who since the rebellion, when his two sons attempted his life, has never quitted the palace-grounds; indeed, so intensely has this act of treachery and disloyalty shaken his faith, and aroused his suspicions, that, like Sardanapalus, he now dreads his own shadow.

Royal granary and summer house.

55. *En route*, we met numbers of old and young well-dressed women, going down to the steamers with different articles for sale— principally rice, vegetables, sweets, *pán*-leaf, betel-nut, and various other minor products. Groups of men were also noticed busily engaged cutting up logs on the stream into small pieces of firewood. The timber being converted, seemed principally *Dillenias, Erythrinas, Gmelinas,* and one or two others; among them were also a few teak logs, but of small dimensions. I was told that seldom any first-class teak reached Mandalay, owing to the difficulty in extraction. None but the King is allowed to possess elephants; buffalo labour has therefore to be substituted, and the logs reduced to dimensions that they can drag. When travelling in the Mogoung District, I had an opportunity of seeing the system on which timber operations are conducted in Upper Burma, and shall have occasion to revert to the subject when describing my journey in those parts.

<small>Sundry observations on vendors and conversion of timber.</small>

56. Teak timber sells at absurdly low prices in the Upper Province, and it would be found a most remunerative speculation to purchase teak up there for the Rangoon market. I have seen timber, averaging thirty-two cubic feet, sold at Rs. 7 per log, and that, too, on the river's bank.

<small>Low price of teak as compared with British Burma.</small>

57. I was not sorry when the Residency was in sight, and I bade my companions good morning, for a more filthy, dusty town than Mandalay it is impossible to imagine. The roads are unmetalled, and ankle-deep in dust; the furrows caused by cart traffic are in many places so deep, as to make it next to impossible for carts to turn without risk of capsizing when once started, or until a cross-road is met, where the opposite traffic works the ridges into an impalpable powder into which the wheels sink axle-deep, often resulting in a block of half an hour or more, while the unfortunate bullocks flounder and strain to get out of their difficulty. All works of public utility represent an equally dilapidated condition. Many of the bridges, principally wooden, are in such a state of decay, that it seems almost dangerous to venture across them; yet no repairs are attempted, plank by plank, and rail by rail, are allowed to rot away, and fall into the stream unnoticed, simply for want of a little of the money now squandered on his Majesty's hobbies, which, like a child's toy, no sooner loose their novelty, than they are forgotten. Everywhere at the capital may be seen machinery of a most costly description lying idle, partly set up, and partly in detached

<small>Condition of public works, roads, bridges, &c.</small>

pieces in various quarters of the town, while some are even still to be seen on the river's bank, exactly in the same places where they were first landed months ago.

58. Such conservancy as there is, has originated in religious scruples, the only scavengers being dogs and pigs, with which the place swarms, and whose lives are spared by order of the King. The Buddhist creed forbids the taking of life, which act of humanity often results in the most revolting spectacles; for though the Burman Buddhist objects to take life, he does not hesitate to commit the most cruel acts, and it is quite a common sight to see dogs going about with sloughing sores, originally brought on by a wound inflicted by an angry Burman, whose impetuous disposition knows no bounds when once excited. Their nature seems a strange mixture of cruelty and kindness: they delight in cock-fighting, but would inconvenience themselves to assist a chicken in distress.

Conservancy arrangements and Buddhist scruples.

59. I reached the Residency about 10 A.M., and after breakfast was shown the rooms that had been prepared for me, in an adjoining house, in the same compound. One wing of the building was occupied by Dr. Johnson, the Residency Surgeon and myself, and the other by the Post-office and the Resident's office, where also the mixed Court sits; the centre hall was unoccupied, and intended apparently for public receptions. This building, as also many other of the European residences in Mandalay, is the property of the King, though, perhaps, the least significant; indeed, beyond the British flag which is hoisted on the roof-top, there is nothing to stamp it with that air of importance due to one of Her Majesty's representatives at a foreign court. The compound is enclosed by a fence of teak framing, with bamboo panelling supported by teak posts. Both gates are guarded by Burmese soldiers, who are supposed to report daily at the palace all matters of importance that transpire at the Residency: but as Burmans find a difficulty in drawing a line of distinction between important and unimportant matters, the system resolves itself into one of *espionage*, and soldiers rather represent a body of spies than a guard of honour. This acts as a barrier to guests at the Residency studying the habits and customs of the people, or, in fact, gaining information of any description directly from them.

Arrival at the Residency; description of the building and Burmese system of espionage.

60. When my baggage came up, I found the Custom-house Authorites had detained my guns, although they were included in the Resident's clearing order, and it was

Detention of fire-arms by Burmese Customs Authorities.

only after some little correspondence that they were delivered. Fortunately, my breech-loader and revolver were locked up, and the three old muskets were undamageable.

61. Adjoining the Residency grounds is the Mission School. The buildings, which are all of teak, include a pretty little church, school, and mission house. The Anglo-Burman class of design has been observed throughout, but the amount of comfort and style displayed in all respects, more closely resemble the modern type of architecture met with in British territory, than what one would expect to find in a foreign land. Judging from the number of boys, chiefly boarders, the institution seemed greatly appreciated by the people, and in a most flourishing condition. Among the scholars were some lads from Moulmein, late pupils of the principal (the Reverend Mr. Marks); their appreciation of his kindness, and confidence in his tutorship had induced them to flock up here to complete their English education. Service is held in the church throughout the week at 6 A.M., when all the boys, both Christians and Buddhists attend. The prayers are read in the vernacular, which is understood by all. An English service is held twice a day on Sundays for the benefit of the Europeans, the pupils also being present, many of whom understand English. It was noticeable how well-behaved the boys were, and what attention they appeared to pay to their books; but this may be accounted for, however, by the whole community being of the one sex. On one occasion, when I had forgotten to take a prayer-book, a little fellow, not over ten years apparently, stepped forward and handed me his; carefully pointing out the place and returning to his seat in a most quiet, orderly manner. The only peculiarity in the service I noticed, was that, when the prayer for the Royal Family was being offered up, His Majesty the king of Burma was also always mentioned. Considering the interest he has apparently shown in the maintenance of this institution, and the very handsome sums he has given towards the erection of the church and other buildings, this addition to the usual form of prayer, perhaps, does not seem out of place.

The Rev. J. E. Marks's S. P. G. Mission School.

62. According to arrangements already made, the day after my arrival I was introduced to His Majesty by the Resident. The hour appointed for the reception was 11 A.M., and a fearfully hot ride we had to the palace, which is about a mile and a half from the Residency. Whether it is considered undignified to be seen galloping up to the palace gate, or whether it is the established etiquette to be accom-

Introduction to His Majesty the King of Burma, and what transpired on the ride to the palace.

panied by a retinue of followers, and sheltered from the sun by umbrella-bearers, I cannot say; but, had my feelings been consulted, I would have much perferred covering the ground with the least possible delay. However, as all was new to me, the solemn pace observed afforded a better opportunity of noting the various matters of interest that presented themselves as we went along. I was immensely amused at the futile attempts made by the umbrella-bearers to fulfil their office satisfactorily, for the heads of the umbrellas, which were of huge dimensions, supported on handles ten feet long, were constantly coming in contact, much to the annoyance of our ponies, which frisked about and cannoned up against one another, leaving us for the better part of the ride exposed to the direct rays of the sun.

63. The city of Mandalay is enclosed by a brick wall about fifteen feet high, with a battlemented parapet, the whole being enclosed by a deep and wide moat, which contains water throughout the year. We entered by the west gate, which is surmounted by a seven-tiered roofed pavilion of the same class of architecture as is observed in the monasteries and other Buddhistic buildings. This led through the principal street to the eastern gate of the palace, which occupies the centre of the city, and is surrounded by a high palisade of stout teak posts. Here we dismounted and parted with our umbrellas. The Resident, however, was still canopied by what resembled an umbrella without a handle, carried by one of the King's officials, who met us at the gate. This honour was not extended to me I am glad to say, or I should have been compelled to be more dignified in my gait, and stared less about me. We were first conducted to a pavilion with an entirely open frontage, evidently a sort of public reception-room, where petitions are also received, and after perusal by the Ministers passed on to the officers to whose department they appertain. That portion of the hall occupied by the Ministers and shared by ourselves was nicely carpeted, and huge cushions provided for the convenience of the former; all others were squatted on the bare floor, petitioners and applicants being in the rear of the court officials, who presented a motley lot, differing notably in age, size, colour, degrees of cleanliness, and general deportment.

Mandalay city briefly described. Also public reception-room in the palace.

64. Now commenced the unbooting process; but having quite forgotten that this barbarous practice was enforced in the palace, I went in a pair of laced boots, which rather threw me out of time when visiting the different officials, before appearing before His Majesty: I

The unbooting process.

was always a few minutes late in entering a place, or some yards behind Captain Strover on leaving. At these odd moments I made the best use of my eyes, for I felt in all probability this would be the last time I should ever enter the palace under similar circumstances.

65. After the usual ceremony of introduction had been gone through, and the Resident interrogated as to my age, qualifications, etc., and other questions of a similarly inquisitive nature, the conversation took a more chit-chat form, and I was asked by one of the Ministers who had recently visited England, whether I had been to London, and seen the different sights he enumerated. Unfortunately I had, at which he seemed both disappointed and surprised. I have often remarked that it affords the greatest satisfaction to Orientals who have visited England to find that they have witnessed sights novel even to Europeans. When visiting the Governor of Mogoung, whose favour I had an object in winning, I lost no opportunity of lubricating the old man's fancies in every possible manner with the oil of gammon, and, of course, always expressed surprise at the wonderful sights his son had seen when visiting England with the Burmese Embassy, but the old charlatan was not easily to be hoodwinked, as will be seen as I progress with my narrative. During the conversation *pan suparee* chewing and smoking was freely carried on by the Ministers, in front of whom were placed silver spittoons, the rest of the officials spitting through the holes in the floor, perforated for that express purpose as previously described. After charging his mouth to an extent that necessitated the thumb and finger process to get the last end of the quid in, I curiously watched one of the Ministers to see what next he was about to produce from the bottom of his handsome gold *suparee* box, when much to my disgust a fowl's feather was leisurely unrolled from a very greasy piece of paper, with which he commenced to tickle his ear; this revolting practice at an end, the feather was carefully rolled up again in the same filthy paper, and put away in its original place. A pair of pincers was next brought out, with which an incessant click-click was kept up, accompanied by two other officials, while they were busily engaged plucking all the hairs out of their old wrinkled chins. Burmans have a great aversion to any hair growing on the face excepting in the form of a light moustache, the reason for this I have been told, is that it is objected to by the fair sex, and interferes with the kissing process, or rather smelling, for the Burmese do not kiss! In the present instance, however, I do not think the old men referred to, could have been actuated by any such foolish motive, for many years must have passed since

Introduction to the Ministers of State and attendant circumstances.

such ideas entered their heads; apparently, it was a mere habit, and a very objectionable one, too, in the eyes of Europeans. Tea, fruit, and sweets were placed before Captain Strover and myself, served on a large silver tray which would have looked a good deal better for a little cleaning.

66. After spending twenty minutes here, we were taken to the chamber of the Italian Consul, who was squatted on the ground, tailor-fashion with his shoes on, and a cheroot in his mouth. The apartment, though large, was the picture of gloominess and discomfort, and sufficiently dingy to have induced the Consul to remark, as I was scanning the walls and taking stock, that a coating of white-wash would be an improvement. Here and there was suspended on the walls a photograph of the great Shway Dagon Pagoda of Rangoon, and one most miserably gilded illustration of the same building, all out of perspective, and evidently the production of some native artist.

The Italian Consul.

67. We had not spent more than ten minutes in the Consul's room when we were summoned to the Grand Hall of Audience. I was now all impatience, for an introduction to Royalty seemed a matter of great importance. The scene of grandeur, however, I had pictured to myself soon dwindled away, as we were (shoelessly) ushered through the dirty, unswept courts and crossings that led up to the Hall of Audience, where we were seated on the dirty, bare teak boards, in the humiliating position of suppliants—an attitude all are subjected to who visit the palace. This apparently was a demi-official Royal reception-hall, at the back of the State-room from which it was partitioned off by wood panelling. The side by which we entered was entirely open, the opposite end being shut in by a crimson curtain. At the back was a raised platform or dais covered with crimson velvet, and finished off in front by a deep gold fringe. Here also was placed a sort of elbow support, in the form of a large square crimson velvet cushion, covered with a white muslin slip, exposing either end, both being elaborately embroidered in gold. That portion of the dais occupied by His Majesty was richly carpeted, and canopied by white cloth, with an open-work valance of the same material all round. The ceiling was of handsomely carved wood, supported on massive gilt columns which now wore a very dingy appearance, but quite in keeping with the rest of the hall, which appeared sadly in want of re-decoration.

Hall of Audience.

Fronting the dais at a distance of about ten yards were arranged in line the Ministers, on their right the Resident, next to whom

I sat. At right-angles to us was a double line of minor court officials. The attitude observed by all but Captain Strover and myself was such as to necessitate sitting on one's own calves, bringing the soles of the feet in line with the back of the head—an almost impossible position for Europeans, who have to compromise matters by sitting lop-sided, doubling the legs under, so that the soles of the feet do not front His Majesty. The Ministers and other minor officials were all dressed in silk *putsoes* of different colours and patterns, and over gowns reaching to below the knees of loose white muslin and *goung-boungs* of the same material; this appeared the half-dress court costume, for I noticed one of the Ministers slipping on this coat just before entering the Audience Hall.

68. After being seated for about ten minutes, a guard of soldiers entered from a door leading into the passage by which we came, and drew up in line to the rear of the minor officials. Their uniform was a coloured *putso* and short jacket buttoned up to the throat, the original colour of which was red I was told, but now it presented that shabby changed appearance which age, dirt, and perspiration are calculated to bring about. Their muskets appeared to be Enfields, but of this I am not certain. Next followed one of the court attendants carrying His Majesty's gold *pān-suparee* box, *lepet* (pickled tea) box of the same costly metal borne on a silver stand, a gold spittoon, and pair of binoculars, all of which he carefully arranged on the carpet after dusting it with the end of his *putso*, and then retired. This being the signal apparently for His Majesty's arrival, the ministers and other minor official discharged their quids through the holes in the perforated floor, and bringing their hands together in front of them, bowed their heads to the ground, in which position they remained until the ceremony was over. A door immediately behind the dais was thrown open, and His Majesty entered with a short, quick step and upright gait followed by one of his little daughters, a child of about seven years old, who waited until her father had settled down, and then seated herself behind him: she was a pretty little thing, and remarkably well-behaved, amusing herself during the interview counting her little fingers, or playing with her handsome diamond necklet. His Majesty has decidedly the Burman type of physiognomy, but is below the average height of his countrymen: he has a pleasing expression, though of a much darker complexion than the generality of the people of this province. He was dressed in a rich silk *putso*, of a vandyked pattern, a white muslin *goung-boung* and jacket of the same material, fitting tightly at the neck, but open below, exposing the chest and stomach.

Ceremony of His Majesty's entrance and exit, and what occurred at the audience.

(39)

His entrance was followed by an absolute silence for a few minutes while he ruffled up his sleeves, surveyed the assembly with his binoculars, myself in particular, and filled his mouth with *pán-suparee*. It was now that I noticed the very shaky state of his nerves, for his hand trembled perceptibly as he shovelled into his mouth the finely-cut *suparee*, with a little gold spoon. The binoculars were once again brought to bear on me, when His Majesty broke the silence by mumbling out something (for his mouth was too full to speak distinctly) intelligible alone to his echo, the *than-daugan*,* the medium through which conversation was carried on between the Resident and himself. The Resident's letter, applying for permission for me to travel through Burma Proper, was now intoned by one of the officials to my right in a clear, well-articulated manner. At the conclusion there was a lull of a few minutes, sufficient to give His Majesty time to deliberate, when he re-opened the conversation with the Resident, which was kept up with some little animation, until, without any previous warning, he rose, turned his back on the company, and walked away. The guard who, during the King's presence, were in a kneeling posture with their guns between their knees, now withdrew, and we also took our departure. I was indeed not sorry when the interview was at an end, for the attitude in which we were sitting was really most trying ; and although I tried my best to remain quiet, I found it impossible, and kept shifting from one side to the other as the perspiration streamed down ; at last I attempted to straighten my leg, for I had an attack of cramp in my hip ; but it was useless, the gentle pressure of something much resembling the butt-end of a musket on my toes, soon made me double up again, as I was not at all certain what might follow, if I disregarded the polite reminder.

69. I shall not attempt to describe the interior arrangement of the palace grounds, for my visit was too hurried to admit of more than superficial scrutiny.

<small>Cursory description of principal buildings in the enclosure.</small>

The most conspicuous buildings, however, were the Palace, the Royal Council-house, the Royal Court-house, the Mint, and a high square tower, where the hours are struck on a large bell and drum, and I was informed that at the midnight watch, a guard regularly went round the moat in a boat to see that all was quiet and orderly. The Palace, which is entirely of wood, handsomely carved and covered with gold-leaf now much tarnished, is erected on a masonry terrace some four feet off the ground. It is of the Buddhistic ecclesiastical type of architecture, with triple-roofed wings and approaches, sending out from the centre a tower with

---

* Receiver of the Royal voice.

seven tiers of roofing, each diminishing in size upwards, and the whole crowned with a gilded *htee*, a privilege alone conceded to Royalty by the Buddhistic creed. The Royal Council-house and Royal Court-house are likewise carved wooden buildings on a masonry base, but there is nothing remarkably attractive about them. The Mint, as well as could be judged from a distance, was entirely of masonry, and not of the Burmanic type.

70. I sadly regretted having to leave the capital without seeing the palace-grounds, more especially the Royal garden; but opportunity did not offer itself I am sorry to say, and I hardly liked to trouble the Resident again to obtain permission for me to satisfy my curiosity, though I fear I threw out one or two broad hints.* The Rev. Mr. Marks very kindly offered to obtain His Majesty's permission for me to go over the gardens; but, from what Captain Strover said, I felt there was little chance of his being able to fulfil his promise.

Failure to scrutinize the palace grounds.

71. On quitting the gate we mounted and returned by the road we came, reaching the Residency about half-past two o'clock. It was a fine broad street down which we passed, but unmetalled and abominably dusty. From the palace entrance to the city gate either side of the road was lined by stalls, in which were exposed for sale all sorts of piece-goods, mock jewellery, glass, lacquer-ware, combs,

Return to Residency from the palace.

---

* Dr. Dawson tells us, the King's garden within the palace enclosure at Mandalay, is in the figure of an irregular parallelogram, and covers nearly two acres of ground. It is intersected by two small sheets of water, in the shape of a Roman Cross. Lying to the north of the palace buildings, you find it surrounded by a fanciful wooden railing standing about three feet high. The diminutive posts of this railing are exquisitely wrought all over with lacquer work, in-laid by variegated glass, representing certain fabulous animals and birds. As you approach this garden, it catches your eye instantly as something pleasant to look upon, and for which there is a fondness even in one's very nature. The walks are all composed of a raised brick-work, and these again are covered in by a coating of firm mortar; facing the garden gate stands the "*garden palace*" which is a light, airy-looking structure, and except the posts, is made wholly of bamboo. Here his Majesty occasionally sits, and receives the officers of his government. A few paces further on to the left of the garden palace, is a beautiful lake, formed by the extension of one of the limbs of the crucial-shaped sheets of water, intersecting the garden. The unrippled surface of this little lake, looks like a polished mirror. On its still bosom, floats a unique and fanciful little bamboo house, which has been named the "*water palace.*" And if there is a cool spot in the capital on a hot burning day with the quick-silver dancing in a thermometer at ten or twelve degrees above "blood heat," it is surely beneath the shade of that little water palace. In the angular spaces left by the position of the sheets of water, the grounds are very tastefully laid out with a great variety of shrubs, plants, and trees, in a manner the best possible for giving effect to the scene. Miniature hills put up in different directions, whose sides are made to resemble, as nearly as they can, natural hills in all their wildness and grandeur. Fragments of rocks crop out, and here and there masses of boulders are seen in the sides of these elevations. In the little hollows formed by these projections and inequalities of surface, plants and shrubs have been set out with considerable skill, whose verdant foliage and variously-tinted flowers, give them a rich and most romantic appearance. On some of these eminences, the tops are surmounted by minature villas, from the windows of which you look out upon a scene which rivals in beauty some of the most vivid and graphic pictures delineated by classic poets as an enchanted ground, or fairy land. It is truly a beautiful garden, and as picturesque as it is really grand.

looking-glasses, scents, knives, scissors, imitation amber ear-tubes, crockery, and so on, giving a busy appearance to the place, which was enhanced by the gaily-dressed crowds that crowded the street. Fronting the houses were nicely white-washed lattice fences, about three feet high, within which were generally observable a few flowering shrubs or fruit trees—*zizyphus*, lime, *papaya*, or pomegranate. This system of fencing off the houses is a royal order of long standing, the object being to keep people at a respectful distance from the king, who is not even supposed to be looked at. What His Majesty must think of our extending this privilege even to a cat, is indeed difficult to conceive.

72. My mornings were generally spent in inspecting the different arts and manufactures, always finding something fresh to engage my attention; and the only matter for regret was that time did not admit of my studying more minutely each branch of industry. Groups of different trades are found mixed with groups of others all over the town, instead of each profession establishing itself in separate streets, as is the case in India.

Arts and Manufacture in the City.

73. Weaving apparently gives occupation to a large proportion of the population at Mandalay, and is, perhaps, one of the most remunerative trades. The raw material is chiefly imported from China, though a good deal of it is indigenous. It is curious to watch the most elaborate designs being worked out all from memory. The rapidity with which the treadles are manipulated, and shuttles changed and rechanged according to the colour required, seems as though the whole process were a mere mechanical art. Even little girls of seven or eight years old I have seen weaving a nine-loom *tamine*, which is considered about one of the most difficult patterns to produce.

Weaving.

74. A few hours spent among the brass-founders will also always repay the trouble. Here are cast in all sizes and orthodox positions gaudamas, elephants, demons, and other monsters, brass vessels of all sorts, and the gongs and bells, which apparently are indispensable at all ceremonies in Burma, secular or religious. The bell-metal has a remarkably sweet tone, and any one with the time to spare and a tolerably correct ear for music, might have the most perfect set of chimes produced: indeed, among the bells exposed for sale I was able to complete all but two notes of the octave. At one foundry a huge gaudama four feet high, in a sitting attitude, was being manufactured to order, at a cost of Rs. 500. The mould was in hand at the time of my visit, so I had an opportunity of

Brass-foundry.

watching the whole process. The design is first fashioned in clay, which is covered with a coating of wax half an inch thick; this is again plastered over with clay, and allowed to dry for a few days: it is then placed in a fierce charcoal furnace; the wax melts and pours out through an orifice left for the purpose, and the mould is ready for the molten metal. It is seldom that the first cast is a success, often there are three or four failures before a satisfactory result is obtained. After the image has been cast, there yet remains to be done the filing and burnishing, which is the most tedious part of the business. Articles for sale are generally exposed in the rough, and worked up according to the price offered.

75. Carpentry is another branch of industry that is largely represented at the Capital, and in the diffierent shops I inspected were some exceedingly good specimens of workmanship exposed for sale at most reasonable prices. A teak box that would cost Rs. 12 in Rangoon can be purchased at Mandalay for Rs. 4. The carving, though well executed, did not come up to some I have seen from Henzada; which place, I believe, is celebrated for this particular art throughout Burma. In the same street with the carpenters, and in many instances occupying a portion of the same house, were decorators and manufacturers of ornamental carved-goods picked out in various patterns, in red and gold and mosaic work in mirror. From a distance this work has a capital effect, but it does not bear close inspection. As a curio, I ordered a *isadike*, or box in which the sacred writings are kept, with a *tazoung* superstructure, after the design of the spire of the palace, for which I was charged Rs. 25.

Carving and Carpentry.

76. Although I went on three different occasions to see the glass-blowers, some excuse was always given which prevented my seeing the process. Captain Strover, however, showed me some very pretty glass marbles, something after the description of those used in the game of *Solitaire*, which, he assured me, were manufactured at Mandalay; but they might easily have passed for English, so perfect were they in all respects.

Glass-blowers.

77. The market-place is about a mile and a half from the city, and situated on one of the principal roads: it is a large square brick enclosure in an unfinished state, with four entrances arranged according to the cardinal points. Within, it is divided into compartments by two roads running the entire length of the building, and intersected by others at equal distances apart. The stalls have thatched roofs, but are not walled in, and each vendor has his

The City Market.

allotted place. Here, is exposed for sale all manner of merchandise, including grain, meat, fish, vegetables, piece-goods, silk, crockery-ware, earthen-ware, brass, copper, and tin utensils, there are also numerous little *olla-podrida* stalls, kept by *Kullas*. There was also a sprinkling of money-lenders and changers here and there, the rate of exchange from Rupees into silver bits being four per cent., and into copper Rs. 3-2. Judging from the large quantity of old silver ornaments that they had exposed for sale (chiefly of Shan manufacture), it would appear the original owners had never been able to redeem their property, which is generally the case when once goods are pledged. I purchased a few combs made from *murraya paniculata* and *nauclea cadamba;* but beyond these I saw nothing sufficiently interesting to add to my curios. From *nauclea cadamba* the clogs of Burma are also made.

78. My attention was now drawn to the hairy family who were standing at a stall, but they were so mobbed, that it was difficult to get a good view of them. They are supported by the king I believe, and have a *carte-blanche* to go to market once a week to obtain what rations they require gratis. To me, the group presented a rather revolting spectacle, more especially the hairy woman, who seemed a most hideous monster; her entire face and head were so densely covered with hair, as to conceal every feature. From Yule's description, however, Maphoon, for that is the poor mother's name, was less repulsive in her younger days.*

The hairy family of Burma.

---

* To-day we had a singular visitor at the Residency : it was Maphoon, the daughter of Shwe Maong, Homo hirsuties described and depicted in Crawford's narrative, where a portrait of her as a young child also appears. Not expecting such a visitor, one started and exclaimed involuntarily as they entered, what at first sight seemed an absolute realization in the flesh of the dog-headed *anubis*. The whole of Maphoon's face was covered with hair. On a part of the cheek and between the nose and mouth, this was confined to short down, but over all the rest of the face was a thick silky hair of a brown colour, paling about the nose and chin, four or five inches long. At the *alae* of the nose, under the eye, and on the cheek-bone this was very fully developed, but it was in and on the ear that it was most extraordinary, except the extreme upper tip, no part of the ear was visible. All the rest was filled and veiled by a large mass of silky hair, growing apparently out of every part of the external organ and hanging in a dependent lock to a length of eight or ten inches. The hair over her forehead was brushed so as to blend with the hair of the head, the latter being dressed, as usual with their country women, *à la chinoise*. It was not so thick as altogether to conceal the forehead. The nose—so densely covered with hair, as no animal's is that I know of, and with long fine locks curving out, and is pendent like the wisps of a fine skye-terrier's coat—had a most strange appearance. The beard was pale in colour, and about four inches in length, seemingly very soft and silky.

Poor Maphoon's manners were good and modest, her voice soft and feminine, and her expression mild and not unpleasing, after the first instinctive repulsion was overcome. Her appearance rather suggested the idea of a pleasant-looking woman masquerading than that of anything brutal. This discrimination, however, was very difficult to preserve in sketching her likeness—a task which devolved on me to-day in Mr. Grant's absence. On an after visit, however, Mr. Grant made a portrait of her, which was generally acknowledged to be most successful. Her neck, bosom, and arms appeared to be covered with a fine pale down scarcely visible in some lights. She made a move as if to take off her upper clothing, but reluctantly, and we prevented it. Her husband and two boys accompanied her. The elder boy, about four or five years old, had nothing abnormal about him. The younger, who was fourteen months old, and still at the

79. The old site of the market-place was being cleared of all its rubbish by gangs of convicts, who were far more heavily ironed than one is accustomed to see in British territory. They looked the picture of misery and starvation. The jail I was informed is an ordinary bamboo building, enclosed by a wall of the same material. At night the prisoners are placed in stocks, and for food they are either dependent on their friends or charity. Deaths from starvation, neglect, or cruelty are of common occurrence, but unknown to the king we are told, who boasts never having ordered one of his subjects to be executed: but if newspapers may be depended on, it would appear from Mr. Marks's speech delivered at Ceylon, that when His Majesty wishes a party executed, he orders that he be put out of sight, and shortly after the mandate, the offender is reported to have died from indigestion!

Convicts and their treatment.

80. North of the town, and just below the foot of Mandalay Hill, is the encamping-ground for Shan and Paloung traders, for whose convenience extensive *zayats* have been built. They commence to arrive from the states east and north-east of the capital about the end of October or middle of November, bringing with them tea, palm-sugar, stick-lac, &c., and taking back other merchandize, principally salt. Everything is carried in pottle-shaped panniers slung either on ponies, mules, or bullocks. I tasted the two descriptions of tea imported—one in the form of balls, and the other compressed in a hollow bamboo; but they seemed wanting in flavour, owing no doubt to the careless manner in which they were originally picked and prepared. Apparently this insipid flavour is most appreciated, for it is quite common to see baskets of tea suspended from rafts and floated down the river, or tied together and allowed to soak in the moat below the Residency with apparently the one object of ridding the leaf as much as possible of all its bitter and narcotic properties. The morn-

Encamping-ground of Shans and Paloungs; their system of trade.

---

breast, was evidently taking after the mother. There was a little hair on the head, but the child's ear was full of long silky floss, and it could boast of a moustache and beard of purple silky down that would have cheered the heart of many a cornet. In fact, the appearance of the child agrees almost exactly with what Mr. Crawford says of Maphoon herself as an infant. This child is thus the third in descent exhibiting the strange peculiarity, and in this third generation, as in the two preceding, this peculiarity has appeared only in one individual. Maphoon has the same dental peculiarity also that her father had, the absence of the canine teeth and grinder the back part of the gums presenting merely a hard ridge, still she chews *pan* like her neighbours. Mr. Camaratta tells some story of an Italian wishing to marry her, and take her to Europe, which was not allowed. Should the great Barnum hear of her, he would not be so easily thwarted. According to the Woondouk the King offered a reward to any man who would marry her, but it was long before any one was found bold enough or avaricious enough to venture. Her father, Shwe Maong, was murdered by robbers many years ago.—*Yule's Ava*, page 94.

ing I visited this locality some fresh caravans from the East had just arrived, but the people were unwilling either to sell or even show us their goods; in fact, it was with difficulty they could be induced to answer the few questions I put through an interpreter The Paloungs are hardly distinguishable from the Shans; they are perhaps shorter, thicker set, and not quite so fair; but in all other respects, either as regards features, costume, or domestic habits, they are identical.

81. Information having been brought me now of some *ficus elas-*
Trip to Mengoon in search of *tica* plantations at Mengoon, I mention-
ficus elastica. ed to Captain Strover my intention of inspecting them; and although he doubted the accuracy of what I had heard, he very kindly arranged to accompany me, and the next morning we crossed over in the Residency boat. Mengoon is perhaps four miles north of Mandalay, on the opposite side of the river, and three from the *Made* creek, where we got on board. The Irrawaddy just here at this season is divided into many arms enclosing islands of considerable size, some permanent and inhabited, others temporary or mere sand-banks of recent formation, which delayed us crossing. Certainly we stopped a few minutes to get a shot at some geese, but what actually impeded progress was the circuitous route and the strong current we had to stem.

82. In the creek where we embarked was lying His Majesty's
His Majesty's State Barge, and State barge, with a handsomely-carved
neglected Steam Saw-mills. and gilded pavilion, and a seven tiered-roof, after the description of the tower in the palace—borne on twin flat-bottomed boats, also gilded to the water's edge, and finished off at prow and stern by leogryphs handsomely picked out in gold and red, and finished off in mosaic work in mirror. I believe this barge has never been used by the King since it was built. Here, also, were the steam saw-mills in course of erection, but from the rusted condition of the machinery it was evident they had been in this half-finished state for months past. The buildings, which were teak throughout and most substantial, had evidently been designed by one who understood the work, for every possible provision had been made, both for launching and landing the heaviest timber.

83. The Resident was quite right regarding the inaccuracy of
Failure to find *ficus elastica* at the report brought me; for after a
Mengoon. most careful hunt all about Mengoon, and enquiries from different people who had resided in the vicinity for years past, we could find no trace of the *ficus elastica* plantations, but were shown some fine specimens of *ficus cordifolia*, which, apparently in the absence of the genuine tree, is equally rever-

enced by Buddhists. The *ficus* group throughout seems to demand homage and respect from all Buddhists and Hindoos, the one most common to the country being that most idolized.

84. After breakfast I took a ramble by myself in search of plants and birds, but came on nothing new. *Ciophytum sensitivum* and *Malpighia coccigera* were every where to be seen amongst the brick rubbish; *Triumfetta rhomboidea*, and *Melochia corchorifolia* were common in cultivated lands; also *Hiptage obtusifolia, Aspidopterys nutans, Elæocarpus varuna, Grewia microcos, Pterospermum, semisaittatum, Sterculia colorata, Capparis flavicans, C. glauca, Cananga odorata*, and a solitary instance of *Eriodendron penlandrum*, evidently cultivated, for it was in one of the orchards of which there are a good many in this neighbourhood. The fruit trees cultivated are, for the most part, plantains, pomegranates, oranges, *papayas*, and custard-apples; I also noticed *Physallis peruviana*—a native of Peru—which was pointed out to me as a weed, but I have nowhere met with it in Burma, excepting in the deserted haunts of man. The only birds I noted were *Corvus impudicus* and *C. culminaius, Palæornis affinis* and *P. torquatus* in numbers; *Ampelliceps coronatus, Carpophaga sylvatica*, and a large number of the *Nectariniidæ* family. Among the ruins I observed some deserted martins' nests literally filled with long-legged spiders *(opilio)*, which, when disturbed, poured forth in myriads, but I did not observe the martins feed on them. Every roof and wall of the old buildings was covered with bats, whose droppings are often converted into saltpetre, for the manufacture of gunpowder, by the poorer classes. The red squirrels with white tipped tails were very common in the orchards, and I amused myself watching their raids on the fruit. Descending from their homes, which were generally high forest trees, they ran across to the orchard, took an observation, foraged, and returned with their booty, repeating the operations of reconnoitering and plundering again and again.

Vegetation and Ornithology of Mengoon.

85. Mengoon, it will be remembered, is celebrated for the pagoda commenced in 1771 by King Mentaragyee, and destroyed by the earthquake of 1839, when but little over one-third completed. Captain Strover and myself took a few measurements, which were found to agree accurately with those made by Yule in 1855. The base was 450 feet square, and height 165 feet, which is 335 feet less than it would have been when completed. There is actually nothing very engaging in the design, though the massiveness of the building cannot fail to attract attention, and create surprise at the money, time, and labour that must have been wasted in the

The great Pagoda, Mengoon.

erection of this colossal edifice, that now lies a heap of ruins, displaying a mass of masonry perhaps unequalled in the world, and serving as a lasting monument of King Mentaragyee's folly. In a tope of mango-trees a little below the ruins is a complete model of what the pagoda was intended to be, and it is from this alone that a correct idea can be formed of the amount of labour and material that yet remained to complete the work. The devastation committed by the earthquake can hardly be described with sufficient effect to convey to the reader's mind the actual amount of damage done. I had read several accounts of the ruins, but none impressed me with the same feeling of wonderment that crossed my mind as I wandered through this sad scene of desolation. The building is rent and re-rent in every direction from top to bottom, tons and tons of solid masonry, hurled some distance by the shock, are everywhere to be seen, while over-hanging the deep yawning chasms are held in suspension by an almost imperceptible tie large blocks of brick work, which are proof of the excellence of the materials used and labour employed. It is not improbable that the effects of the earthquake would have been less severely felt, had the building been supported on a more substantial foundation. Hiram Cox tells us the superstructure rested on covered-in square wells lined with sheet-lead and beams of the same metal five inches square. These wells were filled with offerings of various kinds, such as glass, silver ornaments, mock jewellery, &c., and one of Dr. Priestley's machines for impregnating water with fixed air.*

Towards the north-east these ruins may be mounted by a most dangerous ascent. I ventured three-fourths of the way up to get a good bird's-eye view of the surrounding country, in hopes perhaps of discovering, with the aid of my binoculars, some signs of the *ficus elastica* plantation, but I was disappointed; the scenery was flat and uninteresting, neither was the plantation anywhere to be seen. I now descended, and felt much more comfortable—though considerably blown—when I got to the bottom; for all that supported me were the projecting pieces of masonry that served as steps; but a false selection, and nothing could have saved either my servant or myself from being killed on the spot. The unexpended materials are scattered all about: piles of brick and heaps of lime sufficient to build a handsome mansion, all lie wasted, where they were first thrown. Fronting the east entrance are the remains of two gigantic leogryphs, which, according to Cox, were to have been ninety-five feet high, with white marble eye-balls, thirteen feet

---

* *Cox's Journal of Residency in the Burman Empire*, page 113.

each in circumference. They were decapitated by the earthquake, and the heads now lie in fragments around them.

86. We inspected the great bell, which, with the exception of that at Moscow, is perhaps the largest in the world. It is suspended from three teak beams strapped together with iron bands, resting on teak uprights encased in masonry; these, however, having been thrown out of the perpendicular, the bell has now to be supported on blocks of wood about eighteen inches high. Captain Strover and myself crawled in from below to examine the workmanship, an account of which is given below in the foot-note, as described by that accurate observer and distinguished author, Yule.*

The great bell of Mengoon.

87. Among the most interesting pagodas we visited in the neighbourhood, was that undergoing repairs at the expense of one of the Queens. Its unusual style of architecture cannot fail to attract attention, and as we saw it newly white-washed, and capped with a recently-gilded *htee*, it presented a most striking appearance. It represents a series of concentric masonry circles, each diminishing in size upwards until the seventh tier is reached, and a few feet higher is the *htee*. Each circle is surrounded by a vandyked parapet, with small recesses at equal distances, each being occupied by a marble statuette of gaudama. We mounted the pagoda by a flight of stairs within the building, but descended another way which was evidently intended for egress, the steps leading into the court yard. It was now time for us to take our departure, as we anticipated a few interruptions on the way back. It is fortunate we did not delay; for another quarter of an hour, and the *Made* creek would have been so blocked by boats, rafts, firewood, grass, &c., that it would simply have been impossible to pass up that night; as it was, we were a good deal delayed, and eventually had to make elbow-room for ourselves for; the

Unusual style of a Pagoda in the neighbourhood of Mengoon.

---

* Small ingots of silver (and some say pieces of gold) may still be traced, unmelted in the mass, and from the inside one sees the curious way in which the makers tried to strengthen the parts which suspended it by dropping into the upper part of the mould iron chains round which the metal has run.

The Burmese report the bell to contain 555,555 viss of metal (about 900 tons). Its principal dimensions are as follow :—

	Ft.	In.
External diameter at the lip	10	0
Interior height	11	6
Exterior ditto	12	0
Interior diameter at top	8	6

The thickness of metal varies from six inches to twelve, and the actual weight of the whole bell is by rough calculation, about eighty tons, or one-eleventh of the popular estimate. According to Mr. Howard Malcolm, whose authority was probably Colonel Burney, the weight is stated by the Royal Chronicle at 55,500 viss, or about ninety tons. This statement is probably therefore genuine, and the popular fable merely a multiplication of it by ten.—*Yule's Ava*, page 171.

owners of the rafts and boats refused to make way and seemed amused at our akward predicament. We got back to the Residency about 7 P.M., and I felt deeply indebted to Captain Strover for the delightful day I had spent, and for the vast amount of information he afforded me on all matters connected with Mengoon and its ruins.

88. The following day was spent in talking over my future plans and deciding upon the best course to be adopted in case of misfortune. I was warned at all times to be prepared for difficulties, as the country I would travel over was peopled by wild tribes unamenable to law or reason; and although it was hoped nothing serious would happen, yet I could hardly expect to accomplish an expedition of the nature deputed me, without unpleasantnesses of some sort cropping up. This caution rather gave a zest to my work for I was always fond of a life of excitement, and anticipated some fun with these wild people; however, with a few exceptions, they troubled me very little. Captain Strover next told me he had been making careful enquiries as to where I was most likely to find the *ficus elastica* growing in a natural state; but as the only man who knew anything about the vicinity, was in the King's employ, there was not only a difficulty in getting him to the Residency—without causing suspicion—but also in getting any information out of him. I believe an application was made for some one who knew the country to accompany me, and as there was but this one man at Mandalay, who had worked the *ficus elastica* forests, it was hoped the bait would take, but apparently it did not, for I heard nothing more on the subject. As things turned out, however, it mattered little; for with the information elicited by Captain Strover, and the sketch map prepared from what he had heard, I got on admirably, and was always able to detect any little attempts at deception on the part of my guides, who evidently had been instructed to mislead me. Regarding the distribution of the presents I had brought from Rangoon, I also asked advice, but the Resident considered I had too few things, and suggested I should without delay send off, and purchase a further supply of red and white muslins, beads, &c., which fortunately I did, or I do not know what would have been the consequence: very likely the absence of these things would have been the means of getting me into trouble, for the wild tribes are naturally of a jealous disposition, and troublesome if any distinction is made in the presents.

Future plans discussed with Resident for attaining object of Mission.

89. In the evening His Majesty's royal orders, addressed to the Governor of Mogoung and Bhamo, sanctioning my visiting their districts,

Receipt of Royal Orders to the Governor of Mogoung.

were sent me, under an official letter of instruction from the Resident, which will be found among the appendices.

90. As there yet remained two days before the steamer would start for Bhamo, I determined on visiting Amarapoora, a city though perhaps of no great antiquity, is, nevertheless, one whose past associations lay claim to reflection. Among the ruins of this once-flourishing capital are the relics of past opulence and grandeur that in themselves are most instructive, and cannot fail to excite the interest even of the least curious. King Mentaragyee Phra, fourth son of Alompra, on his accession to the throne, transferred the seat of Government from Ava to Amarapoora, and, it is believed, took possession of his new Palace on the 10th May 1783. He died in 1819, after a reign of thirty-eight years. In 1822 his grandson and successor re-established the capital at Ava, which, with the exception of King Mentaragyee's reign, has continued to be the metropolis for four centuries. In 1837 Prince Tharrawaddie, brother to Mentaragyee, seized the throne, and renewed the seat of Government at Amarapoora, where it remained until the establishment of the present capital, Mandalay.

Visit to City of Amarapoora.

The walled embankments and wooden bridges of extraordinary length, that kept up communication with the city when the overlap of the Myetnye Choung flooded the country to the east and south, are fast being obliterated by age, the embankments in many places are already level with the ground, and all trace of the bridges will be equally extinct ere long. So also will the walls of this once proud city; but there still remains sufficient trace of the gateways to estimate their original solidity and massiveness. The roads, with few exceptions, are a tangled mass of scrub jungle, and the richly carved and gilded buildings are in the last stage of decay, affording but a poor sample of the magnificent spectacle they must once have presented.

The great gun brought from Arakan in the last century, measuring twenty-eight feet nine inches, with an external diameter at the breach of two feet seven inches, and calibre of only eleven and half inches lies spiked and hidden in the grass. It is an unweildy piece of ordinance, being made of a number of pieces of bar iron, bound together by hoops of the same material, and the whole clumsily welded together.

91. Amarapoora, though less densely populated than in the days of its prosperity, still contains a large number of well-to-do-people. The principal street is occupied by cloth merchants and vendors of various other articles, the more wealthy apparently being

Population of Amarapoora.

Mussulmen and Chinamen. These latter ubiquitous people, who carry with them their customs, costumes, and religion wherever they go, are not alone distinguishable by their dress and *pig-tail*, but may be traced by that flat-faced, high cheek-boned, oblique-eyed countenance, so characteristic of their race. Their houses are as a rule of brick, the dimensions being regulated by the owners' means; but, as far as I can remember, in no instance have I seen an example of the Burman type of architecture having been entirely adopted. In Bhamo, Mogoung, and other towns or villages on the Upper Irrawaddy, I have observed, that where a Chinaman's means will not admit of his erecting an abode entirely of brick, the front is always of that material, and the remainder of bamboo and plaster until circumstances permit of the desired addition being made.

92. Here, these people have erected a most substantial temple, which apparently is open to the inspection of people of all religions;

Chinese Temple.

neither was any objection made to my sketching the different articles of interest, though the Chinamen were markedly silent when I elicited information on any religious subject, only noticing my question by a significant laugh. My sketches afforded immense amusement, more especially the one I presented them with, which was done in red and blue pencil, and represented a love scene. I was told it would be kept in memory of me and suspended on the walls of the room in which we sat. I thanked them for the compliment: and thinking the present offered a good opportunity to wedge in a question, I asked which were the appointed days and hours for worship, but no reply was forthcoming, so I gave up all hopes of gaining any information from them on religious subjects.

The temple is a square masonry building with a compartment on each side, an open court in the centre, and roof such as one sees in pictures of Chinese towns. It is entered by a circular gate, which from a little distance has the appearance of a hole in the wall. On either side are two huge marble figures representing some mythological Chinese demon. Round the wall of the vestibule were suspended all sorts of peculiar implements made of wood and covered with silver paper representing the heads of horses, battle axes, crosses, swords, &c., &c.: all these I afterwards noticed being carried at the Dragon festival I attended at Bhamo, and learnt they were distinctive orders of office. Fronting the vestibule was a compartment railed off with gilded iron bars, and a handsome gold fringe of about eighteen inches deep, suspended from the roof, ran the whole length of the rails. Evidently this was the sanctum. Within were two large figures placed in recesses in the wall, and dressed in the most gorgeous Chinese costumes, but whom they were intended to represent I could not find out, probably Fo and Confucius. Between them was the altar, over which was suspended a rich scarlet silk canopy, ornamented in gold and silver work, and hung round with a deep gold fringe.

The altar-cloth was equally elaborate and costly in design : and the paraphernalia, consisting of handsome lamps, candle-sticks, censers, &c., were quite in keeping with the other costly decorations. The remaining portion of the walls was adorned with numerous wooden figures placed in recesses, some representing human-beings, and others monsters of imagination. This place was locked up, and apparently none but the priests were permitted to enter.

The apartments to the right were occupied by the priests who were only distinguishable from their countrymen by a clean-shaved head and white clothes throughout. They were remarkably reticent, and hardly took any notice of me when introduced : it may have been that they were too far lost in admiration of the handsome Chinese lanterns, that had just been presented to the temple, and which they were carefully examining.

93. On the left, as one entered, was seated a party smoking and drinking tea : this was evidently an after-service lounge for all who felt inclined to partake of refreshment. I was invited to join the idlers, and was very politely handed a wee cup of capital flavoured tea, though weak, and a pipe of a most ingenious contrivance—one deserving of the *multum in parvo* name. It was a miniature *hookah*, containing water, tobacco, and lights, all in the compass of an ordinary-sized eau-de-Cologne bottle. The bowl not being sufficiently large to contain over a pinch of tobacco, which is consumed in one breath, the process of cleaning out, reloading from the little reservoir, and lighting becomes very tedious to one unaccustomed to the pipe ; and I only took a few whiffs, though I liked the flavour of the tobacco very much, which, I was informed, came direct from China. The spills were of a sort of touch-paper that remains alight until entirely consumed.

<small>Smoking and refreshment parlours in the temple.</small>

94. The magnitude of the Palo-dangyee cannot fail to attract attention, but its neglected condition points to its unimportance.

<small>Palo-dangyee Pagoda.</small>

95. On the way back to Mandalay, I visited the celebrated temple of Mah-myat-mimi, which contains the collossal brass image of Gaudama brought from Arakan in 1784. This temple is held in

<small>Temple of Mah-myat-mimi.</small>

great sanctity, and draws a constant flow of followers of the Buddhist faith to the shrine, with offerings of all sorts. The idol is seated on a throne, after the design of royalty, and is twelve feet high, with well-proportioned limbs. This is said to be a faithful cast; having been presented to the reigning monarch by Gaudama to compensate for his absence, as he was then about to leave Arakan. It is supposed to have been brought across in two pieces, but there are others who declare to it having been transported entire. The steps leading up to the building are roofed in, and on either side lined with stalls, at which are exposed for sale various articles, including knives, scissors, toys, beads, looking-glasses, crockery, combs, lacquer-ware boxes, &c, &c., all of which seem to find a ready sale among the devotees. There are two high roads leading to this centre of attraction, the eastern and western; I took the latter. It is lined with mendicants, who are entirely supported by charity; and just before coming on the temple, there are some workers in Sagain marble. They seem to have established themselves in a capital position for business, numbers of purchases being made as offerings to the temple by passers-by. I was also induced to invest in a few articles, which I sent to England, where they are greatly admired, especially a little marble elephant, which was a wonderfully-good piece of sculpture. It is really marvellous to see the masterly manner in which these artists hew blocks of marble into all manner of forms and shapes. They have none of the appliances of the modern sculptor, but, seated on the bare ground, with chisel in one hand and mallet in the other, work away at the stone before them, substituting the *crow-bar* for the *revolving-table,* and using their great toes as a substitute for clamps when the block is not sufficiently heavy to resist the blow. They have neither callipers nor graduated scales to guide them, but are entirely dependent on the eye for the symmetrical development of the design, which they have conceived in their imagination. The design having reached a certain stage of completion, the chisel is substituted by a rough, coarse file, followed by a grinding process with fine sand and water. The final polish is given first with finely-powdered fossilized wood, on a wet cloth, and lastly applied dry on the palm of the hand.

96. The eastern road I had intended visiting at some future time, with a view to sketching the *Maha-toolut-boungyo,* and *Maha-oungepeima* buildings, so celebrated for their elaborately-gilded carvings; but I was prevented, having to embark for Bhamo sooner than was anticipated.

<small>Inability to traverse the eastern road to Amarapoora.</small>

97. Beyond the city walls were the remains of an indigo factory,
which, judging from the good condition of the vats and plant, could only recently have been deserted: everything had been started on a grand scale, but allowed to fall through for some unaccountable reason. Indigo was evidently once cultivated in this vicinity, and still continues to resow itself; there was a good crop on the ground when I visited the place.

Remains of an indigo factory.

98. A portion of the road leading from Mandalay to Amarapoora is lined with the most handsome belt of tamarind trees I have ever seen, and which are sufficiently attractive to have engaged the attention of the artists, Messrs. Bourne and Shepherd, who have photographed them. They will be found amongst their admirable collection of views in Upper Burma.

Belt of tamarind.

99. The following is a list of trees, shrubs, and plants noticed and registered: *Cyclea peltata, Argemone mexicana, Papaver somniferum, Nasturtium diffusum, Artabotrys burmanicus, Uraria macrophylla, Unona discolor, Parabœna sagittata, Hypericum clodeoides, Tamarix diocia, Polygala eriptera, P. glancescens, Capparis orbiculata, Cleome viscosa, Atbuliton indicum, Pavonia Zeylanica, Hibiscus vitifolius, Dipterocarpus tuburculatus, Shorea robusta, S. obtusa, Garcinia xynthochymus, Cratoxylon pruniflorum, Helicteres viscida, Bombax malabaricum, Aspidopterys tomentosa.*

Vegetation observed.

100. In fields and gardens, *Portulaca oleracea* birds were scarce; sparrows (*Passer Indicus*), larks (*Alanda gugjula*), *Graculus fuscicollis*, and crows (*Corvus impudicus*) and *C. splendens* being among the most common. The only insects I noticed were of a tropical type, embracing butterflies *Maulis* and *Deptera dytisci*, and *Gyrini* also being very abundant, where there was running water.

Birds and Insects.

CHAPTER III.

Journey between Mandalay and Bhamo, including return voyage.

101. I shall not devote much space to this part of my journey, for the distance has been so often covered, that there is little left, I fear, for me to chronicle of a novel type, while it must also be remembered that travelling by steamer does not offer a favourable opportunity for gathering information. However, there is this satisfaction left me, in knowing that we all do not see with the same eyes; neither does observation consist in the mere noticing of facts that pass before one, but rather in noticing results, and, as Stuart Mill remarks, in his *System of Logic*, to do this well, is a rare talent. I will therefore hope that something still remains to be told of these latitudes, and that I may have been fortunate enough to have gathered a few items of interest, that have escaped the observation of previous voyagers; but if, unfortunately, my narrative proves stale, the reader has always the option of skipping this chapter, and accepting it in the charitable light of a mere connecting link to the remaining portion of my jottings.

Information embodied not of a novel type.

102. On the morning of the 19th December 1873, the *Colonel Fytche*, of 215 tons burden, left Mandalay for Bhamo with the mails, a general cargo, and one flat in tow, laden with cotton. With the exception of another European, the passengers were principally Chinese, returning to their homes in Western China.

Departure from Mandalay.

103. The objectionable habit of opium-smoking rendered these people most undesirable companions on board-ship. No sooner had the narcotic influence of the drug lulled one into dream-land, than another resumed his smoke, until the whole atmosphere in the vessel, throughout the twenty-four hours, was so densely charged with the filthy fumes, that the place became quite unbearable. Any attempt to restrict these men to a particular part of the steamer was altogether out of the question; for they were in such numbers, that they lay packed like sardines all over the deck, right up to the door of the companion-ladder leading into the saloon, down which the clouds of smoke descended, until even that part of the vessel offered no retreat from the sickening fumes. Here a happy thought struck me, and I suggested to the Captain

Objectionable habit of opium-smoking on board.

that if the opium-smokers could not be limited to space, they might be so as to time, and thereby allow Mr. Graham and myself a little time to breathe fresh air. My appeal, however, proved of no avail: the Chinamen had taken first-class deck passages, and could not be interfered with; in other words, these were the paying people, and it would not have been to the interest of the Company to have put their pipes out. Fortunately, habit soon becomes a second nature, and in a couple of days I should not have known, but that I was inhaling the purest of oxygen; in fact, before reaching Bhamo I was induced to try a whiff or so of the poisonous drug, by an old Chinaman who had ingratiated himself into my good books by his charmingly interesting accounts of the jade* trade, and his intended route to Western China *via* Momein; but I vowed never again to try the experiment, for the next morning I awoke with a head no amount of "doctors" or "pick-me-ups" could cure, the only remedy, my old friend suggested, was to repeat the dose of the previous night, but that I declined.

104. I shall not stop here to relate all Iheard of the jade trade, or route to Western China, for it would only be a repetition of what is coming presently. The country between Mandalay and the third defile, not being sufficiently interesting to engage the whole of my attention, I alternately took notes, and watched two Burmans playing chess. Each player seemed perfectly wrapped up in his own line of tactics, and lost to all that was going on around him. Each move was only made after the most deliberate thought; nor was a word exchanged between the players beyond proclaiming check. The game lasted two hours and ten minutes, when the combat was brought to a close in a "drawn" game. The players could now no longer maintain their silence, but joined the spectators in their merry gabble and peals of laughter. Being interested in chess, I made my interpreter teach me the names of the Burmese pieces and their moves; and, before we reached Bhamo, I was sufficiently acquainted with the game to often defeat my Burmese opponents. They seemed, at the start off, amused at my line of tactics, but ultimately acknowledged some of my "mates" capital. Many is the hour at night that I have watched two and three of these Burman enthusiasts, trying to solve some of the problems I had given them. A brief sketch of the game, which differs but little from our own, will doubtless prove interesting. As with us, so apparently with the Burmans, chess is a game more in favour

Burmese game of chess described.

---

* Also called serpentine and ophite. They are all hydrous silicates of magnesia with iron manganese or chrome, and sometimes alumina. Jade corresponds nearly to *verd antique*, which is a precious serpentine, or beautiful and valuable marble mixed with lime-stone.

with enthusiasts than gamblers. With the introduction of this game into different countries, some changes no doubt have been made in the names of the pieces, and their moves. As to its origin and antiquity, doubts still seem to exist: in Hindoostan it is known under the Sanscrit name of *chaturonga*, while the Persians have corrupted the word into *chatrange*, and the Arabs into *shatrange*. By the French it is called *echecs*, by the English *chess*, by the Germans *schach*, and by the Burmese *tsit-da-yin*. On the next page is given a drawing of the pieces and board, which will, with the following description, most readily explain the moves. The game is played by two persons, each having sixteen pieces, rendered distinguishable by a difference in colour. The arrangement of the board, at the set off, is generally as follows; though some say it is not imperative to place the *yattars* and *gnas* on the squares, and that the remaining pieces may be placed at the discretion of the players, provided they are neither in front of the *gnas* nor in line with the *yattars* :—

Arrangement of the Board.

Black.			White.	
Yattars, Squares	1 and 8	... ...	Squares 57 and 64	
Sin ,,	10 ,, 19	... ...	,, 46 ,, 55	
Shimbooyen,,	11	... ...	,, 56	
Tsakai ,,	20	... ...	,, 45	
Min ,,	12 ,, 18	... ...	,, 47 ,, 53	
Gnas ,,	21 to 28	... ...	,, 37 ,, 44	

The moves are almost identical with our own. A *gna* one square at a time, but takes opponent diagonally. The only difference from the English game here is that at the first move the *gna* has no power of advancing more than one square.

A *min* moves exactly in the same manner as a *knight*.

A *sin* moves a square at a time, either diagonally or straight, but retrograde moves must always be in a diagonal direction.

A *yattar's* move is similar to that of a *castle*.

A *tsakai* can only move diagonally one move at a time, backward or forward.

A *shimbooyen's* move corresponds with that of a *king*, and he cannot be *taken*.

Check is called *gna*; double check, *nulchot-gna*; check-mate, *shorme-len*; signifying, *lost*; stale-mate, *tha-ya-the*.

Gnas in squares 25 to 28 and 21 to 24, reaching, respectively, squares 57, 50, 43, 36, and 37, 46, 55, and 64 in the opponent's quarter, can reclaim the *tsakai*, but no other piece. This rule applies equally to either player, and the arrangement of the *gnas* on one side will explain those on the other.

When all the pieces have been captured but the *shimbooyen*, and the opponent has one *tsakai*, a *yattar*, and *shimbooyen* left, check-mate must be accomplished in sixteen moves, or it is considered a "drawn" game. A checkmate of this description is called a *yattar mandalay*.

Forty-four moves are allowed when the check-mate has to be accomplished with a *shimbooyen, tsakai*, and *sin;* this mate is called *sin mandalay*.

Where a mate has to be made with a *min, shimbooyen*, and *tsakai*, sixty-four moves are allowed, and the check-mate is called *min mandalay*.

105. But, to take up the thread of my narrative from whence I diverged. Proceeding northward, up to Singoo, the scenery is flat and uninteresting: the noble Shan mountains still run parallel with the eastern shore, and, though miles inland, continue to be the object of greatest attraction. Singoo, now a village not exceeding eighty houses, has the repute of once having been the fortified capital of an independent state. Whether there is anything on record in the annals of Burma to support this belief, I have never found out; but my own idea is, that the period since the place was of any importance is sufficiently distant to admit of fiction (which grows by age) having gained for it its present repute; and, were the true facts forthcoming it would be found, I dare say, to have been a mere stockaded village of considerable size, and the centre of the holding of some influential Burman; I much regretted not having had an opportunity of exploring the place. A little higher, but on the opposite bank a reef of gneiss-ore and hornblendic rock, with crystalline limestones intercalated, is apparent, but offers no impediment to navigation, as it does not protrude to any distance into the stream. Unfortunately, the navigable channel of the river separated us from the western bank by nearly half a mile: I was thus debarred the pleasure of bagging a few of the blue rock-pigeons that have formed a regular colony in the sandstone cliffs a little above Mengoon. As we progress, the Sagain hills gradually dwindle away to almost the level of the surrounding country, and as they decrease in height, so the vegetation seems to improve. We now noticed a few huts scattered here and there, which my binoculars told me were inhabited by lime-burners. The river thus far has been much subdivided by islands, in all stages of formation, from the sandbank of yesterday's creation, to the island clothed with arborescent vegetation, inhabited and cultivated. It is in such parts that navigation becomes most difficult, and it is only after many years' experience that the eye becomes sufficiently familiar with the upper current to detect the navigable from the unnavigable channel. To

Village of Singoo and navigation of the river.

1	2	3	4	5	6	7	8
9	10	11	12	13	14	15	16
17	18	19	20	21	22	23	24
25	26	27	28	29	30	31	32
33	34	35	36	37	38	39	40
41	42	43	44	45	46	47	48
49	50	51	52	53	54	55	56
57	58	59	60	61	62	63	64

Yaltar	ရထား
Mein	မြင်း
Sein	ဆင်
Satay	စစ်သဲ
Shimbooyen	ရှင်ဘုရင်
Grx	စွယ်

a landsman, I question if the indications would be apparent, even when pointed out; certainly they were not to me.

106. For the last half hour the man heaving the lead may have been intoning *na-ba-tun* (which is intended for "no bottom"), in the most stentorian voice, and the next moment he will be heard to yell in a higher key *sara do balm* (two and a half fathoms); this draws the Captain to the side of the vessel, and the movements of the man with the lead are expedited by a volley of nautical vociferation: *do balm* (two fathoms) is the next sounding shrieked, and the Captain rushes to telegraph "half speed" to the engine-room—*ek balm* (one fathom) is then heard, followed by the order to turn astern full power, but it is too late: we are aground, and many of us on our backs. This is no exaggregated sketch, but one that happens two or three times on a voyage between Rangoon and Bhamo, so treacherous are the channels: still the navigation on this river is not nearly so intricate as that of the river Indus, for I believe the Irrawaddy has seldom been known to entirely shift its navigable course under a fortnight or a month, while a change in the set of the current in the Indus, a few hours after the Pilots have taken their soundings and decided on the course, will so entirely alter the nature of the channels as to render the one first decided upon the most dangerous. There is, perhaps, no river in the world, the fickle nature of whose course and propensity to erode its banks works greater changes, and with it brings more sorrow and ruin on the population, than the Indus. In one season whole villages, and even entire forests, are swept away, and the sites they once occupied transformed into a desolate waste, studded with the *debris* of the gigantic wreck, or converted into a sand-bank covered with a fresh growth of *tamarisk indica*, whose seed has been brought down in suspension by the river which now flows, perhaps, two or three miles from its original course. No analogy can be drawn between the surrounding scenery of the two great waters; for, while the Indus traverses a sparsely-wooded, flat, and uninteresting valley, eroding its steep banks, which may be seen yielding tons of earth and trees to the boiling action of the under-current, the Irrawaddy winds its course through a densely-wooded and mountainous land, whose beauty cannot be surpassed.

107. A little north of Singoo, the river is walled in on either side by a low line of coarse-sandstone hills, which take the form of a series of steps, the lowest reaching the water's edge. This is known as the third defile or *kyouk-dwen*, signifying rock-pond, and extends to Malee, with an average breadth of a quarter of a mile.

The hills are not sufficiently high to give either a bold or imposing effect to the view, though the scenery is rendered remarkably picturesque by the prettily-wooded slopes, from which peep here and there groups of houses in twos and threes, casting half lights, and shadows on the unrippled water, that glides beneath.

108. The most romantic place in this defile is the rock which crops up out of the water on the right bank off the village of Thingadaw. The superstructure of this island is artificial, being made up of boulders of all sizes, and the whole crowned with the pagoda of Thee-ha-dau and a pretty little monastery, in which the priests reside. Palms and *Nycthanthes* have been planted about, and *Fici* and other trees have sprung up either from the droppings of birds, or perhaps from seed contained in the earth, that hold the stones together; the latter have taken a shrub form,—from want of nourishment apparently,—and combined with the ferns, lichens, and mosses, give to the whole quite a fairy-land appearance.

Rock near Thingadaw the most romantic place in this defile.

109. The Captain very kindly stopped here, and gave me a boat to see the celebrated tame fish, that have the repute of answering to the call of *tit, tit, tit*. Evidently, they have lost all confidence in travellers, and require some more substantial proof that they are wanted than mere words, for we used the most persuasive tones, and regulated our call in all keys, but to no avail; no sooner, however, was the water baited than they commenced to come round the boat in swarms; lifting their huge bodies half out of the water, with distended mouths, begging for alms. I am not at all surprised at the poor creatures having become shy, if they are treated by all visitors in the same brutal manner that they were on the present occasion. Had my voyage been at an end instead of just begun, I should have protested against such barbarism; but, as it was, I was obliged outwardly to regard the experiment as a capital joke, by which piece of diplomacy I was allowed to go on shore for a short while, and take a hurried look round me.

Visit to see the tame fish at Thingadaw village.

These fish are said to be of the dog-fish family; some of them, I should say, are quite six feet long. They are scaleless, square-nosed, flat-headed, with mouths even disproportionately large to their size, and forked feelers. Their colour varies from slaty grey to a reddish brown. I offered Rs. 40 for one of them, much to the disgust of the old Poongyees, who told me they were the favoured ones of the deity Phra, whoever he may be!

A fair is held here annually, when I am told all the fish that can be caught by the pilgrims, are decorated down to the shoulders with gold leaf, by the same process followed in gilding pagodas; but I cannot vouch for the correctness of this report : certainly many of the fish had fragments of gold leaf about their heads.

110. The following trees, shrubs, and grasses were either observ-
Trees, shrubs, and grasses.   ed or collected by myself and collector :
dentilloidea, nycthanthes (cultivated), teak, *tectona hamiltonii*, stunted bamboo common, *mollugo, polygonum bombax, cyperaceae, olax, ficus adelia narefolia, mimosia*, and *arundo*.

111. The coal-fields visited by Professor Oldham in 1855, were to
Coal-fields.   the west of Thingadaw. He mentions three different localities in this vicinity, where coal is known to occur; but that eight miles north-west of Thingadaw, he considers gives the best coal, and the most durable.

112. We are no sooner out of the defile, than the river resumes
Natural character of the river.   its natural character : it widens out considerably, and is much intersected by sand-banks and islands of different ages. The surface current no longer presents the smooth, glassy appearance we have just observed; but sweeping onwards, a mighty brown flood, with almost resistless flow, works eddies and whirlpools by its heavy breathings, which add to the intricacy of its navigation.

113. The village of Malee marks the northern limit of the
Village of Malee.   defile; is built on a rocky eminence, crowned with pagodas and monasteries, embosomed amongst trees; and with its prettily-carved minarets and gorgeous *htees*, shooting up through the dark foliage, and the noble Shwe-oo-doung mountains in the distance presents a most pleasing effect. Here there is a Custom-house and police station : the main object of the former,—from what one hears,—is to practice extortion, and the latter to see it enforced. On the western bank, a little higher than Malee, a low line of sand-stone hills skirts the banks for some considerable distance, but on the opposite shore, the hills recede miles inland, immediately the defile ceases.

114. So shallow was the stream soon after leaving Malee, that the
Shallow state of river.   anchor had to be cast and soundings taken. As there was likely to be some little delay before the navigable channel could be determined upon, the Captain very kindly allowed me to go ashore and examine the vegetation. I collected, however, but few plants of interest, the sand-banks giving growth chiefly to *salix, compositæ*, and grasses. The main banks were wooded with an arborescent growth, among which were distinguishable, from the distance, *bombax, dep-*

terocarpus, and *hopeæ*. The wild rose was also common, and here and there hamlets appeared.

Two hours' steaming now brought us to Padepiem, where we remained, to take in wood. On the banks, ready for transport for Mandalay, were a large number of *hopea*, and *depterocarpus* logs, some of the former measuring 39 feet, with a girth of seven feet five inches, and the latter 30 feet long and six feet nine inches in circumference, they were to have been floated down with bamboos, which were also stacked in large numbers on the bank.

115. Besides the trees mentioned, I noticed *dellenia, speciosa, adelia neriefolia, jatropha*, or *coral* shrub, cultivated, as far as I could learn, entirely for its brilliant scarlet corymbs; *vitex, grewia, nauclea*, and *pladera*. To the back of the village, where there is a large sheet of water, and low lying land, *trapas* were common. I also noticed *salvinia, scirpus; stravadium*, and *azolla*.

<small>Other trees noticed.</small>

116. The steamer fuel is of mixed jungle-wood and regarded inferior to that obtained in British territory, but it is supplied at a cheaper rate, I am told, and decreases in price as we proceed northward. This is not attributable to it being more plentiful, for, if anything, the contrary is the case; but labour is cheaper, and *bonâ fide* payment in money better appreciated. Women here bring the wood on board, while the male population line the banks, seated on their haunches, unceasingly chewing *pân suparee*, and lazily looking on. The cheerful, good-natured manner in which the wooding is readily done by the girls, who are full of fun and frolic within the pale of propriety, shows their confidence in the steamer officials, and points to honest payments. Here I am told a wife can be purchased from Rs. 25 to Rs. 80, the price being regulated by the partys' figure, age, complexion, cleanness of limb, and position in life; caste not being recognized in Burma, men of all nations are regarded as eligible husbands, provided the rhino is forthcoming.

<small>Fuel for steamers.</small>

<small>Woman a marketable commodity.</small>

This practice savours strongly of the slave trade, and actually is only a shade removed from it; but it is not exactly that, for the girl's consent is necessary (though woe betide the virgin who declines a good offer), and the money which goes to the parents is looked upon as a sort of marriage dowry. In Burma where the tying, untying, or retying of the Gordian knot is perhaps more easily accomplished than in any other civilized country; the law of Menu regarding man and wife, which is maintained in our law courts in cases concerning people of the Buddhist faith, fully recognizes woman's rights, and in matters affecting property, liberty, and discretion places her on an equal footing with man, thereby screening many a poor creature from a life of misery and bondage, through an unhappy union with a profligate and worthless husband.

117. We had not left Padepiem long, when I noticed seven rafts of teak bound for the capital; the logs were of huge girth, but short, not over fifteen feet at the outside. Timber of this description, I am told, can be purchased here at Rs. 4 per log; evidently the wood was from the forests to the north-west, and floated down the Shweley, which is reported to be a timber-bearing stream throughout the year. Certainly I noticed no such teak along the banks, or at such distance inland as I could examine with my binocular. *Tectona hamiltonii* was, however, common.

Teak timber.

118. Leaving old Pagan and Tagoung to our east—towns of reputed antiquity, though now in their decline—we have the Mengwoon range of hills wooded to the water's edge on the west, faced by a steep sand-stone cliff on the opposite shore.

Town of Pagans and Tagoung.

Steaming past Tagoung, I was greatly amused at the solemn and sincere manner in which my attention was drawn to a certain place by the old pilot, who has been in British employ for many years, and was the first to pilot a steamer to Bhamo. "There" ! he remarked, "resides an all-powerful Nat who is feared and reverenced by all; he has the power of working good and evil: his fame is spread wide and far." The sepulchral tone in which each word was measuredly delivered, and the serious cast of countenance, made me lose all control of gravity, and I burst into a peal of laughter, as Mr. Graham translated for me what the old man was saying. "Ah," he continued," take care, he does not visit his wrath on you, I have known of many similar disbelievers who failed to recognize his great power, and attempted to approach him with empty hands, and who have gone away with stomach-aches from which they have ultimately died." I found I had fallen considerably in the venerable old man's opinion by my flippant behaviour, so I begged the Nat's pardon, and expressed a hope that he would not interfere with my interior economy! Unfortunately, the following day I was laid up for some hours with a sharp attack of colic brought on by going from a warm cabin into a bitterly cold atmosphere to register the thermometer on deck at 6 A.M. The news soon reached the pilot, who called to see me in my agony, shook his wise old head, and remarked, "there is no hope." This will be a capital case for him to cite to future passengers, and with truth he will be able to assert that my cure was effected by *a spirit*, and one, too, which has the power of working *good* or *evil* !!

119. Progressing onwards a few miles, the river is again much sub-divided, and from the size of the trees on the island between which and the left main bank the navigable channel flows, I am inclined to think the river must have entirely changed its course, or the island have existed for the last half century. I could not get any definite information on this subject, for it was not an easy matter to explain the difference between a channel and the river, while the old pilot invariably spoke of the *navigable channel* as the river. The scenery now improves again, especially, as we near the ancient villages of Thingyain and Myalloung. Here still are traceable the remains of forts built by the Chinese of the micacious sand-stone on which the former stands, making a pretty picture with the Ming woon hills for a back-ground. Fortunately, some passengers and cargo had to be landed at Thingyain, which gave me a ramble on shore for a quarter of an hour. The vegetation consisted principally in *bombax, salix, rosa, vitex, gardenia, depterocarpus, terminalia-chebulia salicata, ranunculaceæ, campanulaceæ* (or the hare-bell order), *illecebraceæ,* bamboo, and grasses A few cultivated palms were also observable.

Villages of Thingyain and Myalloung.

120. Here, what in Burma is known as a crucifix was pointed out to me, but the corpse of a criminal, once exhibited on it, had long since returned to dust, and the bones lie bleached on the ground. I should much have liked to secure the skull, which seemed rather a perfect specimen, but the Captain seemed horrified at the very idea. Why the name crucifix has been given to the staging to which the corpse is lashed, I never could understand, unless indeed it be by the *law of contrary,* for it has not the least resemblance to the cross on which the Roman criminal was condemned, nor does the attitude in which the malefactor is secured, license the term. I have somewhere seen in print the following sentiments associated with this subject: "The details of a crucifixion being painfully associated with the last scene in the life of the founder of Christianity as to divest the barbarous custom with interest." I fail to trace the analogy. The body is lifeless before it is suspended, and the exhibition is not entirely devoid of moral influence on all passers-by, this is to my mind a spectacle no more revolting than the system of hanging in chains in England, which practice prevailed among us not so very long ago.

Burmese crucifix.

121. At 8 A.M. of the 22nd December we were abreast of the Shweley river, the first tributary of importance we have passed since leaving Mandalay. At the mouth it appeared 600 feet wide, it narrows considerably

Shweley River.

above and at this season not more than one-fifth of its bed is covered with water. I am indebted to Mr. Graham, for information regarding the character of its windings in the interior, which he obtained from some Shan passengers we had on board, who had often followed it down from its rocky home, to where it discharged itself into the Irrawaddy. The stream is tortuous in its course, becoming more winding east of the Naumeil creek. Throughout the year it is a timber-bearing stream, and teak trees and bamboos floated down it. For boats in the low season Naumeil is the limit to which it is navigable, but during the floods, it may be ascended a few days' journey higher. Its banks are populated by Shans, but the frequent raids committed by the Kakhyens of the neighbouring hills, render life and property unsafe.

122. Onward we speed, and in a few hours are abreast of the prosperous and well-populated town of Katha, where we stop a quarter of an hour to land some Chinese passengers and cargo. The town is established on a commanding eminence, composed of dark red beds of tolerably hard ferruginous conglomerates, and pebbly sandstones, irregularly distributed, or developed, in thick masses of sand, and soft sandstones of a yellowish colour. It were almost needless to remark that emblems of the Bhuddist faith, are as prominently represented here as elsewhere, and, as seen from the river, grouped among groves of plantain, mango, jack, tamarind, and other wide-spreading trees, above which tower the graceful areca, cocoanuts, and borassus, present one of the most picturesque and striking views we have yet seen.

Town of Katha.

To the back of the town are extensive paddy-fields, which extend, as well as the eye can judge, to the foot of the high hills in the far west: the remaining three sides are more or less surrounded with vegetation, of a scrubby or arborescent nature. The pagodas are somewhat of a different style of architecture to what I have hitherto noticed. They are more of a spiral type, raised on a square base, the first convolution above the plinth being made up of a series of recesses which are filled with marble statuettes. A brisk trade in paddy is carried on here, and a ready sale is found for general merchandise, which is chiefly in the hands of Chinese and natives, representatives of the firms at Mandalay. The cutlery here is also regarded remarkably good.

123. *Hopea*, sprinkling of teak, small and gnarled, *T. hamiltonii, Shorea robusta, Fici, Gardenia, Bauhinia, Rosa, Vitex, Salix, Andropogan,* (lemon grass), *Arundo,* bamboos (small variety) *Myrtaceæ, Randia oliginosa,*

Vegetation.

Terminalia chebula, Pentapetes, and *Depterocarpus :* also cultivated limes, oranges, pomegranate, and *Carica papaya.*

124. Before the next village of Moda is reached, which has
Village of Moda.
occupied five hours' steaming, the river becomes much broken up by low grassy islands and sand-banks, and the only navigable channel is so narrow as to render rounding the elbows a difficult matter, and even with our little steamer, the stern generally bumped the opposite bank. To the west, the permanent banks of the river are lined with miniature Mississippian cane-brakes—but to the east the country from Katha, northward represents a vast Savanna.

125. The sand-banks in places are covered with waders of
Birds observed on banks of river.
various species, also ibis, adjutants, pelicans, cormorants, bitterns, and what appeared to me a flamingo ; but I cannot speak positively ; unfortunately, the bird was out of gun-shot.

The small mountain stream known as Koukway *choung* now empties itself into the river to the right. Its banks are sparsely populated by Kakhyens, who bring and barter with the people of the plains, gums, honey, ivory, and *pwaingzet*,* for whatever they require. Ivory, I am told, can be purchased here at Rs. 5-4 per viss, but that, in the interior, splendid tusks will readily be exchanged for some trifling article of merchandise.

126. So dense was the fog on the morning of the 23rd, that we
Arrival at Shwegoo.
were detained for some hours, shortly after leaving our moorings of the previous night. This suited me capitally, for it brought us into Shwegoo about 3-30 P. M. too late to admit of another start after wooding, yet early enough to give me a long ramble on shore. Fuel was shipped here at Rs. 8 per 1000 billets.

Shwegoo another village of considerable size and importance, owing to the large quantity of grain it exports, is situated on the high alluvial left bank of the river, which is ascended by a flight of steps reaching to the water's edge. The houses are all enclosed in a bamboo stockade, with a gate at either end of the principal road, which runs north and south. These are closed shortly after dark, on account of the raids committed by the Kakhyens, who are held in great dread by all inhabitants of the plains. The villagers seemed remarkably sociable, and ready to offer information on all subjects. At one house where I stopped to admire a handsome *Thunbergia* covering the verandah trellis, the owner very politely insisted on my accepting some cuttings, remark-

---

* A sort of wax elaborated by the *Tringona læriceps.*

ing that he was not quite certain whether they would strike, but that if I would call in on my downward trip, he would have some layers ready. I accepted his kind offer, and sure enough on my return voyage I found my friend had not forgotten his promise, and the plants now thrive at the Government plantation at Magayee. I presented his daughter with a few silk handkerchiefs and some scent, in acknowledgment for which, she very modestly placed before me the wreath that entwined her hair, apologizing that time would not admit of her gathering fresh flowers. I would have capped the compliment; but unfortunately words failed me. I must not forget to mention that in this house I also noticed a very healthy young *Ficus clastica* growing in a pot said to have been brought from Mogoung last year, when but a seedling of a few inches high.

127. The blowing up of a very influential Hpoongy was to have taken place the following day, and I much regretted time would not admit of my remaining to witness the ceremony.

Funeral obsequies of a Hpoongy at Shwegoo.

This process of cremation is the one usually followed in the case of the priesthood or people of rank; but among all other classes, the body is placed in a coffin, and buried in the ordinary way. The bier from which the remains of the old hpoongy were to have been disposed of, was a most gorgeous affair, standing twenty-seven feet from the base. It was after the design of a seven-roofed *thain*, constructed of skeleton bamboo-work, decorated with tinsel, lace, and a diorama illustrating the life of the priest. Each corner was guarded by a figure having the combined form of man and cock, the upper portion representing the former, and the latter finished off with a fine display of feathers. The coffin was to have occupied the uppermost tier, and the remaining six to have contained varying proportions of gunpowder. This ceremony is generally attended with some serious accidents as the process of igniting the powder by means of rockets is most dangerous. To all four sides of the bier, long ropes are attached as rocket slides, extending to the spectators, but it very often happens that the rockets get disengaged and shoot into the crowd, which, on occasions of this sort, is very dense. The ceremony, throughout, is a most interesting one, though I do not feel at liberty to give a more lengthy description of it at present.

128. Here I made my first acquaintance with the Kakhyens, who evidently had been attracted to the river's bank by the shrill steam whistle. There was a group of seven men and five women. The former averaged about five feet eight inches in

First acquaintance with Kakhyens.

height, and the latter perhaps over five feet two. They were a weak, insignificant, miserable, dirty-looking set, with dark complexions, hair cut square over the forehead like that of a Rembrandt's child, in both sexes, notedly silent and presenting that wary, suspicious cast of countenance, which is characteristic of all wild tribes. The men were all armed with guns and swords; to their girdle was suspended a powder-flask, a bullet-pouch made of rattans, and a few other paraphernalia connected with their flint-guns; from their shoulders was suspended a dirty home-spun linen bag, containing a *pán-suparee* box, and other odds and ends. The women carried on their backs a basket, pottle-shaped, but terminating towards the apex more abruptly; it was suspended by beautifully cane-plaited straps to a yoke somewhat similar to that used in England to carry beer, or milk cans, with an extra strap to bring over the forehead, on which a portion of the weight is borne. A few of the women were carrying children on their backs, suspended in a cloth sling brought over the shoulders and tied in front. Their clothes consisted of a coarse home-spun blue cloth, with red border, reaching to the knees, below which, they wore a collection of rings made of cane, each of the thickness of an elephant's hair, which I first mistook them for, on account of the black shiny appearance produced by the *thitsee* oil with which they are varnished. The women also wore similar ornaments round their loins, together with girdles made of small cowrie shells, which they greatly prize; their jackets, which were of a finer material, and likewise decorated with these shells, only concealed their breasts, the remaining portion of the body, from navel upwards, being exposed. My subsequent life with these wild tribes, taught me that the people I have just described were a branch of the Maroon clan. Further on in my journal, I shall have occasion to enter more fully in the manners, habits, and customs of these people. I need not, therefore, occupy more space here with this subject.

129. Before proceeding to describe the river further on, I must not forget to mention having seen a number of mango trees, whose trunks had been hacked to a height of three-feet six inches from the ground, with a view, I learnt, to pomological improvement; the tree, though blossoming abundantly, casting its fruit before ripe. As may be supposed, I was not a little surprised to find the rude Burman had so far reaped the benefit of observation as to intuitively resort to a violence which serves to check the cresive energies of the tree, and thus bring the fructiferous for reproductive essences into action.

Intuitive knowledge of Burmese pomology.

130. Opposite Shwegoo is a sacred island of the same name literally covered with pagodas and Buddhistic buildings. It sub-divides the river; and shortly after the streams unite at the northern apex of the island; here the second defile is entered. There is something profoundly grand about this cutting of nature, something irresistibly impressive, that wraps the mind in wonderment at the great changes worked by the action, re-action, and combination of the physical forces. Neither is the scenery less striking or romantic. The river here changes the character by which it has hitherto been marked, and becomes more confined and tortuous in its course; indeed, between the entrance and exit, the compass might have been boxed. In its rapid but undisturbed flow, it acts as nature's mirror, reflecting her many charms in their most faithful colours. Each bend, like the turn in the kaleidoscope, reveals fresh beauties, until after two hours and twenty minutes' steaming through an amphitheatre of hills, either mantled with a luxuriant growth of vegetation reaching to the water's edge, and concealing beneath their shade a few fishermen's huts, or presenting huge masses of displaced rock, resting one upon another in all possible positions, that great geological changes could alone produce; we find, at a moment least expected, the gorge is at an end. This abrupt termination, coupled with the geological formation of these hills, which in general terms may be described as representing carbonate of lime, varying in colour, according to length of exposure, from greyish black to a reddish tint, veined with calcspar, with serpentine cropping up in odd places, and all resting on a substratum of bluish clay, sufficiently accounts for the present course of the river. We all know that the action of water on rocks may take place either by actual solution or decomposition, or by loosening the cohesive force of the particles, and allowing them to disintegrate, or both, or principally by acting mechanically upon them, removing portions to a distance, rubbing and rolling them one against another. The mechanical action may be the result of various causes, which need not be explained here. Among the many examples of the eroding power of running water, I would draw attention to Sir C. Lyell's account of the excavations by the Simeto of Sicily, whereby in about two centuries, a passage was opened through *a lava current* measuring from fifty to several hundred feet wide, and in some parts from forty to fifty feet deep. Lava is a compact homogeneous mass of hard blue rock, and in no part porous or scoriaceous. How much more rapid, then, must have been the action of the water in the present instances?[*]

---

[*] Professor Austen on Geology.

The sight that unfailingly attracts most attention is situated, perhaps, about mid-way in the defile. Here, supported on a limestone pedestal, whose precipitous drop cannot be under 150 feet, rises, at a single leap some 600 feet from the base, what appears the half of a great mountain, whose smooth, bare, shining face, polished by atmospheric influence and repeated washings of the river, affording no footing to plant life, other than *Cryptogams*, or slender creepers, whose habit of life have taught them to delight in such escalading, overhangs the silent stream threatening each passing traveller with instant destruction.

This picture is rendered still more romantic by the little pagoda, which stands on the very brink of the pedestal, embowered in a mass of rich green foliage, as though it had been built by some genii-architect as the watch-tower of a guardian angel.

> "Not vainly did the early Persian make
> His Altar the high places and the peak
> Of earth—o'er gazing mountains, and thus take
> A fit and unwall'd temple there to seek,
> The spirit, in whose honour shrines are weak,
> Uprear'd of Human Hands, come and compare
> Columns and idol-dwellings, Goth or Greek
> With nature's realms of worship, earth and air,
> Nor fix on fond abodes to circumscribe thy prayer!
>
> BYRON.

131. The only animals we saw were some fine specimens of domestic buffaloes, whose forest life had, however, evidently reduced them to a wild state, and two varieties of monkeys; the light coloured *Gibbon*, whose wailing cries take the full compass of an octave, and warned us of his existence in the wood long ere we saw him, and the fisher monkey *(Muos cercopethecus,)* an uninteresting brute in comparison with the rest of his family; excepting when after sport, and then it is indeed amusing to witness the caution he displays in handling a crab, or moving a stone in search of one. These brutes were generally seen in large numbers around the fishermen's houses.

Animals seen in second defile.

132. Here the fish are caught in nets similiar to those seen at Ostend, on the Malabar coast, and at Ceylon, though, of course, of a more primitive type. Two bamboo bows, of perhaps, fifteen feet, are placed across one another at right angles, and to each end is attached a corner of a net sufficiently large to form a good deep hollow; a bamboo of sufficient length to extend some distance over the water, is then lashed to a tree and supported by a bracket from below. To the end of this pole, the net is suspended by a long rope, and so let down or pulled up at convenience. The net is weighted by few pieces of rock thrown into it.

Manner in which fish are here caught.

(71)

133. With the exception of a few water-hens (*Plotus vaillentii*) and fish hawks, the pass seemed devoid of birds; it is not improbable, however, that they were scared by the noise of the steam whistle which was constantly sounded as a warning to downward vessels.

Scarcity of birds.

134. The following trees and shrubs were observable :—*Tectona hamiltonii, Conocarpus acuminatus, dillenia, Sterculia colorata, bombax malabaricum, dipterocarpus, Teak* (stunted), *Nux vomica, Campanulaceæ*, plantains wild, and cultivated near houses, bamboos and climbing plants in great variety including *Bauhinia, Clerodendron*, and *Thunbergia*.

Vegetation.

135. Immediately on clearing the defile, the hills to the east gradually recede until quite lost in the far distant haze; and shortly afterwards but a faint blue out-line marks the far-off mountains to the west. Tsenkan is now reached, situated on the banks of a stream from which it takes its name. Here I noticed a large number of bamboo and teak rafts said to have been brought from five miles inland. The timber was of large girth and straight; but in very short lengths, not averaging over fifteen feet. Between Tsenkan and Koungtoung, the permanent banks of the river continue well defined, rising in places forty to fifty feet above the level of the water; at this season (December), they are for the most part alluvial, displaying in places an excess of black or white sand. Just above Partha the navigation is somewhat complicated owing to a reef of rocks jutting out from the left bank, at an oblique angle with the stream, leaving but a small passage for steamers to pass.

Brief history of Tsenkan.

136. North of Koungtoung the river widens out considerably, and presents a net-work of channels up to Bhamo. Both banks, since leaving the defile, have been fairly wooded, but I had only an opportunity of noting the vegetation in odd places. It for the most part consisted of *Salix, Rosa, Bombax, Marantaceæ arundo*, and bamboo cultivated *Vitex trifolia, Punica granatum, Jatropa multifida*, plantains, cocoa-nuts, and *Borassus flabelliformis*, on the sand-banks, *Cyperace, Companula, Crotalaria*, and *Graminæ*.

Vegetation.

137. From Mandalay to Bhamo the wind has steadily blown from the north-east, dense fogs up to 10 A.M. and thermometer from 6 A.M. till 6 P.M. averaged 76·5F. Throughout the day a great coat was acceptable, and hot grog at night looked forward to. The voyage occupied from 9-30 P.M. of 19th December to 5 P.M. of 23rd.

Indications of thermometer on the way from Mandalay to Bhamo.

138. The return trip occupied from 8-30 A.M. of 29th April to 6 P.M. of 30th of April. There was a marked change in the weather. Strong winds blew from the south-west accompanied by sand storms, the last we experienced, just before reaching Mandalay, necessitated our stopping, for it was impossible to see a yard ahead, this was followed by a shower of rain, which reduced the temperature three degrees. From 6 A.M. till 6 P.M. the thermometer averaged 95·5F. One felt thankful there were no ladies on board, and *pyjamas* and a thin shirt was the recognized costume, excepting at meals. In place of hot-grog for a night-cap all our ingenuity was employed to securing a cool " B." and " S.," the great pick-me-up of eastern climes ! Before closing this chapter I must record my sense of gratitude to the commander of the *Colonel Fytche* for the kind manner in which he afforded me every facility to gain information, without in the least interfering with the interests of the company.

<small>Return trip, and change in the weather.</small>

CHAPTER IV.

Bhamo, including a trip to the Kakhyen hills viâ *the Taping river.*

139. *December 24th.*—It was too late to land last night, so I
postponed the pleasure of calling on
the Officiating Assistant Resident un-
til this morning. Before leaving the steamer, however, Mr.
Cooper came on board, and very kindly invited me up to the Residency, but expressed his regret at not being able to extend his
hospitality, as he had run short of stores, and did not intend re-
plenishing them during the remainder of his stay, which was not
for long. This was of little consequence, for I was well supplied
with provisions, having already been warned of the difficulty I
should experience in this respect after leaving Mandalay, and further cautioned at all times to be independent of the villagers for
food, quarrels often arising from over-zealous servants forcing the
people to sell against their will.

Delay in landing.

140. Mr. Cooper had evidently come on board charged with in-
dignation, for barely had the usual
civilities been exchanged, than he expressed surprise at not having received
earlier notice of my coming, the first intimation given him being
that conveyed in the mails we had brought up. He seemed still
more astonished at the weakness of my escort, and the absence
of a guard provided by His Majesty the King of Burma. He spoke
of the disturbed state of the country, and the great risk I ran in
attempting to travel among the wild Kakhyen mountaineers until
peace had been restored; and even went so far as to protest
against my leaving Bhamo until he had communicated with the Resident at Mandalay, placed him in possession of the correct state
of affairs, and pointed out the imprudence of allowing me to
go amongst these wild people, who were up in arms, and had
placed the Burmese Government at defiance. I was sadly disappointed at the unfavourable turn things had taken, for it appeared
as though I was not to be permitted to carry through the work
I had so aspired to. Fortunately, however, after a patient hearing,
I was able to fathom the secret of Mr. Cooper's grievance, and satisfactorily explain the unavoidable circumstances under which I
had been thrust upon him so unexpectedly; this had the desired

*Mr. Cooper notices certain irre-
gularities of procedure.*

effect, and I was permitted to proceed, though he resolutely determined to represent matters at head-quarters, and thereby relieve himself of all responsibility. Having so far gained my point, I changed the topic, as I find it necessary now also to do.

141. Bhamo, which is a corruption of the Shan word *Manno*, signifying *water-pot village*, is situated on a high cliff of yellow clay on the left bank of the Irrawaddy, 200 miles N.N.E. of Mandalay, in Latitude 24° 16' north, Longitude 96° 53' 47" east. It is the great emporium of trade with Western China, and to this it principally owes its importance. With the exception of the river-frontage, the town is enclosed by an irregularly-shaped stockade of teak logs about ten feet high; loop-holes are cut in the timbers for musketry fire, and watch-towers occur at intervals. During a night engagement, we are told, the enemy are illuminated by torch-light, the flambeaus being made of finely-chopped decayed wood, saturated in wood-oil, and wrapped in the leaves of *Licuala peltata*. The river here divides into three channels; that on which Bhamo is situated is the widest, and about 700 yards broad; the entire width of the river from bank to bank is about a mile and a half. There is a difference of sixty feet between its rise and fall, and, for the convenience of the people to fetch water &c., flights of bamboo steps are constructed at intervals along the bank, which, even at the highest floods, are some feet above the level of the water.

Bhamo, situation and description of.

142. The palisade was originally intended as a protection against the raids committed by the wild mountaineers, but these attacks being now less constant, the defence has been allowed to fall into great disrepair, so much so, that it is not an uncommon occurrence for tigers or leopards to enter the stockade at night and carry off dogs and pigs, and sometimes even human-beings. The long-established practice of closing the gates at sunset still continues, after which no Kakhyens are allowed inside; at 9 P.M. the gong is struck for the second time, when all ingress and egress is prohibited, lights and fires extinguished, and the patrols commence their rounds.

The palisade—a protection against raids of wild mountaineers—and its subsequent disrepair.

143. The town stretches along the river bank for, perhaps, about a mile and a half, but its average breadth does not exceed a fourth of that distance, narrowing in some places to fifty yards, where the palisade has had to take a sudden bend to avoid a ravine. The ground is tolerably high and well-drained,

Former elaborate buildings, and construction of kyoungs and pagodas.

and the swampy ravines and water-courses that have unavoidably been included are spanned by wooden bridges, now in a most dilapidated and neglected state; few are even safe for foot-passengers. The remains of these once elaborate buildings,—with their massive carvings and handsomely-turned—balustrades, and those of the pagodas and *zayats*, go to show that works of public utility no longer share the attention of the Authorities; though they point to the prosperity of the town in days gone by. The decline is attributed to the constant raids by the Kakhyens, but it might more justly be traced to the evil effects of an unjust Government. The thought uppermost in the reigning Governor's mind, would seem to be the construction of *kyoungs* and pagodas, in the hope of establishing a repute in this world for charity and good works, and securing blissful repose in his future existence. Though formerly a gay young man, he now gives out that he has lost all interest in mundane affairs, and finds comfort alone in contemplation, and preparing for a stage of sanctity which will fit him for that absorption into the essence of Buddha which is the one aim of all good Buddhists.

144. Within the stockade, I was informed, there are 700 houses and 4,200 inhabitants, made up of Shan-Burmese, Chinese, and a sprinkling of Mahomedan and Suratee traders, representatives of Mandalay firms. The sanitary rules, referred to at page 18, are here also strictly observed, excepting in the Chinese quarters, where these people object to conform to the rule which necessitates their sweeping up and burning all rubbish that has accumulated in front of their houses the day previous. The population appears to have been somewhat exaggerated, but it is next to impossible to obtain any reliable information on such subjects from the officials. The houses occupied by the Shan and Burmese portion of the community, are bamboo buildings raised off the ground three feet, and thatched with *saccharum spontaneum*. They have a tidy, cheerful appearance, and are arranged, with some attempt at method, along the main and intersecting roads, some of which are paved with burnt bricks set on edge, and all avenued by fruit or ornamental trees, consisting of *Anona reticulata*, *A. squamosa*, lime, sweet-lime, mango, guava, pomegranate, *Carica papaya*, *Hibiscus mutabilis*, *Jatropha multifolia*, and *Bauhinia acuminata*. I also noticed one apple tree and nine peach trees; of these latter, there were also some trees in the Residency compound, but in neither case could their origin be traced. The fruit is of a flat variety.

Observance of sanitary rules; description of houses, and roads avenued by fruit and ornamental trees.

145. The bulk of the male population earn a livelihood, either by cultivation or boat hire; but, judging from the number of idlers one sees loitering about, it appears as though employment was scarce. This, however, is not the case, it is the cheapness of living that stimulates laziness—the earnings of a month keeping them in idleness for about half a year, and so long as they are possessed of sufficient to buy a meal, they will not work. There are a few Burman petty traders, who carry on a small business up river, in grain and other minor indigenous products, but these are being thinned out, by the demand for brokers, now that a royal monopoly is gradually being established on all articles of commerce, which are collected through a European firm at Mandalay, who have guaranteed to the King a fixed annual revenue on all articles specified in the contract. Professions are limited to jewellers and carpenters, both very mediocre, the demand for first-class workmanship being small.

Means of livelihood among men, and mode of living.

146. The silversmiths find employment chiefly in smelting and adulterating silver, which is the only currency of the country north of the capital. The legal amount of alloy is noted below, but there is good reason to believe the prescribed standard is not in every instance adhered to. Buying and selling by this process is both tedious and wasteful, not only do those unfamiliar with the quality of the metal suffer, but great waste occurs in chopping off *wee* pieces from the ingot, to obtain the required weight at which the article to be purchased has been valued. This mode of exchange necessitates every one being possessed of scales and weights.

Legal amount of alloy in silver.

Nga-yay, very rough, contains ...	...	{ 1 tikal silver
		  ¼ ,, lead
		  ⅜ ,, copper

Ah saik-gnway, rough, contains	...	{ 1 tikal silver
		  ⅜ ,, lead
		  ¼ ,, copper

Hnit-mat-gnway contains	...	{ 1 tikal silver
		  ¼ ,, lead
		  ⅛ ,, copper

I am indebted to Captain A. B. Bower's Bhamo Expedition Report of 1868 for this information, which precisely corresponds with the currency of the present day.

147. The women are remarkably industrious and ever busy with their domestic duties, in which they display the greatest interest and exercise supreme control. It is seldom they are seen entirely idle, even their little flirtations are carried on

Industry of women, and system of mattrass-making detailed.

while at needlework or when seated at the loom—occupations taught them from their earliest years. Here also I noticed them engaged in mattrass-making, a branch of industry I had not hitherto observed. The system consists in a process of quilting which obviates the necessity for "ticking," the mattrass having the appearance of corduroy, each rib being about four inches wide. These beds are remarkably comfortable and peculiarly adapted for travelling, owing to the facility the ribs offer for packing into a compact space. They are made as follows :—Bamboo spikes, a little thicker than a pencil and three feet long, are driven into the ground four inches apart, on these, a net-work of cotton is worked by running the thread in and out of the stakes; this web is not over a few inches from the ground. A layer of finely carded cotton half as thick again as the intended depth of the mattress, is next laid on the net, and gradually beaten down into a consolidated mass by small switches; the whole is secured by a net similar to that at the bottom, and the sides fastened by cutting the upper and lower meshes and tying them together. The quilt is now ready for covering, the ribbing process being subsequently performed by needle and thread.

148. Besides the indigenous labour, immigrants from the Hotha and Latha valleys come and settle down here from October till April as brick-makers and blacksmiths. They are a quiet, orderly set, and always appear to find plenty of employment; strange to say many of the *dahs* they manufacture are sold to the *Kakhyens* with the consent of the Burmese authorities. These people are Shan-Chinese but have more of the Chinese type of feature and habits than the genuine Shan, who again nearer approach the Burman. Their costume consists of a huge *pugorie*, short jacket, and trousers which do not extend below the knees; the remaining portion of the leg is covered with bandages of the same material as the rest of the costume, which throughout is dyed blue. I was surprised to notice among other pieces of old iron that had been given these people for conversion, English weights, and what closely resembled some of our defaced marking hammers.

Description and occupation of immigrants from Hotha and Latha valleys.

149. The Chinese quarters occupy the middle of the town, and their houses are either entirely of sun-dried bricks with tiled roofs, or merely the front wall is of that material, the remaining three sides being of bamboo matting plastered with clay. Their temple is a *pucka* building, after the orthodox design, answering the double purpose of a guest-house and place of worship. The decorations, images, and paraphernalia of religious office are

Detailed account of the Chinese quarters.

less elaborate than those of the Amarapoora Temple; neither is the court-yard nor out-buildings generally kept as clean. The entrance is through a hole in the wall, this circular gate-way being apparently peculiar to the Chinese ecclesiastic type of architecture. The Chinese community, I am told, are represented by a head-man who is selected by the Woon with the consent of the people, and is consulted and entrusted with all matters that concern them. There is a great sameness about their shops, and nothing is exposed for sale, but the owner or his representative may be seen seated at the window smoking, and ever ready for a chat with passers-by to whom he enumerates his goods in the best-natured manner. For the most part they consist of tea, sugar-candy, silk, cards, straw hats, Manchester piece-goods, opium, apples, preserved oranges, vermillion, gypsum, yellow orpiment, Chinese medicines, and body colours in large variety, lead, copper, and various other odds and ends. Since my arrival Messrs. Sutherland and Co. have established an agency here, much to the disgust of the Chinamen, who find they are being considerably undersold. The gentleman who represents the firm, informed me that his principal business would be among the people north of Bhamo, with whom he intended carrying on a system of barter, exchanging twist, cloth, thread, or whatever they required for ivory, rubber, wax, gums, amber, &c. This he said would entail a certain amount of risk, as a credit-system would be necessary, but that the profits would be so considerable that a bad debt now and again would little matter. Before I left Bhamo my informant had commenced his speculations on a somewhat extensive scale, and he told me that the people he had to deal with—Kakhyens included—were remarkably honest, and seldom failed to fulfil their promises: in some instances, he said, he had advanced Rs. 500 worth of goods, and that on his next visit to the village the equivalent was always forthcoming.

150. The Governor's private residence and court-house are within the same enclosure, and situated on one of the by-streets east of the main road, the building and out-houses have a shabby, untidy appearance, and no attempt at decoration has been made, not even has the spiral-tiered roof been adopted, to which a Governor is entitled. The enclosure is a bamboo mat fence, with a few rusty old pieces of ordnance at each gate, weapons that should most be feared by the gunners!

Governor's private residence and court-house.

151. The only building within the palisade that really attracts attention is a seven-roofed teak *thain* of recent construction, the religious bequest of a Burman who has spent his

Specimen of Burmese ecclesiastical architecture described.

last rupee on the building; certainly it is the most exquisite piece of Burmese ecclesiastical architecture I have seen. The carving bore the closest inspection, and the ability of the artificers and designer improved on study, neither was the excellence of the workmanship confined to the outside, for the paneling of the ceiling presented an open net-work of floral designs, enclosing birds, animals, and grotesque figures most carefully carved.

152. Within the stockade, and to the east of the town are four large *Ficus elastica* trees of the following dimensions:—

Ficus Elastica trees.

No. I.—Height .... 82 feet
Circumference of main trunk .... 72 do
Ditto   inclusive of aërial
  roots round trunk .... 117 do
Area covered by crown .... 627 do

There were 69 aërial roots, the three thickest representing, respectively, 5 feet 2 inches, 4 feet 9 inches, and 4 feet 2 inches; these radiated in various directions on reaching the ground, but remained close to the surface, exposing one-third above ground. Those immediately round the trunk and which had inosculated into one mass, took the form of buttresses on reaching the ground.

No. II.—Height .... 79 feet
Circumference of main trunk .... 74 do
Ditto   inclusive of aërial
  roots round trunk .... 107 do
Area covered by crown .... 592 do

Aërial roots 74, the three thickest being respectively 4 feet 10 inches, 4 feet 2 inches, and 3 feet 7 inches. In all other respects the habits of growth of this, and the following trees, are identical with No. I.

No. III.—Height .... 70 feet
Circumference of main trunk .... 69 do
Ditto   inclusive of aërial
  roots round trunk .... 98 do
Area covered by crown .... 597 do

Aërial roots 62, the three thickest being respectively 4 feet 6 inches, 3 feet 10 inches, and 3 feet 5 inches.

No. IV.—Height .... 68 feet
Circumference of main trunk .... 65 do
Ditto   inclusive of aërial

roots round trunk .... 89 feet
Area covered by crown .... 573 do

Aërial roots 59, the three thickest being, respectively, 5 feet 6 inches, 4 feet 7 inches, and 3 feet 10 inches.

These were all said to be seedlings of two years old when obtained from Mogoung in 1856, which would have made them about nineteen years old when measured by me. Not much reliance, however, should be placed on this information, for I much question whether any one here was sufficiently interested with their introduction to have been impressed with the date on which they were planted. They have never been transplanted since first established in the ground they now occupy, which is a well-drained elevation of yellow clay, resting on a blue sub-stratum of the same formation. Their present unhealthy, exhausted appearance, has resulted from excess of tapping and indiscriminate amputation for cuttings which are planted along the suburban roads, where they thrive capitally. Cuttings of three years' growth average nine feet high, with a handsome well-formed crown, and stem one foot three inches in circumference. It is questionable, however, whether the parent trees will survive such unnatural treatment much longer. Neither season nor system is observed in tapping, but whenever the Governor receives instructions from the Palace to collect caoutchouc, orders are issued to indent on these trees, and the operation is performed by hacking them all over, and collecting the milk in hollow, pen-fashioned bamboo tubes that are driven into the lower end of the cut, which generally is made obliquely with the limb operated on. The people about here tell me, from December to March is the best season for tapping, but that during the rains the flow of milk is more copious, though the yield of the coagulated substance is less. Two years ago these trees are said to have supplied 60 viss of caoutchouc per annum, but now not more than 35 viss a year is reckoned on. These statements, however, must be taken for what they are worth, for the Burmans are ever ready with an answer, and have a decided turn for invention, which often carries a certain amount of weight from the plausible, well-measured manner in which the information is tendered.

153. The Residency, which has been built at the expense of our Government, occupies a capital position on a piece of rising ground about two miles above the town. It is fronted by the river, and at the back—at a distance of some two miles—is a bold range of mountains rising to an altitude of perhaps 5,000 feet. The architecture is of the Anglo-Burmese type, but as I cannot say much in

Detailed description of the Bhamo Residency.

favour of the workmanship, my description must be limited. No doubt, during my stay there, in December and January, I saw things under the most unfavourable circumstances, for Mr. Cooper had made no attempt to study comfort during his short stay, and this large rambling, unfurnished building, presented the most dismal, melancholy appearance possible to conceive; I was not in the least surprised to hear my host complain of depression of spirits, as he sat of an early morning in an easy chair, muffled up in a large fur-skin in an atmosphere of dense fog, that had penetrated the building through the open space between the walls and roof. The liver, as a matter of course, was accused of bad behaviour; in fact, of sulking at the isolated life it had to lead; but I should have traced the origin of his malady to another cause, and I am certain, had I remained in Bhamo another month under similar conditions, I should have been equally as bad. The only improvement Mr. Cooper seemed interested in, was the construction of a front entrance to the house, being under the impression that the more wealthy and important people of the place shunned the Residency, having to enter the building from beneath,—a practice Burmans in position have a strong aversion to. I am here reminded of an amusing anecdote corroborant of this peculiar antipathy, in which, during the earlier part of our conquest, it was found necessary to haul a Burman of position through the window of a high official, on whom he had occasion to call, but objected to enter from beneath the building! This prejudice, I am told, becomes stronger when the inhabitants are not confined to the male sex. The enclosure to the Residency is a bamboo mat fence, and at the front entrance there is a guard of twelve sepoys and a havildar, more for show, I presume, than protection.

154. It was fortunate both Mr. Cooper and myself were fond of out-door pursuits, so that the absence of comfort at home little mattered. An hour or so after breakfast I always started on my rambles, and seldom returned before 6 P. M. Mr. Cooper could not always accompany me in the early part of the day, for he had his office work to attend to; but we generally managed to have our evening shooting together. Sport is not plentiful in the immediate neighbourhood of Bhamo, for the painted partridge, jungle fowl, and pheasants are too extensively snared, and deer and hog so hunted and worried with dogs throughout the year, that but few are met with on this side of the river; still we seldom returned without something for the pot, which the absence of animal food necessitated our shooting for, quite as much as the mere love of sport. For deer shooting we generally had

Excursions with Mr. Cooper, and account of the sights.

to employ some Assamese and their hunting dogs, to run down the wounded animals, for we were only shooting with No. 3 shot to avoid accidents, there being a good many people about. I must confess, when first I saw the dogs I was incredulous of all that was said in their favour; certainly their looks belied them: poor, miserable, half-starved-looking wretches, with crouching gait, and tail well between their legs, only too glad to bolt on the approach of a stranger, I thought it impossible they could be good for much; but I was vastly mistaken; for, no sooner was a deer wounded, than they were on the track, and seldom failed to run it down. The cruel manner in which the poor brutes were belaboured with kicks and blows when the huntsmen came up to find they had already commenced to devour their prey, was a most distressing sight, and I was only surprised to find such cruel treatment had not utterly ruined the pack for sport. The greatest havoc we committed was among the ducks and geese; of these, we generally managed to kill sufficient of an evening for ourselves and followers. Fortunately, the natives show a preference for the more oily and fish-tasting water-fowl, and at all times prefer quantity to quality—a pelican being more acceptable than a duck; so we had little trouble in supplying their wants in this respect. I also managed to make a couple of tolerably good bags of snipe (fifteen, and twenty-four and a half couple), among which were a *solitary* bird, two painted, and seven jack: a list of the remaining variety of birds I collected here, will be found at the end of the first section of this chapter. The only animals I bagged, or even saw, were some deer, a wild cat (*Felis javanensis*), a handsome brute about the size of a dog, yellow ground and black spots, and remarkably fierce; a red squirrel (*Sciurus ferrugineus*), also *S. barbei*, and a flying squirrel (*Pteromys petaurista cineraceus*); tigers, and leopards are also common, and are often heard at night within a few yards of the Residency, but I never saw any. In the neighbouring mountains we hear game of all sorts abounds, including elephants, bison, pig, bear, samber, and those common to the plains.

155. Christmas day was entirely devoted to sport, as the most pleasant amusement we could select. Our start was delayed by some Chinese visitors, who had come to call on the Assistant Resident; they spoke with confidence regarding the speedy suppression of the Panthay war, but said until all was quiet again, it would be unsafe to continue the cotton export trade with Western China. They mentioned that Tussa Cone's army had been reduced to 1,200, and were surrounded by 30,000

Conversation of certain Chinese Visitors on Christmas day.

Chinese troops, the Commander-in-Chief of the force having promised the Chinese Government, to have peace restored within three months. They also gave, as their opinion, that immediately the war was at an end, the Chinese would merely reside at Bhamo during the business season, making Momein their head-quarters for the remainder of the year. They seemed opposed to the idea of opening out trade with Western China, and pointed to the insuperable difficulties that presented themselves. This objection was but natural, considering the proposed scheme would have interfered with their interests, they now being the only people in the field; but, as regards the obstacles, they were immensely exaggerated, beyond doubt. It was fortunate these men could not understand Mr. Cooper's Chinese (which he afterwards told me was a peculiar Court dialect unknown to the masses), or I should have lost the benefit of the interesting conversation, that was now carried on through an interpreter.

156. During our rambles we came on a large pagoda in course of construction, which we were informed was being built at the expense of the Governor; enquiry, however, led to the disclosure that the labour was gratuitous (which really meant forced), and the material supplied on the same principle, so that this building, which was intended as a lasting memorial of his good deeds and munificence, resolved itself into a monument of his oppression and injustice. The building was surrounded by eleven young *ficus elastica*, reared from cuttings taken from the trees in the stockade four years ago, just on the first burst of the rains: they averaged eleven feet high, and looked remarkably healthy.

Pagoda intended as memorial of Governor's good deeds.

Our eagerness for sport had led us to misjudge the distance we had come, and it was long after dark before we got back to the Residency. The long walk and bracing atmosphere had fully prepared us for dinner, and after drinking to absent friends and enjoying a pipe or so, we were literally driven to bed, by the clouds of smoke from the wood-fire lighted in an earthen pot in the absence of a more suitable fire-place. I would have preferred an extra great cost, to the stifling atmosphere we had to breathe, but my companion suffered so much from the cold, that I could say nothing. The thermometer stood at 47° F. in my bed-room, where there was no fire. Although we had not a very good day's sport, we enjoyed ourselves immensely, and gained much valuable information regarding the manners and customs of the people, and their state of contentment: they appeared generally to be satisfied with their condition, but unanimously protested against the acts of extortion committed by income-tax collectors, who, in their demands, doubled the original burden, which, in the first instance, was very fairly regulated according to the position of the rate-payer.

157. According to arrangements already made, Mr. C. very kindly accompanied me on an official visit to the Woon. After the usual complimentary salutation, I handed in His Majesty's passport, granting me permission to travel through the Bhamo district, and directing I should receive all assistance necessary. The order was written on a palm leaf (*corypha talina*) with a style, formed into a hoop, and enveloped in a second leaf, the ends of which were secured by a piece of old red cloth, and stamped with the arms which are represented by the peacock. The seal was broken in our presence, and the order read aloud by the senior secretary, in the usual chanting tone; the document was then returned to the Governor, who very politely consented to afford me every assistance in his power immediately I would give him a definite outline of my plans, which I agreed to do in the course of a few days, after talking the matter over with the Assistant Resident. Unfortunately both Mr. C. and myself were dependent on interpreters, which made the interview less interesting and instructive, than doubtless would have been the case, had we been able to exchange our views direct. The Governor was notably gentlemanly in his behaviour, though reserved and cautious in his own conversation. He shook hands with us both on entering and leaving, and seemed in no way put out at our entering with our shoes, though they were hardly in a state to tread his nicely-carpeted floor after our walk through the town, which was ankle deep in dust. The reception hall was merely a portion of his private apartment curtained off, the floor being raised about eighteen inches higher than that on which petitioners are allowed; on our side was a stand of arms, among which I noticed two double-barrelled breach-loaders, six double-barrelled percussion rifles, and nine old *Brown-Besses* with bayonets: these were all tolerably clean, but the array of arms that stood in the covered square fronting us, appeared rust-eaten and neglected.

The whole six Court officials were present at the interview, but never spoke, excepting to confirm the Governor's views or to whisper a suggestion in matters that had escaped his memory. I am told the officers are, as a rule, appointed by the King, and that they change office on the transfer of a Governor. No state documents either, I believe, are considered valid unless

Official visit to the Woon.

bearing the signature of the *quorum*, besides that of the Woon. Within his own District, a Governor's sway is absolute, he can impose what taxes he thinks fit, the King looking to him for an ever-increasing revenue. The present incumbent, I heard, was more popular than his predecessor, from whose acts of oppression, tyranny, and extortion the poor have barely yet recovered. At present taxation depends a good deal on the means of rate-payers, but I am told Rs. 12 per annum is the minimum rate fixed.

158. Passing down China street on our return to the Residency, we saw some Chinamen having a game of shuttle-cock, substituting their elbows and knees for a bat, the use of the hands being prohibited. The cock consisted in a bunch of fowls' feathers fastened into the square hole of a China pice brass coin. Next we came on a number of Burman lads, amusing themselves with foot-ball. The ball, but little larger than a cricket ball, is hollow, and of open rattan net work. The game is generally played with sides, but occasionally each party plays independently. The ball must never be touched by the hands, but kept bounding from one to another by means of the feet, knees, or thighs, some rules even admit of the arms and shoulders, but this is not general. It is remarkable to see the skill sometimes displayed: a good player may often be seen, on the ball approaching him, to take a spring, perhaps some four feet off the ground, clap his feet together, and send the ball flying to the opposite side with a blow from the sole of the foot. This, game though unknown in India Proper, may be regarded one of the national sports of Burma, and extends far south. Wallace, in his charmingly instructing work on the Malay Archipelago, mentions having seen a similar game played in the Aru Islands.

<small>National sports of Burma described.</small>

159. I now heard from the Assistant Resident that private information had reached him, to the effect that the King had issued a royal mandate prohibiting the collection of *Ficus elastica* seedlings; and he assured me his informant could be depended on. This was bad news, for the motive of the order was too apparent; however, I was quite prepared for little difficulties, and resolved to overcome them if possible. The order had not been sent direct to the Woon, but circulated through the royal poongies, a channel generally adopted when secrecy is to be observed. Evidently my visit to the capital had excited suspicion, and influenced the rubber trade, for immediately after my interview with His Majesty, the price went up 20 per cent., and con-

<small>Royal mandate prohibiting collection of *Ficus elastica* sucklings.</small>

tinued to rise, until the King proclaimed *caoutchouc* a royal monopoly.

160. I here had the good fortune to form the acquaintance of the late Reverend Dr. Mason and his wife, who had come up to Bhamo, in hopes of establishing a Kakhyen Mission, and gradually instructing the wild mountaineers in the Christian faith. Dr. Mason was busy studying the language as best he could, picking up a word here and there as opportunity offered; and I believe before he returned to Rangoon, his collection of words had sufficiently accumulated, to admit of his publishing a text-book on the subject. Mrs. Mason, ever ready to assist her husband in his good works, expressed a desire to go among these wild people by herself; for she felt the poor old gentleman—now over seventy years of age,—was too feeble and delicate to accompany her. I was glad to find, however, neither the Assistant Resident, nor the Governor, would for a moment listen to such an unreasonable request, which would unquestionably have led to most undesirable complications, if not to her death: the good lady's wanderings were therefore confined to the suburbs, and a short trip up the Taping river. Dr. Mason evidently had not received much encouragement from the Burmese Government; there was first a difficulty about a grant of land, and then other obstacles were thrown in his way, that might easily have been overcome had the King been disposed to support the scheme.

Mission of Rev. Dr. Mason and his wife.

161. Later on I made the acquaintance of a Roman Catholic Priest, who had also come to Bhamo to work among the Kakhyens. After a very limited experience, even of the more civilized highlanders,—who come down from the hills occasionally to barter goods,—he told me it would simply be working against his own interest to thrust himself too suddenly on these people in their mountain homes, and that he intended gradually to pave the way to a good understanding, by throwing himself among those of the tribe who visited the plains, and then step by step, teaching them, through free intercourse, to appreciate the object and unselfishness of his cause. Apparently this gentleman had come up here by permission of His Majesty, for no difficulty was experienced in finding a site for him to build on, or workmen to run up his little bamboo cottage. Under other circumstances I should have felt disposed to attribute a political reason, to the King's aversion to the establishment of a Protestant mission at Bhamo, but his recognizing the introduction of a Roman Catho-

Arrival of Roman Catholic Priest at Bhamo.

lic institution, leads to the belief that he gives a preference to the latter faith, as nearer resembling Bhuddism, in the matter of continence, self-denial, poverty, and humility.

162. Having finally settled on the route I intended to take, and made all necessary arrangements for my journey, I sent my compliments to the Governor, asking his acceptance of a few presents, and soliciting the favour of a private interview on the morrow. I received a very polite message in return, thanking me for the presents, and saying he would be delighted to see me at any hour that might best suit my convenience. The following day, about 11 A.M., I called, and received a most hearty welcome; I was met at the door by the Governor himself, who shook hands and ushered me into the reception-hall, keeping my hand in his till I was seated; he was less reserved and more communicative than on the last occasion, and expressed a desire to know the *real object* of my mission; I quite satisfied him on this subject, but mentioned that besides gathering information connected with the habits of the *Ficus elastica*, I intended collecting specimens of all plants of interest, or that were valuable for medicinal or other economic purposes. He seemed interested in my description of our system of distinguishing plants, and immediately sent for a few leaves said to have medicinal properties, with a view to gaining my opinion, he politely put it, though no doubt, his object was to test my knowledge of the subject. Fortunately, the three specimens were *Azadirachta indica*, *Calotropis gigantea* and *Bixa orellana*, all of which I was familiar with, and able to describe their different uses. A medicine chest that had been presented him some time ago, was next produced, but none of the bottles had ever been opened, for no one knew the use of the different drugs; this I explained, and had the proper doses written on the bottles in Burmese. When we came on the quinine and ipecacuanha, I rather surprised my friend by telling him that we had already commenced to cultivate these plants in British Burma; he at once begged a few for the king, which I promised, immediately after our experiments had reached a certain stage of success. I now solicited some information regarding his district, and a map was produced, drawn something after the fashion of one illustrating altitudes; the whole plan being covered with hills rising one above the other, and the principal roads and rivers being made to run through a most impassable line of country. The approximate distance of the different places were judged by the lines, and cross-lines with which the map was covered, each square being intended to represent ten

Private interview with the Governor.

miles either way. I had the promise of a copy of this marvellous drawing, but it never reached me, neither did I expect it would, for the authorities are cautious how they supply information of this nature.

163. No sooner had I definitely fixed the date for my departure, than the Governor showed signs of wavering, and expressed his regret that I should attempt the journey when the country was so unsettled and life not safe, and hoped I would postpone my tour for about two months. This I told him was quite out of the question, and that I felt there was little to fear, when travelling in the districts of such a well-organized Government. Seeing I was inflexible and bent on going, he consented to arrange for two boats, and an extra crew for the Residency's boat, which had been placed at my disposal; he also promised to send an intelligent guide with me, on whose advice I was at all times to act, which, of course, I consented to do, though I had fully resolved to use my own discretion in all matters of importance, and in which the interests of my mission were concerned. Fortunately my *cicerone* turned out a most tractable old party, and let me do pretty well as I liked, provided he was allowed plenty of food, *pán-suparee*, and cheroots, which I was careful to see he was never in want of. The interview was brought to an end over tea and sweets; and to all outward appearance we parted the best of friends: certainly the politeness and assistance I received throughout my stay in *Day-myo* district has left no room for doubting his sincerity; of course, he had a part to play, as others similarly placed would have had, but that part, so far as I was concerned, was performed in the least objectionable way. Two days subsequently, the Governor sent the whole of his Court officials to visit me, and intimate his intention of calling the following day. They brought me a small branch of the wild tea plant, which they said the Woon had obtained from the hills to the east of Bhamo. The leaves were coarser and smaller than those of the cultivated variety, and both entire and serrated. It is neither used by the Chinese nor Kakhyens I am told. The boats and boatmen were reported to have been arranged for at one rupee per man per day, and an extra rupee for each of the boats hired. I fixed the day after the arrival of the mails for my start, as I expected some botanical boards and paper by that steamer, which I had telegraphed to Rangoon for from Mandalay, finding the supply I had started with insufficient. The visitors did not leave a very favourable impression, for they were sadly wanting in manners, and dirtily dressed: however, they had every courtesy shown them, and the usual civility and mark of hospitality in the form of tea and biscuits was observed.

Subject of my approaching departure.

164. According to appointment the Governor called the following day, and I made it a duty to show him the same cordial welcome he had extended to me. We chatted away over tea and biscuits for about quarter of an hour, the conversation chiefly being of an official nature. He reiterated his regret at my determination to travel among the mountaineers, and offered some really very good and sound advice, in case I should fall into difficulties. I was glad he had found time to return my visit, or I should have been disappointed in the character I had formed of him;—certainly he was by no means called upon to show me a civility, he had up to that time, not even extended to the Assistant Resident, and I was told not to expect it of him.

Governor's visit.

165. In the evening Mr. Cooper and myself as usual went out shooting, and I was sorry to find on our return that two of my peons—the party already spoken of as a debauchee, and his companion, an equal sybarite—had disarmed some Shans and shown them over the Residency! I was greatly put out at this, and requested Mr. Cooper to have the men confined in the guard-house till next morning, when they had twenty-four stripes each administered, and confined to the Residency compound for the remainder of their stay at Bhamo. I was not aware native liquor was procurable here, until Mr. Cooper informed me that *shumshoo* was openly sold by the Chinese, and that it was not very long since that he had to punish one of his guard for getting drunk; had I only known this, I should have been on the *qui vive*, knowing the character of my escort.

Misconduct of two Peons.

166. In the course of my wanderings through the suburbs I came on a number of Kakhyens encamped under a wide-spreading *Ficus elastica*. The party consisted of thirty;— fourteen men with their families—who had come down from the neighbouring mountain to barter fire-wood, pigs, silver, rice, bark of *cinnamomum cassia* (which is used as a substitute for *C. zeylanicum*), and other natural and cultivated products of the hills; for salt, *suparee, cowries (cyprœa moneta)*, cotton, gaudy cloths, beads, &c., &c. They were busy cooking opium in a small brass spoon, sufficiently large to hold half a wine-glass of water; a piece of the drug, about the size of an ordinary pill, was thrown in, and allowed to simmer for a few minutes; the liquor was poured off and fresh water added; this process was repeated three times; when the pill was thrown away, and the liquor boiled down to the

Observations on the Kakhyens found encamped under a Ficus elastica tree.

consistency of treacle, and spread on plantain leaves, which were finely cut up and smoked in bamboo pipes.

167. The men were middle-sized, well set-up, and muscular, with small waists, broad chests, and the lower limbs powerfully developed, befitting genuine mountaineers. They had no beards or whiskers, and the few hairs that served as an apology for a moustache were well waxed and brought to a straight point. They are more hairy however about the body, than either the Shan or Burman, who, as a rule, are remarkably smooth-skinned. The women were good-humoured and amiable-looking, with large mouths, moderately thick lips, high cheek-bones, narrow eyes, small, straight noses, and low foreheads. The very young girls are even pretty, with rosy cheeks and dark olive complexions, but hard work, exposure, privations, drink, and early marriage, soon deprive them of whatever beauty or grace they may have been possessed. The old women are thorough hags. The costume of both sexes, the fashion of dressing the hair, and the weapons of the males correspond with those described at page 68. They were a dirty lot, begrimed with filth and smoke. Unlike most other wild tribes, the male Kakhyens are content to decorate themselves with a cock's feather stuck in their hair, or a tiger's tooth with part of the jaw attached, fastened to their sword-belts; leaving all other ornaments for their women, who, apparently, they are fond of seeing gaily decorated. The female ornaments, though simple, inexpensive, and peculiar in design, become these wild people, and add considerably to the picturesqueness of their *tout ensemble*. The ornaments generally consist in *cowries*, sown about the jacket or arranged as girdles, necklets, or ear-pendants; beads and bugles are also much in favour, and a good deal of taste is often displayed in their arrangement for the article required. The more wealthy families—which signifies those who have committed the greatest depredations—also wear silver jewellery in the form of large hoops round the neck, cylinder-shaped ear-tubes, five inches long, with a bunch of hair, dyed red, protruding from one end, and bangles round the wrists; some also wear flat pieces of silver sown on to a piece of red cloth by which it is suspended from the ear. The unmarried girls were remarkably shy and timid, quite the reverse of what they are in their mountain homes, and, strange to say, immediately Mrs. Mason approached, they made for the nearest jungle with the fleetness of a deer, and could not be prevailed on to return till she had left their camp. Inquisitiveness

Description of the Kakhyens with their dress and ornaments.

was a marked feature in the character of these people, they carefully examined everything about me; the lightness of my *solátopee* was not only wondered at, but the elastic sides to my boots struck them dumb; and when I pulled out one of the rubber threads, and explained, through an interpreter, that this was only one of the many uses to which we put *caoutchouc*, they gave a significant look at one another, and the silence that followed for a few minutes was first broken by a couple of old hags pulling away at my trousers, to test—I presume—whether these were elastic also: fortunately I had braces on. I was told that the *Ficus elastica* was not known in the mountains to the east of Bhamo, but that a stray tree here and there was to be met with, in villages skirting the foot of the hills:—evidently these must have been planted.

168. The Tswabwa or chief of the party, was a middle-aged man, and wore a disagreeable, cadaverous expression, and never opened his mouth throughout the interview, until just towards the last, he proclaimed himself Tswabwa of the Latoung hill, and invited me up to his village, some thirty miles distant, guaranteeing perfect safety to myself and people. I had to decline the invitation, however, for the journey would have occupied a longer time than I could spare, as it was quite uncertain when the steamer would arrive. Subsequently I learnt it was within this man's Tswabwaship, that a Governor was killed not many years ago; but the stigma still remains, and is told as a lasting disgrace against this tribe. There is little doubt, however, but that these savages were goaded on to the crime by acts of official tyranny, which are of such common occurrence as to have engendered a lasting and most bitter feeling of hatred between the two tribes, to which may be traced in most cases, the frightful murders and outrages committed by the Kakhyens. Even in the matter of barter, they get most unjustly imposed on by the Burmese, and seldom receive half the real value of their goods. Though an uncivilized, wild people, they are not ignorant of this fact, and seek the first opportunity to repay themselves by raids and plunder. I once was told by a Kakhyen, that he was always careful to press down in the scales whatever he purchased from a Burman, in the same manner that they compressed into the smallest space whatever they obtained from them. Though I attempted to explain to the poor fellow, the delusion under which he was labouring, and the object the Burman had in purchasing by bulk and selling by weight, he persisted in being satisfied with his own *coup de maitre*.

The Tswabwa of the Latoung hill.

169. The country surrounding Bhamo presents one vast plain, with cart-tracks radiating from the stockade in different directions; some of these are exceedingly pretty, reminding one of English lanes, in their windings through the copse-wood, that has replaced the timber trees which have long since been felled, to secure a commanding view of the surrounding country; low, swampy ravines intersect the country to the east, and here, also, is an extensive marsh and *jheel*, where water-fowl of sorts abound, and aquatic plants, including *Trapa bicornis*,* *Nymphæa pubescens*, and *Nelumbium speciosum* grow in luxurious abundance, their tubers and water-beans are sold as food, and the gorgeous flowers serve as sacred offerings at the pagodas.

Country surrounding the town.

Here and there patches of jungle are partially cleared for cotton crops, but no care is bestowed on the culture, and the result is a short and coarse staple. The seeds are dibbled in with intermediate sowings of *Hibiscus sabdariffa*, and the crop left to stand its chance with the surrounding weeds and copse-wood, by which it is soon over-topped. The cotton that is exported to China comes from Mandalay and southward; but there is no reason why Bhamo should not meet the demand were only a little care and trouble bestowed on its culture. Both the soil and climate are well-suited to the plant, and I believe it was not far north of this that the *nankeen* cotton was once produced with great success and largely exported. Here, as elsewhere throughout the whole province of Burma, paddy is the staple crop; it is the most easily cultivated and the principal food of the people.

170. To-day (28th December), a Chinese official, a Mandarin of the red button—now on a private visit to Bhamo,—called to invite the Assistant Resident and myself, to the Dragon-festival. In this man, Mr. Cooper recognized the party who had treated him so badly when travelling in China; evidently the Mandarin did not remember his victim, or it is hardly likely he would have attempted so unblushingly to " beard the lion in his den" after the attempt he had once made on his life. I am inclined to think, my friend mistook his man,—not at all a difficult matter considering the awkward circumstances under which they met, and the great sameness of features, expression, deportment, and general appearance that prevails among the Chinese. We accepted the invitation; but owing to some blunder on the part of the Chinese interpreter, we

Account of the Dragon-festival.

---

* The *Trapa bicornis* bears a remarkable fruit, resembling a buffalo's head, and is called *chuay-gong* in Burmese, and *ling* by Chinese.

arrived earlier than was expected, and consequently everything was in a state of confusion. Carpets, however, were soon spread on benches, and tea and pipes handed round until the Mandarin was ready to receive us. The entertainment was in the temple, and prayer was being conducted in the chamber, over the entrance to the inner court, when we arrived. The ceremony apparently gave employment to four priests : one was reading the law out in a loud voice for the benefit of those busy in the court below ; another punctuated the sentences, by knocking a couple of ebony rules against one another ; a third rang a bell at given intervals ; and the fourth was engaged, fumigating the chamber with incense.

After an interval of a good half-hour, the Mandarin sent word to say he would be glad to see us. He was living up-stairs in one of the guest-rooms round the outer court of the temple ; and a filthy, dirty little den it was ; filled with all sorts of lumber, our host's bed and table, occupying an extreme corner. After more tea, pipes and sweets, we sallied forth to watch the procession, pass down the main street, which it occupied two hours in doing. Some twenty yards in advance of the principal group were a few skirmishers, who kept the way clear by discharging blunderbusses, loaded with sufficient powder to give the report of a cannon ; next in order came a body of gaily-dressed men, marching at a slow, measured pace, with eyes fixed on the ground, and carrying the different insignia of office, referred to at page 51 ; then followed the expounders of the law, the senior priest reading aloud from a roll of paper, and the others either ringing bells, striking sticks together, or swinging the incense-pot to and fro, as they progressed. There was a break now of about five yards, and then came the band, which consisted of fifes and bones, making the most discordant noise possible to conceive ; I was astonished to find that a people in other respects so civilized should continue to have such a barbarous idea of music. A group that presented themselves to my mind as jesters, were the next in the train ; their faces were disfigured by paint, false moustaches of unnatural length, and large round spectacles, while their costume was equally ludicrous with the rest of the get up ; their principal office appeared to consist in trying to excel one another in buffoonery, and apparently they were commanded by a stout party mounted on a pony, who would have made a capital Guy Fawkes. Perched on a bamboo about fifteen feet long, was a boy disguised as a girl, he looked quite pretty as he gracefully kept fanning himself, and smiled on the admiring crowd. He was in a standing position, and borne in turns by volunteers from the crowd ; but the surprising part to me was, how the child preserved his balance, and yet looked so comfortable. The procession now was a repetition of what had gone before, only the order had been exactly reversed. We dined with the Mandarin in the evening, and although I ate sparingly of the greasy food placed before us,—under the plea of want of skill in handling the chop-sticks,—yet I very indiscreetly took a glass of *shamshoo*, which I had occasion to remember for two days afterwards: both Messrs. Cooper and Graham, however, were in favour of the liquor, and partook of it freely without any evil effect.

171. Here also I witnessed the Water-festival, a ceremony with which the Burmese new-year is ushered in. Deluging one another with water, is the great diversion at this anniversary, which is even more childish by far than a carnival. At an early hour on the first of the new year, guns are fired from the Governor's house, and the salute taken up by *feu-de-joie* throughout the town, accompanied by shouts of "*Thayia ming kia bin*," which, I am told, signifies "Indra has descended." All now sprinkle newly-drawn water in front of their house, and a processof drenching one another and passers-by —irrespective of caste, religion, or position—with syringes or even *chatties* is kept up for three days, during which period no one is supposed to take offence, it being considered an honour to be thoroughly immersed.

Account of the Water-festival.

172. Before proceeding to a description of my trip into the Kakhyen Hills *viâ* the Taping, I must not forget to mention that, on my return to Bhamo, I found Mr. Cooper had been succeeded by Captain C. B. Cooke. The Residency now no longer assumed the wretched scene of discomfort it presented when I was last there; a transformation scene had taken place; and everything was the picture of neatness, and as comfortable as it was possible to make such an uncheerful building. I take this opportunity of recording my thanks to that Officer, for the great kindness and hospitality he showed me, during my stay with him at the Residency.

Succession of Captain Cooke to post held by Mr. Cooper.

VEGETATION—INDIGENOUS AND CULTIVATED.

Biophytum sensitivum, Oxalis corniculata, Tribulus lanugenosus, Aspidopterys nutans, A. hirsuta, Reinwardtia indica, Elæocarpus wallichii, Corchorus capsularis, C. urticæfolius, Triumfetta rhomboidea, Grewia humilis, Columbia floribunda, Buethneria pilosa, Melochia corchorifolia agati, Citrus medica, Cordia myxa, Taliera, Bixa orellana, Phyllanthus, Pentapetes phœnicea, Eridendron pentandrum, Thespesia populmea, Hibiscus solandra, Sida corylifolia, S. glutinosa, Hopea odo-

rata, *Dipterocarpus tuberculatus, D. incarnus, Sauranga macrotricha, S. armata, S. punduana, Gordonia, Campanula arenosa, Ammannia rotundifolia, Azolla, Salvinia, Cyrilla, Serpicula, Nauclea, Lagerstræmia parviflora, Combretum, Michelia champaca, Dillenia indica, D. sarmentosa, Ranunculus diffusus, Clematis bracteata, Melodorum verencosum, Aspidocarya uvifera, Brassica campestris, Viola Palrinii, Drymaria cordata, Tamarix diocia, Marsilea, Thunbergia, Clerodendron, Calotropis gigantea, Artocarpus integrifolia.*

BIRDS.

Motacilla madraspatana, Henicurus immaculatus, Orthotomus longicandata, Larbivora cyana, Chæmorrornis leucocephata, Pratincola rubicola, Grandala cælicolor, Copsychus saularis, Oriolus melanocephalus, Jora zeylonica, Otocompsa leucogenys, Hypsipetes psaroides, H. McClellandi, Malacoeircus canorus, Sibia capistrata, Trochatopteron lineatum, Garrulax alboyularis, Pomatorhinus erythrogenys, Suthora nipalensis, Planesticus abrogularis, Geocichla citrina, Petrococeyphus cyanus, Niltava sundara, N. grandis, Cryptolipha cinereocapilla, Leucocirca albicollis, L. aureola, Myiagra azurea, Pericrocotus flammeus, P. brevirostris, P. peregrinus, Pephrodornis pondiceriana, Lanius erythronotus, L. nigriceps, Upupa epops, Arachnechthra asiatica, A. pectoralis, Coccystes jacobinus, Cyanops asiatica, Megalaima marshallorum, Yunx torquilla, Brachypternus aurantius, Gecinus occipitalis, Picus brunneifrons, Palæornis affinis, Ceryle rudis, Alcedo bengalensis, Collocalia linchi, Hirundo fluvicola, Athene brama, Ascalaphia bengalensis, Otus vulgari, Elanus melanopterus, Circus æruginosus, Aquila bifasciata, A. fulvescens, Micronisus badius, Tinnunculus alandarius, Talco jugger, Plotus melanogaster, Graculus fuscicollis, Seena seena, Dendrocygna arcuata, Ardea purpurea, Mycteria indica, Carpophaga sylvatica, Euplocamus lineatus, Gallus ferrugineus, Glareola orientalis, Lobivanellus atronuchalis, Gallicrex cristata, Alcedo asiatica, Pelargopsis burmanicus, Halcyon smyrnensis, Coracias affinis, Nyctiornis athertoni, Strix indica, Ninox hirsutus, Harpactes erythrocephalus, Xantholæma hæmacephala, Upupa ostris.

On my return to Bhamo, I was sorry to find that two large cases of birds and plants I had left there for safety during my absence, had been utterly destroyed by insects and white-ants.

SECTION II.

173. In consequence of a robbery of fifty bales of royal cotton,

Robbery of cotton.

en route to Western China, the through trade had been suspended for the last month, and the Governor had ordered that the roads should remain closed until the loss had been made good, half by the Kakhyens, and the remainder by the Chinese community of Bhamo, who had guaranteed its safety. The latter now craved the interference of the Assistant Resident, denying that they had ever accepted the responsibility, and pointed to the serious inconvenience and loss they had already sustained by the issue of this despotic order. The quantity of cotton collected at Tseekaw, ready for transport to Momein, by mules, was reported to be 1,500 bales. The Governor, on a reference from the Assistant Resident, explained the circumstances under which he had found it expedient to take stringent measures, but positively stated that trade had been re-established some days ago. These statements were so very contradictory, that Mr. Cooper determined to take a run up to Tseekaw, the next day (29th December), and ascertain from the people direct, the correct state of affairs. Having nothing more to do at Bhamo, and there being no probability of the steamer arriving for another week, I thought the present would be a capital opportunity of extending my knowledge of the country, and accordingly asked permission to accompany my friend, to which he very kindly consented.

174. To avoid the monotony of the first part of the journey, the boat was started at 10 A.M., with instructions to meet us at Mata, a small hamlet some two miles from the mouth of the Taping. At 4 P.M. we shouldered our guns, and took the bridle-path that leads through a dense thicket to Tsain-pen-ago, thence proceeding to Suseenah, on the banks of the Taping, and within half a mile of its junction with the Irrawaddy. Here there are some two or three hundred pagodas, all more or less in ruins, and overgrown with bamboo and arborescent scrub; but still the site maintains its original sanctity, and continues to draw large numbers to the sacred annual festival. Continuing to skirt the banks of the river, in hopes of bagging a few ducks and geese we reached our destination for the night, about 6 P.M., some time before the boat came up. It was too late to continue our rambles, so we sat down, and, as is not an uncommon practice under similar circumstances, appealed to one another for a probable solution of the cause of delay, forgetting that neither of us could possibly be wiser than the other as to the reason of detention; but still there is always some little satisfaction in the vague speculations offered, however remote the conclusions arrived at may prove. An hour had elapsed, and there was still no signs of the boat, so I strolled back in the direction of the Irrawaddy, to see what had happened; I had not far to go, however, before the voice of my old cook urging on the crew was distinguishable, and in another half hour we were comfortably housed in our little cabin. It was a clear starlight night, and the thermometer stood at 50·5 at 8 P.M., in the open.

Excursions at Bhamo.

175. Mr. Cooper considering that there was no immediate hurry for reaching Tseekaw, we determined to make a thorough examination of the country *en route*, and share the benefit of each other's note-books at the end of the day. We generally left the moorings of the night previous at 6 A.M., and so arranged that the first halt should be at some place of interest, where we could wander about, and pick up information until breakfast; after which, we parted company for the remainder of the day, taking opposite banks—knowing that the Taping was sufficiently tortuous in its course to admit of our excursions extending some distance inland, without fear of being headed by the boat which had orders to follow us up.

<small>Further examination of the country.</small>

176. The entire distance by water from the mouth of the Taping to Tseekaw, has more than once been computed by different travellers at twenty-one miles, though I am inclined to add another eight to the estimate. Tamine, situated on the right bank, was the first village of importance we stopped at, for breakfast. It contains about a hundred houses, each enclosed by a high bamboo fence, and the whole surrounded by a double stockade eight feet high of the same material. These palisades, I am told, are not regarded as impenetrable, but rather intended as a protection against sudden attacks, and to allow the inhabitants time to defend themselves in cases of unexpected raids by the Kakhyens, who are much dreaded in these parts. Judging from the comfortable appearance of the houses, and the numbers of well-dressed people we saw, this village no doubt is in a prosperous condition. The population are entirely Shan-Burmese; the male community gain a livelihood by cultivating paddy, and the women find employment at the loom, at which they spend their leisure hours weaving the gay *tamines* and *putsoes* worn by themselves and family.

<small>Village of Tamine.</small>

Within the stockade I noticed mango, *Carica papaya, Anona cliculata, Ægle marmelos*, oranges, sweet-limes *(citrus limetta), Punica granatum,* tamarind, *Anacardium occidentale, Bauhimia, Jatropha,* and a very fine specimen of a *Granadilla* growing over a house.

177. Some 150 yards beyond the stockade were two *Ficus elastica,* even more luxuriant in habit than those noted at Bhamo, which I account for by their never having been tapped. Of their history nothing could be ascertained, and when I asked permission to take some cuttings, I was refused, and told the trees were the sole property of the Loogyee, who was absent on a visit to the Woon. Though

<small>Two *Ficus elastica.*</small>

I doubted this statement, I accepted it, there being no immediate hurry for the cuttings until I returned to Bhamo. However, on revisiting the village; seeing no one near at hand to ask permission of, I reluctantly acted on my own responsibility, and being a rather hot day, my interpreter recommended that the branches should be carefully stowed away in the cabin, to protect them from the sun ; his idea was *concealment* no doubt, but I fear something more than *sol's* rays prompted the suggestion ; as nothing more was heard on the subject, I conclude the operation was a success, and that neither the people nor the trees missed the limbs we took away. Both specimens were growing on an alluvial deposit resting on gravel ; the finer tree measured—

	Feet.	Inches.
Height	110	0
Circumference of main trunk	80	0
Ditto including aërial roots	150	0
Area covered by crown branches	690	0
Circumference of three aërial roots taken at five feet from the ground	5	2
	4	7
	2	9

178. At 4 P.M. we made fast for the night at the Shan village of Sinekau, and were most hospitably received by the head-man, who placed his house at our disposal, and rendered all possible assistance in providing for our wants. The population were entirely of the agricultural class, and apparently well to do. The village was surrounded by a double bamboo stockade in capital condition, and had been unmolested by the Kakhyens for the last two years. The principal cause for dissatisfaction was evidently the oppression committed by the subordinate officials, whose only means of subsistence would appear to be the pickings they derived in the discharge of their duties. We spent the evening in an excursion to the *Jheel* west of the village, and managed to bag a few snipe and teal ; there were also large numbers of other water-fowl, including geese, *Carbo nudigular*, *Pelican*, *Terns*, *Tulica atra*, water-hens (*Gallinula javanica*), and *Nycticorax grisesus*, white paddy-bird (*Herodias allia*), and *ibis*.

Shan village of Sinekau.

The aqueous vegetation was principally represented by the *Nelambiaceæ* order ; I also noted *Myrophyllum tetrandrum*, and a *Salix* was conspicuous on the banks. Here, also, I noticed paper being manufactured from *Daphne cannabina*, the only difference in the process followed from that described at page 14, being that the bark was boiled with wood ashes prior to conversion into paper stock. The paper was tolerably fine and used for writing. I did not see the plant growing, but had specimens brought me, and was told by the people that it grew on the hills to the east, though I never noticed it in my wanderings. Our guide begged of us to hurry back, as it was getting dark, and there were a good many tigers about—only the night previous an old woman had been killed within the stockade, he said, and this we found to be correct. The alarm was too promptly raised, and the brute was unable to carry off his victim, for the people were too soon to the rescue; he dropped the body in the act of clearing the stockade, which stood nine feet high.

179. In proof that the Shans are not entirely devoid of affection, and forgetful of those who have gone before, I relate the following circumstance. Walking round the village, I observed an old Shan smoking an exceedingly pretty pipe, the bowl was of silver nicely carved, and the stem a well-selected bamboo root, highly polished from long smoking. I offered to purchase the article at the man's own price, but he declined to part with the bowl at any figure, saying it was the only memento he had of his old wife, who had died some two years back; the stem, however, he was willing to part with for Re. 1, remarking he had cut that for himself, and could get plenty more like it.

Instance of Shans' affection.

180. The next morning we could not get away before 8 A.M., so dense was the fog. The thermometer at 6 A.M. stood at 52° outside the house. The river here is about 200 yards broad, and the banks, which are twelve feet above the present level of the water, are, we learn, during the freshes often submerged to a depth of two feet. At 11 A.M. we passed a small hamlet of eleven houses, snugly embowered in a grove of plaintain and lime trees; the people were Shan-Burmese. This little community had been planted under the auspices of the Kakhyens to the east, with a guarantee of protection, on the understanding that, immediately the people had fairly established themselves, each house was to pay a yearly fixed tax in the shape of grain, vegetables, or any other article stipulated for. The people seemed quite contented with this arrangement, and had taken no precaution of protecting themselves from the raids of the surrounding mountaineers; indeed, it was the absence of the stockade that first attracted our attention, and led to the enquiry, which elicited the foregoing information. From here, the configuration of the left bank gradually begins to change; the mountains to the far east send out spurs which, in a series of undulations of varying altitude, eventually reach the water's edge; these again give off spurs at right-angles, until the whole country gradually

Further observations during the excursion.

working from E. to N.W., as far as the eye can reach, presents one vast mountainous system, densely wooded, and intersected by rugged gorges and fertile valleys. The hill sides are dotted with Kakhyen *toungya* cultivation, which has rather a pleasing effect amidst the luxuriant and noble arborescent foliage.

181. A little further on, and the Manloung stream empties itself into the Taping on the right bank. It takes its rise in a lake of the same name, situated to the west of Tseekaw, and also receives a constant supply of water from a branch-stream given off by the Taping two miles higher up.

Manloung stream.

182. At the junction of the Manloung with the main river, there are a number of old ruined pagodas, which mark the site of the once influential town of Tsain-pin-ago, a place of anterior date by many centuries to the city of the same name near Bhamo.

Town of Tsain-pin-ago.

183. By 5 P.M. Tseekaw was reached, and, as might have been expected, we found two of the Governor's court officials had preceded us by a day, evidently with a view to gag the people, and watch the Assistant Resident's line of action. It is a mistaken idea to suppose that, in a place like Bhamo, a single movement of a British subject—much less of a Political Officer—can be concealed from the Governor; nor is it the least improbable that a system of espionage is maintained through one's own domestics,—for where is the native who is not open to a bribe? even those we have placed the most confidence in, and elevated to positions with emoluments that should have rendered them proof against corruption, have at last been detected red-handed. After we had settled down in the house that had been prepared by Mr. Cooper's Kakhyen interpreter, who had been sent on ahead for this express purpose, the two officials presented themselves with trays of sweets and fruit: they were remarkably polite, and gave the Resident to understand that they had been sent by the Governor to see all our wants provided for, and to render us every assistance necessary. The object of our visit was then cautiously solicited, but the question was equally cleverly parried, and Mr. Cooper proceeded to enquire about the probable distance to which the Taping was navigable, as we intended proceeding onward the following day. Of course, endless obstructions were at once thrown in our way; the first difficulty was our boat being too large, then it was doubtful whether canoes could be obtained, and lastly, the danger of encountering the blood-thirsty Kakhyens, who, but a day previous, had been reported to have plundered two Shan villages

Return to Tseekaw.

on the banks of the Taping only a few miles further on, and killed three of the inhabitants. The crowds that had by this time surrounded our house, were ready to corroborate all and every statement made by the officials, and, strange to say, the relations of the deceased were present, and implored of us not to venture such a hazardous trip, if we valued our lives. We were not, however, to be thrown off the scent in this manner, and expressed determination on going under any circumstances : after a little more *palaver*, it was agreed that the canoes should be in readiness the next morning at 6 A.M., and that the Governor's representatives would accompany us. The officials had not very long left, when I was sorry to find Mr. Cooper change his mind about going, but very kindly gave me permission to do as I thought best; of course, I was resolute, feeling the present excursion could hardly present the dangers and difficulties I would have to encounter later on in my travels, and besides which, this offered a capital opportunity of testing what my escort were made of. Having been debarred the pleasure of my friend's company, was a matter for regret, for it is always more agreeable and satisfactory to have an extra pair of eyes when exploring a country; however, Mr. Cooper could not be persuaded to alter his mind again, for he had a double motive, I was informed, in remaining behind—in the first place, he did not consider it correct to risk his life, and thereby involve Government in political difficulties; and, secondly, he was in hopes that, if the two officials accompanied me, he would be better able to extract information from the people in their absence. The grounds of his first objection I quite concurred in ; but as regarded the second, I was satisfied there was not the least chance of his hopes being realized ;—neither were they, for only one of the Governor's Officers accompanied me.

184. Before proceeding with an account of my journey further on, I must give a description of the physical aspect of the country between Bhamo and Tseekaw, and also allude to the village we are now in. The Taping is one of the principal tributaries of the Irrawaddy. It takes its rise in Western China, and in its mountainous course is a mere magnified mountain torrent running down through narrow gorges. Quitting the hills, it assumes the character of a large river sweeping down in a tortuous course through a fertile valley, and navigable for boats of three feet six inches draft up to Tseekaw throughout the year. Ascending this river, its large expanse of water gives the impression that it is navigable for a considerable distance, but one is

Country between Bhamo and Tseekaw.

astonished at the shortness of its course from where it first quits its mountain home, to its discharge into the Irrawaddy. Either bank has long since been denuded of all arborescent growth, with the exception of a few *Bombax, Fici, Dipterocarpus grandiflora,* and *Erythrina,* which are scattered here and there over the extensive belt of *Saccharum spontaneum* that extends to some distance inland on both sides of the river. These vast savannahs are annually flooded by the overlap of the Taping, and utilized for rice culture, but not to the same extent as of old, when this productive plain was densely populated. The traces of old cultivation are everywhere to be seen, and the sites of the numerous deserted villages still distinguishable by the orchards and groves of plantains which, from neglect, have long since ceased to fruit or flower. The origin of the decline and depopulation of the country, the people attribute to the repeated raids of the Kakhyens, whose acts of ravage and plunder were, and still continue to be, passed unnoticed by the Government. There is no question of this being the true cause, nor is proof wanting up to the present day of the absence of protection to life and property in Upper Burma. In many of the more recently abandoned paddy-fields, I found the land over-grown with plants of the *Zingiberaceæ* order, and also noticed *Portulaca obracea, Viola batrinii, Gynandropeis benlaphylla,* and a wild insipid strawberry *(Fragraria indica).*

185. Tseekaw is situated on the right bank of the river; it contains a mixed population of Shan-Burmese and Shan-Talokes, and numbers about a hundred and fifty houses, the whole being enclosed in a double bamboo stockade. The houses are slightly different to those I have hitherto seen; each has a large balcony in front with a bamboo trellis or mat parapet, about three feet high. Mr. Mason tells me this is the usual style of building common to Toungoo—a part of British territory I regret not having seen. Within a separate enclosure, but only a few yards distant, the Chinese have established a small community of their own, and erected cotton godowns, and a *shamshoo* distillery; they also carry on an extensive business in salt, which is bartered for other articles. The Burmese law regarding the slaughter of cattle and sale of liquor are, I believe, equally rigid; the former is in a measure observed here, but the latter openly disregarded, and liquor sold to any one who can pay for it. The result is, that the Kakhyens are fast becoming dissatisfied with their own brews of rice-toddy, and spend all they have in this highly-intoxicating liquor, under the influence of which, generally their most desperate deeds are committed. It is quite a common occur-

Village of Tseekaw.

rence to find men (generally Shans) lying on the road dead drunk, and robbed of everything they possess, including their clothes.

186. I had an opportunity of seeing *shamshoo* manufactured at Tseekaw, and will here describe the process. In a large wooden bucket, made of toon, rice is first steeped in water, with the addition of a herb to promote fermentation; the herb I did not recognize, nor could I obtain its name, but was told it was imported from China for this express purpose. Immediately the liquor has reached the correct stage of fermentation, it is transferred to an iron cauldron, covered with an inverted pail, the two being tightly secured by a paste of flour and water, and allowed to boil on a slow fire. In the lower part of the pail, is inserted a hollow bamboo, four feet long, this connects the apparatus with a double-walled vessel, the inner compartment being, constantly kept cool by fresh supplies of cold water, and the condensed liquor passing through the inner-walls pours into the vessel placed below ready to receive it. The first quality sells at Rs. 2-8 per bottle; the second, which is only the old material with an addition of water redistilled, at Re. 1-8 per bottle; and the third at Re. 1. The first and second qualities burn with a bright blue flame immediately lighted, but not so with the third, for which I am told there is hardly any sale, and is, therefore, generally used to adulterate the first qualities.

Process of manufacturing sham-shoo.

187. To the west of Tseekaw is the lake of Manloung—said once to have been the old bed of the Taping—an idea supported by the configuration of the country—that now disgorges itself by a stream of the same name, into Taping at old Tsain-pin-ago. At this season the expanse of water does not exceed over three-eighths of a mile broad, two miles long, and fourteen feet deep in the middle; but during the monsoon it is said to present one vast sheet of water for miles. To the west, the Manloung stream divides, uniting again some little distance south, and forming the island now occupied by the Shan village of the same name, and numbering some seventy houses. On the highest ground are situated the pagodas and monasteries, looking quite pretty, clustered in groves of that noble bamboo, the *Bambusa gigantea*, plantain, mango, jack, and other fruit trees; indeed, the village throughout, has a snug, prosperous appearance, and the people seem contented and happy. The male population are entirely of an agricultural class, while the women busy themselves with the domestic affairs, devoting their spare hours to the manufacture of *putsoes* and *thamines*, for which they find a ready sale; every house has its loom, and the bulk of the raw cotton is said to be the pro-

Lake of Manloung.

duce of the Kakhyen hills. East of the lake the country is comparatively marshy, and the arborescent vegetation was principally represented by stunted *Fici, Dipterocarpus grandiflora, Bombax, Strychnos, Nux vomica*, and *Licuala peltata*. The water and banks were covered with birds in large numbers, among which I noted snippets and sand-pipers in great variety; *Phæopus vulgaris, ibis* (black and white), *Leptoptilos argala, Ardea fusca, Herodias alba, Pigrisoma melanolopha, Nycticorax grisens, Rhynchops nigra, Pelican (Pelicanus onocrotalus), Carbo lancogaster*, geese, duck (of four varieties), snipe, and in the vast paddy plains stretching far away to the north, *Grus antigone* and jungle fowl were common. It was a most difficult matter to get within shot of the cranes, and after a hard day's stalking, I only managed to bag two, both unfortunately females.

188. On the 1st January 1874, I started on my excursion up the Taping, accompanied by one of the Governor's officials. The canoes were cut out of a single teak log, and only sufficiently broad to admit of us sitting in line; even a change of position, necessitated the greatest precaution for fear of a capsize, so cranky were these little cockle-shells. At the start, I was under the impression that these boats had been provided with a view to intimidate me, but before we reached the rapids I found the journey could not have been accomplished in any other way—so strong was the current. Up to old Bhamo, the banks remained unchanged in character, but the river was much divided by sand-banks, the principal channel not being over twenty feet wide and two feet deep. Here the course abruptly changed from N.N.E. to S.S.E., and we found ourselves gradually being walled in on either side by high hills, densely cloaked in evergreen forests, passing into almost pure bamboo and plantain jungle, as they neared the water's edge. We had entered the defile; and here the stream narrowed to sixty yards, increasing in velocity as we ascended, and decreasing in breadth as the high sand-stone cliffs converged into a narrow gauge, through which the rapids poured over huge boulders, leaving in places a channel of not over three yards for the water to pass. The first obstacle that necessitated us leaving our canoes was a dislodged block of rock that had settled in the centre of the stream. It was larger than any ordinary house, and stood nine feet out of the water. Tradition has christened it the "*zoorjee zone*," or the sorcerer's mortar. The hollow in the centre is supposed to have been the saucer from which he drank, and is called "*zoorjee zoon*," while the third cavity represents his foot-print, we are told, though it least represents that part of

Excursion from Tseekaw up the Taping.

the human body. The detached square block, which lies a few yards below, is called the "*zoorjee thittar,*" which signifies the box of this great personage. I now proposed a tramp over the hills before we returned; the first ascent was sufficient to pump the Burman minister, and of his own accord, he suggested that myself and party should ferret about by ourselves. I continued to follow the river up for some miles, but found it unchanged in character from where the rapids first commenced, obstructions were quite as frequent, and the precipitous cliffs on both sides continued to be fringed with sombre vegetation, damp and dripping with moisture, and covered with pendulous mosses, lichens, and ferns. We are told by those, however, who have crossed the Taping still further east that it is a river of considerable breadth. Before returning, I managed to bag a couple of peacock-pheasants and three jungle fowl; I also got a shot at a splendid leopard, but unfortunately missed him. Porcupine quills were constantly being picked up, and one of my peons caught a chameleon alive, which was preserved in spirits when I returned to Tseekaw. Before I rejoined the minister, the sun had nearly set, and he was in a great state of mind; I fancy the old gentleman had never before in the whole course of his life been picketed out in the heart of a forest under such uncomfortable circumstances. Before quitting the defile, we came on a band of armed Kakhyens crossing the river on a raft of bamboos. No questions were asked, nor the men interfered with, though I was afterwards told they were a gang of dacoits evidently on their way to plunder some village.

189. I parted company with my *keeper* at old Bhamo, and returned to Tseekaw by land. On my way I passed several little hamlets, and among them was a Shan-Taloke colony, who had settled down here only a fortnight ago, having been driven from their homes near Momein by the outrages committed by the Chinese and Panthay armies. In mode of living and general appearance, these people nearer resemble the Chinese than Shans; yet, in disposition they differ from both. They are a mild, inoffensive, industrious tribe, and though so cut off from the civilized world, they rather court than avoid intercourse with Europeans who are kindly disposed towards them. When I entered their village, I found many of the men engaged making buckets of *toon* wood, the hoops being of thin strips of plaited rattan. They told me they had to leave their homes with as few things as possible, and were consequently obliged to work by moonlight to supply themselves with the articles in daily requirement.

Return by land to Tseekaw, and observations during journey.

They appeared remarkably skilful coopers, and quick workers, completing a pail in a day. Singularly enough, I met this same party at Pegu on my return to British Burma, and was immediately recognized by the late Tswabwa's wife, who now represents the head of her village. Before reaching Tseekaw, we came on a drunken set of Kakhyens, who brandished their swords about, and were otherwise insulting, refusing to make way, and demanding opium of us, but we continued our path with apparent disregard, keeping an eye on them, lest they might carry their threats into force; however, all passed off quietly, and in another half hour I was within the stockade, and found Mr. Cooper pacing the main road in a great state of anxiety about me, for it was now past 9 P.M. We had a long chat at dinner over our day's doings, when he told me, the cause of the traffic having been suspended here, he ascertained to have emanated in an order from the palace, with a view to securing a more ready sale of the royal cotton that had been sent to Momein by another route. He also put his *veto* on my extending my travels into the hills in this vicinity as I had originally intended to do, giving as a reason that he had been credibly informed, I would be killed if I went among the Kakhyens in the present disturbed state of the country. I was immensely put out at this, as it simply meant my mission was to cease at Bhamo, for the entire country through which my work lay was more or less peopled by these much-dreaded mountaineers. I therefore requested he would kindly commit to paper whatever he had to say; for my orders from the Local Government and Resident at Mandalay were definite, and I hardly felt inclined, under the circumstances, to abandon my original plans. It was rather an amusing sight to see us corresponding with one another across a table 3′ × 2′ 6″, but official etiquette demanded this burlesque; only three tetters, however, were exchanged, and mine was the last, wherein I recorded in mellowed official terms that it was hardly likely I had been sent up here at the jeopardy of my life, and that as my work lay entirely among the Kakhyens, I thought it better I should face all difficulties at once, and begged in this matter to be allowed to exercise my own judgment, and take care of myself. To this I received no reply, so I accepted silence as consent: Mr. Cooper wished me "good night" with a few admonishing words, and I proceeded to catalogue the plants I had collected, which are enumerated below:—

190. *Tectona grandis* (scarce and small), *Fici*, chiefly epiphytical, *Erythrina, Bauhinia microphylla, Diospyros, Bombax malabaricum, Dipterocarpus incanus* (small), *Butea fron-*

Catalogue of plants collected during adventures.

dosa, cedrela toona, Borassus *flabelliformis,* and *Cocos nucifera* (stray trees, cultivated in the plains, both stunted in growth and barren); *Aspidopterys tomentosa, Elæocarpus varuna, Reinwardtia indica, Hiptage obtusifolia, Buettneria pilosa, Melochia corchorifolia, Pterospermum acerifolium, Sida corylifolia, Hopea odorata, Schima mollis, Sauranga armata, Drymaria cordata* (in garden in plains), *Brassica campestris, Viola patrinii, Aspidocarya unifera, Delima sarmentosa, Dillenia indica, Ranunculus diffusus,* bamboos, wild plantain, and *Areca,* a sort of grass growing epiphytically on a stunted *Phœnix,* and *Bauhinias buteas, Robinias urceolas,* canes, and other giant-creepers span the forest with their huge limbs in strange fantastic shapes and forms joining tree to tree. These, again, are clothed in moss and decorated with *parasitical orchids* and the more delicate of the *Orontiaceæ, Bignoniæ,* and *Convolvulaceæ* groups, which add materially to the richness of the forest drapery—the whole presenting a scene as grand as any pictured by *Salvator rosa.*

191. *2nd January 1874.*—This morning Mr. Cooper enquired
Preparations for another excursion. whether I remained unchanged in the views expressed last night, and on replying in the affirmative, he said I would have to arrange for a Kakhyen interpreter, as he could not spare the man attached to his Office: at 11 A.M. he started for Bhamo, and I was left alone to mature my own plans. The absence of the Government Kakhyen interpreter —whose services, in the first instance, I had been promised—was my greatest difficulty, for I knew not where to look for a substitute and to attempt an excursion among the mountaineers, *without* some one who could speak their language was altogether out of the question. Just then, Yan Sing, my Burmese interpreter, made his appearance, and on consulting him, he said he had over-heard the whole conversation that had transpired last night,—as he lay in bed in the compartment next to where we dined,—and had already anticipated my wishes in the matter of arranging for a man to accompany us, who could speak Kakhyen, Shan, and Burmese; this was capital news, and my spirits rose from zero to zenith at once. He further went on to say that he had been told that the Governor regarded me a *harmless traveller,* and that the Court officials had left instructions with the Loogyee to render me every assistance, and had also provided an escort of six men, if I determined to explore the neighbouring hills. What more could I have wanted ? —so I dismissed Yan Sing, with instructions to mature his plans, and immediately developed, to bring all concerned before me. This was a most anxious time for me, knowing that if anything went wrong, I should be doubly blamed, and perhaps given my *conjé :* but

I had determined to carry the work through at all hazards, and have done so, I hope, to the satisfaction of the Local Administration and Supreme Government. Late in the evening, Yan Sing appeared again, and reported that all was ready for a start next morning, but that the Loogyee, and his satellites, wished to talk matters over with me before finally arranging for my escort. Of course, I understood what this meant, and was perfectly willing to pay my way, provided that the demand was not exorbitant. The Loogyee was accordingly sent for, and received with much politeness ; and, after a few friendly greetings, we all (eleven) lighted cheroots and commenced to blow a cloud that very soon nearly filled my shanty to suffocation. I had been coached up in the etiquette to be observed, and consequently remained silent, while the old gentleman leisurely looked round the room, and apparently took stock of my *lares et penates ;* he then commenced the conversation with a string of absurd questions, regarding my age, and pay, and as to whether I was married or not,—and in either case how many children I had,—why I risked my life for a *Ficus elastica*, and so on ; then followed the intermediate course of palaver, and after a little more beating about the bush, he came to the point, and gave me to understand what I would have to pay my escort and the guide, which latter would serve also as an interpreter ; as for his own services, he remarked, nothing was expected, unless I felt disposed to assist a poor married man, with many hungry mouths to feed. He next stipulated that no payments were to be made to the parties he provided, excepting through him. I agreed to his plans throughout, and the party were promised to be in readiness to start on the morrow at 8 P.M. The assembly now broke up, and I was heartily glad when they were all gone, for I know of nothing more tedious than an interview of this nature, but it has to be gone through,—and with an apparent relish too,—if there is an object to be gained.

3rd January 1874.—Dense fog up to 8 A.M. Thermometer, 51°25′ F. at 6 A.M. I had to be up at early dawn to superintend the packing of my kit, for it was important the loads should be light, and nothing more taken than was absolutely necessary. Each follower had to carry his own requirements ; this ensured no extravagance in the form of luxuries, which are generally included when their loads are carried for them ; but this arrangement also necessitated my provender being kept locked up ; for on a previous occasion, and under similar circumstances, I found myself without anything to eat, the cat *having emptied the biscuit tin and replaced the cover !* By 7 A.M. everything was ready, but we did not get away until the fog had commenced to lift, for the people have a strong aversion to leave their houses these misty mornings; and I thought it best not to be too exacting at the start off. At nine o'clock, the old Loogyee made his appearance with four coolies, and the Interpreter. The latter had instructions to pick up two policemen from each village as we went along, until the full complement of six were made up. After a good deal of talk and grumbling, the loads were allotted each man, and by ten o'clock a start had been accomplished. By police it must not be understood that my escort were selected from an organized or paid corps; they were merely villagers, who had to provide their own arms and ammunition. Their swords were the ordinary *dahs* of the country, and guns, old rusted match-locks that evidently had not been fired out of for years. In this instance, I was looked to for powder and bullets, but as I had none of the latter that fitted their guns, B.B.B. shot served as a substitute. There was always some little delay in recruiting, but once to the front, the people took good-naturedly enough to their fate, and gave no more trouble. It was far too cold for my people to continue their national light and airy costume, so they made their first appearance to-day in Shan jackets and pants, white stockings with red tape garters, and red woollen night-caps; certainly they had a comical enough appearance. We had not gone, far before I noticed an unfortunate Shan lying dead drunk by the road side; he had nothing on, and the basket these people carry their provisions in, lay empty by his side; evidently he had been robbed.

192. Our course now lay in the direction of old Bhamo,* which, as I have already mentioned, is situated on the banks of the Taping; nothing however, now remains to mark the site of this once flourishing town but the ruins of its walls, which are a mere heap of bricks, covered with earth, and overgrown with jungle. Here we diverged north-west and by north, until the large Shan-Burmese village of Seitket was reached. It is situated at base of the Kakhyen mountains, and is the guard-mounting station for the out-pickets posted on a spur of the main range. The village was strongly barricaded; but I was told the safety of the people mainly consisted in keeping on good terms with the mountaineers, and meeting their demands as far as possible; this entailing extra expense, the inhabitants are exempt from all taxation by the Burmese Government. We rested here at the head-man's house for half an hour, and were most politely received. I was seated on a nice new rug, and cheroots,

_{Start in the direction of old Bhamo, and stay at village Seitket.}

---

* I find old Bhamo has been incorrectly placed on the map: it should have occupied the place of the second *e* in the word *Seekaw*; it was there that we left the Taping, and struck off in a north-west by north course.

pán suparee, and a huge silver water-bowl, with a cup of the same metal floating in the centre, placed before me ; however, I required refreshment of a more substantial nature, and proceeded to breakfast off a few hard-boiled eggs and biscuits with which I was provided. The people seem exceedingly happy and contented ; the house was large, substantially built of boards throughout, and remarkably comfortable within; well furnished, and provided with those extra little fittings and appointments that add to comfort according to a Burman's idea. The lady of the house was busily employed hackling thread, but found time to join in the conversation, and with woman-like inquisitiveness wanted to know full particulars regarding myself and the object of my visit. She was full of kind advice and cautions, and particularly warned me against making the Kakhyens drunk, or remaining among them when inebriated, as they were then unappeasable, and disregarded the lives even of their own clan. At the opposite end of the verandah the eldest daughter was seated at the loom ; she, however, remained silent throughout the interview, but made the best use of her bright black eyes ; this probably being the first time in her life that she had set eyes on a European. It was now noon, and we had still ten miles to accomplish before evening, so I took my departure, thanking the host and hostess for their hospitality.

193. The ascent was commenced in a north-easterly direction,
<small>Obstructions during the ascent in a north-easterly direction until arrival at Ronelein.</small> gradually working round to the east till Ronelein was reached. The track meandering round the spurs, would only admit of us proceeding single file, and some of the steeper ridges were exceedingly slippery and difficult to clamber over. My first dilemma was having to cross the neck of a ravine spanned by a single stem of a fallen tree. I had my doubts of being able to walk it, yet to be supported was showing I was in a measure at the mercy of my followers, so I resorted to the very undignified position of sitting straddle legs across the tree, and propelling myself by an action easier to imagine than describe. My own people were evidently bad climbers, and begged a halt of a few minutes at every brook we came to; however, they improved as we went along, learning to substitute the short elastic steps of the mountaineer, for the long, swinging gait they had been accustomed to in the plains. Continuing to ascend, the vegetation became more dense and noble : trees with straight shafts, some naked with grey or pale-brown bark, others literally shrouded up to their crowns with *epiphytes* now towered over head on either side of the narrow gorge we followed, while among the sub-arborescent growth, the plantain was the most

conspicuous, growing in luxuriant profusion, and its graceful foliage contrasting notably with the smaller leaved plants among which it nestled. Here and there, from some prominent craig, a *coup d'œil* of the low country could be had, and the Taping—which appeared as a mere silver thread—might be traced in its tortuous course along the valley, from the Irrawaddy to its *embrochure* from the mountains. The forests now echoed with the peals of laughter and the wild songs of people fast approaching us. I was told these were our much-dreaded enemies, evidently drunk, and cautioned to pass them on the side their swords were suspended; the reason for which I afterwards learnt was to avoid the first cut, which is always a horizontal sweep made in the act of unsheathing the sword. In about quarter of an hour, we had met; the party was made up of twenty young Kakhyen men and women, all remarkably well dressed in the costume previously described, but the latter appeared to have more silver ornaments about them than I had hitherto noticed on these people. The former were armed with guns, spears, swords, crossbows, and poisoned arrows, and wore a couple of cock's feathers in their hair, which added to their wild appearance. They stopped to demand of us whence we had come, and where we were going, but refused to answer any of our questions. Their eyes were fixed on me the whole time, and after a few more questions, they took a hurried look round at all we had, and started off with a fiendish yell, which might either have been intended for contempt or respect—I expect the former.

Next we came on thirteen Shan-talokes on their way from Sanda to Bhamo ; they had been robbed of everything they said, with the exception of what they had on, and begged assistance of me : under any other circumstance, I would gladly have acted the good Samaritan; but travellers are always liable to be imposed upon, so I thought it as well to say I had nothing to spare. A short halt was made at the stream where they were resting, to let my people quench their thirst, while I listened to the full particulars of the robbery. According to their account, it appeared they started from Sanda a party of eighteen, with a quantity of silver, which they had intended to exchange at Bhamo for cloth and other articles, this being the trade they had followed for the last three years. As was customary, they took an escort from village to village, and paid the usual blackmail of Rs. 1-8 per man, or silver to that amount. Shortly before reaching Malan, which from their description lies north-east of Ronelein (the village I was on my way to visit), they were attacked by a large body of Kakhyens, overwhelmed, and robbed of all they had, besides losing half of their party who were killed in the engagement. They seemed to treat the matter in a most philosophical manner, and said it was hopeless to look to the Burmese Government for redress, or to expect ever to recover any of their property. I was obliged now to push on again, for we had yet a couple of miles to get over before reaching the picket, where I had arranged to rest for the night; this we accomplished by 5 P.M., and glad enough did my followers appear when the guard-house was in sight.

194. This was the first plateau of a series of hills, emanating from a spur given off by the main range of Kakhyen mountains. The barometer showed an altitude now of 950 feet. The picket consisted of thirteen Shan-Burmans (including a sergeant), armed with flint-guns and *dahs*; they are relieved once a month, and paid a basket of paddy for their service. The sergeant, who is generally an influential man, commands three reliefs, which exempts him and his relations from taxation. These men are not trained soldiers, but of the same stamp as my police escort, and are enrolled under similar conditions having to supply their own arms and ammunition. The building was of the *zayat* or rest-house type, a wooden platform raised three feet off the ground, planked in on three sides, and thatched with grass. It was situated on a cliff, over-hanging a vast valley, and surrounded by a dense, dark forest. The barricade consisted of three walls of stout logs four feet apart, and the intermediate spaces filled in with timber transversely piled; still, did the Kakhyens feel so disposed, nothing would be easier than to set fire to the whole stockade, and burn the guard to death within their own stronghold; but, from what I afterwards saw, it was quite apparent that peace and order were alone maintained by allowing the Kakhyens entirely their own way : the slightest opposition on the part of the soldiers, and they would be massacred to a man; wisely, therefore, they feign friendship and good-will towards these savages, and carefully avoid offending them. I was surprised to observe that the Shan-Burmese at this picket, who are professedly Buddhists, had in a measure retrograded into *nát*-worship, offering to the spirits of the forests, the mountains, and elements a portion of their early meal before it touched their lips. Perhaps this was more in the form of exorcism and propitiation than actual worship, but certainly I had noticed the practice nowhere else observed by Buddhists.

Stay at the picket.

195. I had now to consider how I should introduce myself to these wild people, in the least unpleasant manner, for they had received no prior warning; and, to thrust myself and party too suddenly on them, would have been most unwise.

Information to the Tswabwa at Ronelein of my intended visit.

I consulted with the sergeant and others, who were unanimous in the opinion that I should proceed on the following morning, and that, if the Tswabwa was displeased, I could easily return. This was an easy way of disposing of the question, but a very imprudent one, it appeared to me; so, after a little more parley, it was decided my plan should be acted on, and accordingly the sergeant, my Kakhyen interpreter, and two other Shan-Burmans were dispatched for Ronelein, with a message to the Tswabwa, saying with his permission I would call on him the following morning at any hour he would appoint. The distance to Ronelein had been computed at seven miles up a stiff ascent, so I hardly expected to learn the result of my message before midnight; though the sergeant assured me he would be back by about 10 P.M.; this did not seem probable, for it was now half-past five, and allowing an hour for the interview, they would have had to walk at a good three miles an hour to accomplish the journey in that time; certainly half the distance was down hill, which these people descend at a very rapid pace. During their absence, time passed slowly enough; so slowly, that more than once I listened for the tick of my watch to see it had not stopped. About ten o'clock we saw a party descending the hill by torch-light, and immediately concluded that they were my messengers, but I was disappointed; they turned out to be a party of young Kakhyen girls and boys out for a midnight ramble and flirtation, which I am told they prefer carrying on in the depths of the forests to their parental homes. They presented a most savage, yet picturesque group as they approached, brandishing their torches over one another's heads, and singing and capering about with wild delight. My suspense was soon brought unexpectedly to an end by a shout from the sergeant ordering the guard to open the gate, and in a few minutes more I was introduced to three Kakhyens (an old man with silvery-white hair cut square over the forehead, the Pomine of the village, and a lad of about seventeen), who had been sent by the Tswabwa to make careful enquiries as to the true object of my visit, and to bind me over to certain promises, before they consented to my visiting Ronelein. They were all armed with *dahs*, spears, and guns, and each had brought some trifling present for me in the form of yams, beans, and other vegetables, which I accepted as a good omen. After answering all their questions, which were put in a most studied and measured manner,—an interval of two or three minutes often occurring between each interrogative—I was asked to bind myself not to proceed beyond their village, nor assist their neighbours with whom they were at war; not to come with more than six armed men; and lastly, not to cast the evil-eye on them, nor cause the ground on which I trod to be rent asunder as some other white men had done when travelling through their relations' country.* I agreed to all they required of me, but even that was not sufficient; they next turned to the sergeant of the guard, and asked him to stand security, which he consented to do; and they then agreed to my visiting Ronelein next day. I presented them with Rs. 3-8 in silver bits, and promised not to forget the Tsawbwa on my visit: they then took their departure; and we all turned in for a few hours' sleep at 1 A.M. I laid down in my clothes, for the thermometer stood at 45°, and I had nothing to put over me but a light rug; my people kept themselves warm by nestling into one another and sharing each other's blankets. The novelty of my position and want of confidence in those around me interfered greatly with my rest, and I was glad when the time came for us to be on the tramp again. The watches had been changed every third hour and the relief signal given by a boisterous shout that rang through the forest and was echoed back by the surrounding hill; with this exception, all was profound silence, and none but those who have been similarly situated can realize the grandeur of such perfect stillness; the impression it leaves, or the past associations it developes with a rapidity that could alone be portrayed by a dream.

196. The second ascent was commenced at 6-30 A.M., there was a fresh crispness in the air, and the thermometer stood at 41° F., my people looked miserably cold, but a glow was soon produced with the stiff climbing. The path which still lay up steep ridges was very slippery, and in places only passable from the hold afforded by interlacing roots of trees. We had not gone more than a couple of miles when a halt was unanimously suggested, and my attention drawn to a grand bird's-eye peep of the low country or, rather, the sea of mist floating 1,300 feet below us, the tops of the trees being sufficiently high to give them the appearance of shrubs studded about the deceptive element in well-arranged groups. The hill sides, as we progressed, were cleared in detached patches here and there, and terraced, this being the style of cultivation followed by the highlanders. A fresh clearing is generally made every third year, and the abandoned area allowed to lie fallow for ten. This system appears to serve as a

Commencement of second ascent and arrival at Ronelein.

---

* Evidently they were referring to the same circumstance narrated by Dr. Anderson at page 366 of his report on the expedition to Western China; he writes: " It is stated that eleven villages have been destroyed by land-slips in the Sanda valley, and that nearly all the villagers have been buried in the ruins : these sad catastrophes are ascribed to some evil power possessed by us, and we are told that a portion have died in every village we visited."

sort of chronologicial register to these people, for no Kakhyen can tell you his age but will always give the number of clearings he has survived. They are not dependent on the rains, but irrigate by the mountain streams, which are so skilfully brought under control as to admit of the water being turned on, or off at pleasure: excess of rain is therefore always more dreaded than drought. Approaching Ronelein the path gradually narrowed, until it became absolutely dangerous, and there was barely room for two people to cross one another. To the left, was a perpendicular side of the hill; and on the right, a sheer drop of some hundreds of feet that made one giddy to look down. Here my Kakhyen guide told us to keep a sharp look out, as it was a favourite place of the mountaineers to commit plunder: they either fired down from above, or hurled large boulders down on passers-by,—not an enviable position evidently my Burmans thought, for they pushed on with fresh life, not forgetting to do as they had been recommended. The path terminated in a dislodged block of sandstone twenty-nine feet high, said to have been hurled down on a rich Chinaman, whose wealth was buried with him, and still remains beneath the stone. Over this we had to climb by means of the niches made as substitutes for steps, but they were so shallow and narrow, that I was obliged to perform the feat without shoes or socks,—the only possible way I could have got across. On the opposite side, the path was most ingeniously faced with stone, and in places where the earth had been partly washed away, the repairs were quite recent; this continued to the base of the last ascent, where I observed a cradle suspended to a tree, with what I supposed to be the corpse of a child,—so carefully were the contents rolled up in clean white cloth, and prettily decorated with flowers, and canopied by a white sheet;—but I was mistaken, it turned out to be an embalmed dog, a bi-monthly offering to the *nât* who is supposed to reside in this spot, and ward off all evil-disposed persons. Ronelein stands at an elevation of 1,850 feet, and occupies the highest point of this range; the thermometer registered in the shade 69° 5' at 10·30 A.M., when we reached our destination. A more romantic spot it would be difficult to imagine, the houses are not huddled together as we had been accustomed to see them in the villages of the plains, but the *htay* (house) which affords accommodation to a whole family,—from the grand-parents downwards,—has its separate little plot of land sufficiently cleared to admit of cultivation round about, without the entire area having being denuded of its trees; and when situated on the ledge of a hill-side, the banks are carefully fenced with stone to protect them from being washed away by rain. The first *htay* we came to was the residence of the old patriarch whose acquaintance I had formed last night, but it was considered etiquette first to call on the Tswabwa, before entering any other house. His *htay* was the last we came to, situated on a slightly higher eminence than the rest. Immediately my arrival was announced by the jemadar, I was invited in and seated on a brand-new rug in the guest-room, my followers having a few mats spread for them. It was some half hour before the Tswabwa made his appearance, which afforded me a capital opportunity of studying the style of building and interior arrangements. The entire length and breadth of this *htay* was not under two hundred feet by sixty feet: it was raised off the ground six feet, and the flooring was of bamboos, with walling of the same material flattened out and plaited. The lower part was barricaded up to the floor and used as a pen for live-stock, including large numbers of fine white pigs, with ears over-lapping the eyes—a variety I have seen nowhere else in Burma, and am inclined to think the breed has been introduced from China. The roof was thatched with grass and shaped after the form of a turtle's shell, the eaves extended to some two or three feet beyond the walls, and either end formed into a sort of verandah. The interior was divided down the centre lengthways, one side being intended for guests, and the other for private use. At the entrance, a portion of the guests' room was walled off as a sleeping apartment for all male and female adults, and the opposite end devoted to *nat* worship, where there was a little shrine, and all the other paraphernalia associated with fetichism. It is in this part of the house, also, that the embalmed corpses are kept until the nearest relation is in a position to kill a buffalo, and feast the whole village on the burial day. I once had the misfortune of having to sleep for a night in close proximity to one of these putrid bodies, as will appear further on. The portico was decorated with the numerous buffaloes' skulls that had been slaughtered on gala days, and trophies of *shikar*, including the horns of deer, and skulls of tigers and boars: these latter animals abound in the hills, and often cross-breed with the domestic pig when feeding in the forest.

197. The room presented a most curious collection of things, which evidently must have been plundered property: there were two very handsome China vases, three carpets, one of those utensils included in a toilet service (of rather a unique blue, gold, and white pattern,) which now served as a receptacle for chillies, two handsome *dahs* with carved ivory handles, one velvet table-cover, a cashmere *choya*, a large bunch of human hair, intended for *sazoos* no doubt, and nine double-barrelled percussion guns.

Collection of things in the Tswabwa's house.

198. At last, the Tswabwa made his appearance from the private apartment, followed by a crowd of men, women, and children; we exchanged looks, but not words; nor was a syllable spoken for about five minutes after he was seated. He was a middle-aged man of about five feet eight inches, thin but wiry, rather narrow in the chest, and small arms and wrists, with notably large hands and feet. The face was narrow, and flat-nosed—small, deep, but not obliquely set eyes, no beard, and but very little moustache. The hair was cut short and squared over the forehead. His organs of observation and destructiveness were large, and cerebellum small; his general expression was cadaverous and unpleasant. He wore a blue cloth round his loins, which extended to the knees, the upper and lower borders being wove in red and coloured wool. A white quilted jacket, and white muslin *gong-bong* or head-dress completed his costume. His ears were pierced, and a bunch of *Celosia* and *Tagetes erecta* made to serve as ornaments; below the knees were a number of the thin cane ring described at page 68. Tatooing is not practised by the Kakhyens until we get much further north, and then the women are tatooed in bands below the knees to the ankle, which is exactly the reverse of the Burman custom.

Interview with the Tswabwa, and description of him.

Silence was now broken by my Kakhyen mouth-piece entering into an explanation as to the origin of my visit, he having previously been told exactly what to say. The Tswabwa was remarkably taciturn, merely signifying approval by a grunt and a nod, leaving all the talking to his *Pomine*, who was loquacious in the extreme, and rattled away with questions at a great pace; the womenfolk also joined in the conversation, and of course were still more inquisitive than the men, wanting particularly to know all about our women, over the customs, in respect to marriages, how many wives we had, and various other questions, some of which verged on the naughty, I am afraid. I was recommended not to take notes in the presence of these people, neither to be too prying nor pressing in my enquiries, so I could gain but little information regarding many subjects on which I should have liked to hear their views Their religion is demonology, and naturally they are extremely superstitious, always consulting omens, and the most trifling circumstance will determine the fate of a dozen or more lives, or some equally important event. They speak of once having had a Bible and a written tongue of their own, but are strong in the belief that the former was written on leather, and eaten by a hungry Kakhyen or *Thainbore* as they call themselves; and with its disappearance the alphabet was lost.

199. They glory in their life of freedom, scorning the idea of being subjects of the King of Burma, or having to pay tribute or vassalage to him; all they give is voluntary, and not compulsory they say; but of this subject and others connected with the manners and customs of these people, I shall treat more fully in the next chapter, when comparing the different classes of this interesting tribe.

Manners and customs of these people to be subject of next Chapter.

200. Breakfast was now served, on nice clean plantain leaves in bamboo baskets, which acted as a table. The meal consisted of boiled rice and various stews and curries, but what the ingredients were, I could not venture to say. I only tasted one, and that was evidently pure *capsicum* stew, for it nearly skinned the roof of my mouth. Everything was presented in the most cleanly manner, but the fronziness of the inmates—both in appearance and scent—was so very forbidding, that I could only manage to play with the meal out of mere compliment to the people. My party fortunately were less fastidious, and called for a second helping. No people could be more hospitable to their guests than these mountaineers are to all who take shelter under their roof, and it is a popular idea that, so long as the sword is suspended in their house, they will never abuse the confidence placed in them; excepting in their cups, and then they are ungovernable even among themselves. Next followed a part of the entertainment I most dreaded,—the passing of the "flowing bowl," but to refuse, would have been regarded a marked insult by these people, who are true believers in the old Latin proverb *in vino veritas*. I had to caution my peons; but the sergeant of the guard assured me the liquor was merely fermented rice-toddy, sweetened with a little *jaggery*, and had no inebriating effect, unless taken in very large quantities, with the express purpose of getting intoxicated, as the Kakhyens are in the habit of doing. Myself and followers having each been supplied with a bamboo vessel of this vile beverage, one was handed to the Tswabwa, who put the cup to his lips, as a signal for all to follow: nor did any but myself fail to empty the goblet in a draught; *heel taps* evidently being regarded bad form, but I found it impossible to swallow more than a mouthful or so of the filth, which, to my palate, resembled what I would imagine sweetened putrid water to taste like; however, I kept the cup to my mouth the whole time the others were drinking, and by a sham gulping process, led the Tswabwa and his friends to imagine I was equally enjoying the beverage. The goblets consist in a joint of a bamboo about three inches in diameter and a foot long, they are cut through at two-thirds of their length, the lower portion serv-

Observations during breakfast.

ing as a cup, and the upper as a cover. To prevent spitting, they were neatly banded with cane plaited rings coloured with black varnish, which gave them the appearance of being hooped with japanned iron rings; they contained about a quart each. After the liquor had gone the second round, I commenced to distribute the presents among the women and children, consisting of two and four-anna bits (which are used as necklets), beads, needles, and thread; to the men I gave pieces of white and red cloth for head-dresses. The Tswabwa was, of course, the first served, and received a double share; I had to be careful that no difference was made in the description of presents, for fear of generating discontent; even as it was, some of the women came to have their necklets exchanged, because, perhaps, the beads were differently shaped or varied in colour from those presented to others. The younger and unmarried portion of the female community (who are alone distinguishable from the married by the absence of a turban, for they are mostly all mothers), were most importunate in their requests for more beads, and would give me no peace, until I satisfied them that my stock was exhausted. It is a remarkable fact that the children of unmarried girls are accepted as the gift of the "virgin's guardian spirit," and the fresh arrivals supported by the parents of the young mother. With these tribes flirtation has no bounds up to marriage; but when once a woman has elected a husband, which is always proclaimed at a large public feast, adultery, if committed without the consent of that husband, is punishable by death. Liquor was now again introduced, but as we had yet other calls to make, I ordered my followers to abstain from drinking any more. As a parting gift, the women presented me with a complete set of their own ornaments, and three bamboo drinking cups; and the men gave me a cross-bow and poisoned arrows, but declined to divulge the process of poisoning them. A similar programme was followed at the different *htays* we visited; each host and hostess trying to excel the other in hospitality and liberality in presents. It is a point of etiquette with these people on the occasion of the first visit to leave the *htay* by the door you entered at, and likewise quit the village by the road you came. The last house we called at therefore was the first we came to on our arrival, and will be remembered as the residence of the old man who called on me last night. Evidently the old fellow had been imbibing freely, for he was most loquacious, and even went so far as to tap me on the back, and as a particular mark of friendship, gave me a piece of a creeper that had formed itself into a strange knot, and like the ring of Gyges was supposed to confer invisibility and preserve me from all harm. On parting, he cautioned me never to make friends with the

Kakhyens, remarking they were a bad lot, and would one day cut my throat. I must not forget to mention that on leaving Ronelein the senior female representatives of each *htay* presented me with flowers and hard-boiled eggs, which I am told is a token of sincere friendship! On the whole, the inhabitants of this village appeared a remarkably healthy set of people, especially the younger portion of the community up to the age of twelve. Cholera is unknown among them, small-pox apparently being the only epidemic, and it is surprising that this scourge does not commit greater havoc among a people who never take to water for purpose of ablution, and in other respects are equally dirty in their habits of life. Immediately a person is affected, however, with this disease, he is taken into some distant part of the forest, fed daily, and not allowed to return until well; in this position many are carried off by wild beasts, for which the *nâts* get the credit. *Ophthalmia*, dysentery, fever, and cutaneous diseases would appear to be their most common ailments; and their only remedy, invocations to the *nâts*.

201. Round the homesteads are grown yams, gourds of different descriptions, tobacco, poppies used for opium, Indian corn, potatoes,* fig, plantain, sweet-limes, *papaw, sesamum,* and a number of peach trees, which latter, however, are alone valued for their flowers; the fruit is never eaten by the people, nor could I trace from where the seeds were first obtained. *Physalis peruviana* grows everywhere about, and the fruit is eaten; the yellow raspberry, wild rose, and *Osbeckia* also became common as we neared Ronelein. I also noted a number of old familiar annuals: *Carthamus, Tagetes, Guinia, Datura, Celosia,* and *Amaranthus.*

Different growths round the homesteads.

202. We returned in a South-South-West direction, down a most steep descent and at a very rapid pace, but not without a good many tumbles. I was constantly losing my footing, and performed a good part of the journey on my hams; so steep and slippery were the rocks in places, that even the sure-footed highlander often found his legs slip from under him. Seekaw was reached by midnight, and the next morning I started for Bhamo in the Residency boat, (which had been sent to await my return), where I arrived on Tuesday, 6th January 1874.

Return to Seekaw, and ultimate arrival at Bhamo.

---

* Some potatoes, grown by the Kakhyens in the hills, were brought as a present to the Assistant Resident at Bhamo, when I was there. They were small, but capital eating.

CHAPTER V.

From Bhamo to Mun-tsoung (latitude 26°) and back via Mogoung.

203. It appears to me advisable to submit this chapter in the form of a diary, which will convey more clearly and impressively the main features of this portion of my journey, and also form a more handy guide to those who may at any future time feel inclined to follow in my wake.

204. *Saturday, 10th January 1874.*—All arrangements were now complete for my start, and I left Bhamo this evening at 4 P.M. My followers suggested a postponement until to-morrow, as it would be dark—they remarked—before we were out of sight of the Residency: however, as it was only after much difficulty that I had managed to get all on board, I was determined to sever them from their town entanglements as far as lay in my power, for I too well knew that if there was to be a repetition of the leave-taking scene, the probability would have been that I should see nothing more of them until the same hour to-morrow. As mentioned elsewhere, I had three flat-bottomed boats, each of 400 baskets burden, and drawing three feet of water when laden; the complement of each crew, five men, three of whom were slaves who had been purchased from the Kakhyens, and could speak their language thoroughly. The Residency boat was occupied by myself, interpreter, and the *cicerone* provided by the Governor, the remaining two boats being set apart for my followers and stores. The early part of the day was taken up superintending the shipment for Rangoon, per steamer *Colonel Fytche*, of the *Ficus elastica* cuttings and plants I had collected. On my return to the Residency, I found no attempt had been made to take any of my kit on board the boats, and half my peons were absent: this was most perplexing, for the days were now short, and the luggage had to be conveyed a considerable distance, the river at this season being separated from the main shore by a sandbank some three-fourths of a mile wide. The Assistant Resident very kindly sent for my peons who were captured in different parts of the town, and brought back the picture of dejection and disappointment. It is the exception when a Burman will hurry his actions for any one, but when they are forced to work against their will, they are aggravatingly perverse and lazy, and I should not have been able to get off this evening had not Mr. Cooper very

kindly engaged all the coolies procurable, and thus frustrated the little game of my people, which was to have another night with their friends. There was so much delay in getting off, that it was too dark to proceed, before even the mouth of the Taping was reached, and we were compelled to make fast for the night at a sandbank some two miles above Bhamo.

205. *Sunday, 11th January 1874.*—Left our moorings at 7 A.M.; thermometer 51° Fahrenheit: dense fog up to 8.30; remained at Sinking for half an hour, and took a ramble on shore. This village numbers some forty houses occupied by Shan-Burmans of an agricultural class; it is situated on the left bank, and opposite are the hamlets of Kannee and Coongyee. Here the river is sub-divided by an extensive island of recent formation, and submerged during the inundation. It was covered with *Graminæ, Compositæ, Campanula,* and *Tamarisk* of a few months' growth. Shot *Dendrocygna arcuata, Halcyon smyrnensis, Lobivanellus atronuchalis,* and two geese. The riverbanks now gradually became more defined, and the stream narrows from 500 to 350 yards, with a proportional increase in the depth and velocity of current, which is, as a rule, regulated by the expanse or contraction of the stream. Skirting the left bank are a low range of lime-stone hills covered with bamboo (small variety), *Bombax malabaricum, Dipterocarpus tuberculatus, Chikrassia tabularis,* and *Conocarpus acuminatus.* Small clearings are also here and there apparent where the Kakhyens carry on their *toungya* cultivation.

206. We now came on the Moh-loy *choung,* bearing north-east at its junction with the Irrawaddy; it is a hundred yards wide, with five feet of water in the deepest part. It is said to be navigable during the rains, for boats of considerable size, to a distance of a hundred and five miles. A little further north, and on the same bank, is the village of Nga-pyen-law ; quarter of a mile further on, and we crossed over to Kyoondate on the opposite bank, which represents a vast alluvial plain, susceptible to the annual floods, and stretching for miles inland to the base of the limestone hills in the far west. From Mya-za-dee we recrossed to Thaphan-bin or Lebaing (as it is sometimes called) where we made fast at 3 P.M., and remained for the night. The river here is much contracted, and the water changed from a muddy brown to a deep sap-green. The remaining hours of daylight I spent on shore ferreting about the surrounding country. I came across nothing new in arborescent growth, with the exception of a solitary *Pierordia lapida; Oxalis corniculata, Biophytum sensitivum, Triumfetta rhomboidea,* and *Asparagus acerosus* were common : *Sesamum indicum* is extensively cultivated and finds a ready sale, the oil expressed from the seed being

used for culinary purposes. Cocoanut, *Papaya*, *Ægle marmelos*, jack, mango, *Areca catechu*, and plantains were among the cultivated varieties. I bagged *Chalcophaps indica*, *Urocissa occipitalis*, *Carpophaga sylvatica*, and four *Gallus ferrugineus*, which latter feed near villages, and I am told often interbreed with the domestic variety. Thaphan-bin is enclosed in a treble stockade, the intermediate spaces between the bamboo palisades being planted with spikes of the same material, in addition to this precaution, each house has its own separate bamboo enclosure—so great is the dread of Kakhyen raids. The village is picturesquely situated at the base of a low range of hills, the most prominent having the repute of being pervaded by a *nát*, and on which account is exempted from *toungya* clearings. It was long after dark before I got back to my boat, and my people expressed delight at seeing me return alive, for they had been hearing all sorts of exaggerated accounts from the Shan-Burman villagers of the acts of atrocity committed by the Kakhyens, and the unhesitating manner in which they took life for the mere love of the sport!

207. *Monday, 12th January 1874.*—Detained starting this morning till 9 A.M., so dense was the fog. Thermometer at 6 A.M. 49° Fahrenheit in my cabin. Before our departure Moung Shwe Dway, the *Loogyee* of the village, called on me with a present of fruit; he seemed a civil, intelligent fellow, and ready to give information. According to his account there is a prosperous trade in paddy, bamboos, and teak carried on between this village and Bhamo. Teak, he said, of eighteen feet long and six feet girth realized Rs. 8 at Bhamo, and paddy, Rs. 1-2 per basket. He likewise mentioned that teak was sufficiently seasoned to float in nine months, if girdled when the tree is in flower, felled three months subsequently, and allowed to dry with butt-end supported at an angle of 45° with the horizontal line. Before taking his departure, he asked for some medicine, as he and many others in his village were subject to fever, for which they could find no remedy though they had been unceasing in their invocations and offerings to the *náts*. I gave the poor fellow a little quinine, for which he seemed immensely thankful, more especially when I told him the probability was, all signs of the malady would have left after the third dose. I was also visited by a Kakhyen who introduced himself as Poung Kullo, brother of Kummiong, a Chief of Nee-wah-toung: he was accompanied by some half a dozen followers. Their costume, mode of wearing hair, and class of arms corresponded to those of the same tribe already described, with the one exception, that Poung Kullo wore a necklet of yellow clayey-looking beads, which is not only a distinctive mark of rank and family, but is alone worn

by *Humars, Tswabaws,* or *Powmines* or their nearest of kin, and is supposed to protect the wearer from evil. Like other wild tribes, they were most inquisitive, and if let alone, nothing would have escaped fingering; but I had to keep them out of my cabin, and satisfy their curiosity with a description of all articles they referred to. They seemed pleased when I mentioned having recently visited some *Kakhyen* villages, and spoke of the great civility and kindness that had been shown me: but evidently the idea brought a spirit of jealousy to the surface, for Poung Kullo immediately invited me up to his brother's village, with every assurance of comfort and safety. He resides in the hills to the north-east some fifty miles off, and the journey to and fro can be accomplished in a week. Time would not admit of my availing myself of his offer, or I should have done so, with every confidence. I presented Poung Kullo with a white muslin *gong-bong*, and his principal attendant, with a couple of yards of Turkey red, with which they seemed perfectly satisfied, and took their departure. After they had left, the guide provided by the Governor, sent word through my interpreter to say I had been most indiscreet in allowing these treacherous people to come on board; their only object being to estimate the amount of plunder and arrange for an attack at some future time. I believe this is a system they carry out among Burmese traders, but merely in retaliation for similar acts of dishonesty. I firmly believe the Kakhyens are honestly inclined when only fairly dealt with: it is seldom one hears of their breaking faith in trading transactions; in fact, so much reliance do traders place in their word, that large advances are made on goods promised.

208. In half an hour we were abreast of Shoay-boo, where some half dozen Kakhyen houses peeped through the densely-wood slopes on the right bank, and added materially to the poetry of the landscape, which was hourly becoming more imposing and grand. I landed here, for about half an hour to get a shot at some peacocks, but only managed to bag one after a good deal of trouble: with *Gallus ferrugineus* I was more fortunate, and brought away three and a half brace. I also saw a fine *Buceros rhinoceros*, but did not manage to get him. *Centropus enrycercus, Palæornis magnirostris,* and *Coracias affinis* were also noticed. Teak is common, but of small proportions; and the following trees &c., occur: *Pierordia lapida, Cordia myxa, Lagerstræmia reginæ* (stunted); *Conocarpus acuminatus, Calophyllum, Dillenia aurea, Aspidopterys nutans,* and *Sida corylifolia* : bamboos also were plentiful.

209. In the centre of the stream is a huge mass of serpentine rock, standing ten feet out of water, it is known as the *Lubine kin* which signifies " porpoise guard," this being the northern limit

of this fish it is believed. The mountain slopes continue to be densely wooded to the water's edge on both banks. *Gibbons* are common, and the forest echoes again with their wailing cry. *Muos cercopithecus* were also conspicuous.

210. The celebrated pagoda of *Shoay-chet-ake* next attracts attention; it is situated on the right bank on a spur of rock that projects into the water some little distance. The golden cock is supposed to sleep here, and feed at Amarapoora, where, it will be remembered, a pagoda has been dedicated to it: the building is maintained in a state of good repair. Not quarter of a mile further on, is the site of old Thapahin, which was plundered and burnt down by the Kakhyens last year. Here again the river is divided by a block of serpentine 150 feet long, the channels on either side not exceeding 50 to 80 yards, that to the west being the broader. By 4 P.M. we had made the village of Thaminagyee occupied by Pwons—a tribe allied to the Shans and speaking a dialect of their language. In type of feature, the two people are identical, but the former are of a darker complexion, and inclined to be more hairy about the limbs. Their chief means of livelihood consists in the sale of teak and bamboos, on which the neighbouring Kakhyens levy black-mail. The village contains about forty houses of the Shan type, with a slanting thatched roof, and elliptic gables. The whole are enclosed in a double wall bamboo pallisade. The place had recently been attacked by the adjacent mountaineers, but the Pwons were able to hold their own, though I am told there was a great loss of life on both sides: they were now in hourly dread of a second raid, for the Kakhyens are notedly revengeful, and never forgive their enemies unless handsomely compensated for the killed and wounded of their party; and even then merely await an idle excuse to wipe out the (supposed) disgrace by the sword.

211. I remained here for the night. Quarter of a mile inland I came on a party of Pwons burning lime. The kiln consisted of a hole twenty feet deep and eight feet in diameter; it was situated on a steep incline; the mouth of the furnace was below, and supported by a rubble arch. The kiln is charged with alternate layers of lime and wood, and finally covered in with earth. After lighting the fires the people return to their village for the night; the slaked lime is taken to Bhamo, and bartered for cloth or articles of food. The late Mr. Graham, agent of the firm of Sutherland and Mackenzie, joined me here; he was hurrying up river in a *loung*, to establish a bartering system of trade with the people, which he seemed to think would prove a most remunerative business; he

had with him a good supply of Manchester piece-goods, twist, thread, &c., which he intended advancing—as he went along—on promise of ivory, rubber, amber, &c., &c. We parted company in the morning.

212. Two fine young *Ficus elastica* trees were offered to me here, but unfortunately they were too large to carry away, so I arranged to purchase them on my way back. Shot a *Loris tardigradus*, some painted partridge, jungle fowl, a *Ketupa ceylonensis*, two otters (the flesh of which my Burman peons regarded a delicacy), and a leopard-cat, which came at me like a young tiger when wounded, but the second barrel put an end to his bad intentions.

213. *Tuesday, 13th January 1874.*—Started at 7 A.M., but only to cross the river for a short excursion inland. Themometer, 50° at 6 A.M. Dense fog for an hour after landing; returned to boat by noon. It had at first been my intention to send on the boats, but on second thought, I hardly considered this wise, for it was not at all certain the distance they could make, and very doubtful whether I could reach them anywhere else within the defile, for the river was now hemmed in on either side by perpendicular scarps of serpentine and lime-stone rock, in places over eighty feet high.

214. My trip was unsatisfactory in the extreme, for I saw nothing sufficiently interesting to compensate for the trouble and fatigue I had to undergo, clambering over the huge boulders that lay across our path. Vegetation throughout, though dense, had a stunted appearance from an absence of surface soil. Massive, disengaged blocks of serpentine lay one upon another in all forms of disorder, some merely maintained in their position by the Goliathan embrace of parasitical *Fici*. Under the ledges bees' nests of a conical shape were common—some were three feet long and as broad at the top. The honey is much prized, except at certain seasons, when it is said to be piosonous. The fact of honey being poisonous at certain times of the year is borne out by the fate of those in the retreat of the ten thousand, who partook of the honey which was said to be posioned with the flowers of *Rhododendron ponticum*. We came on a party of Pwons from Shweminwoon, who informed us that they were on their way to visit a rich merchant who had just arrived at Tha-mine-gyee. I explained that *I* was the party they referred to, and was on my way to call on them. I was surprised at the rapidity with which the news of my arrival had been circulated; nor could I obtain from them whence they received their information. Three of the party returned with me to their village, and were most pressing in their invitation for me to stay the night. On leaving, I

was presented with a number of hard-boiled eggs, and yams: the former, I have been told, is a mark of sincerity with the Kakhyens; but whether it is intended as a similar token with these people, I cannot say. Their hamlet consisted of seven houses; but was stockaded. This settlement had been established here by the Kakhyens, who levy a black-mail for the protection of the people. They had small areas under *toungya* culture, but their chief business was in the teak and bamboo trade. When we first came on the party, they were busy hanging little scraps of rags on the bushes before visiting me—votive offerings no doubt for their safety.

215. Vegetation noted :—Teak abundant, but of poor growth; *Gmelia arborea, Dipterocarpus alata, Calophyllum, Albizzia, Conocarpus acuminatus, Dillenia* (fruit eaten by the natives), *Strychnos, Nux vomica, Nauclea, Careya, Blackwellia tomentosa, Rhamnoides, Rosa, Phyllanthus. Rumex, Deymaria cordata,* and *Aspidocarya uvifira:* also bamboos.

216. Returning to my boats I found a large number of Kakhyens and Pwons awaiting my arrival; my people seemed to have had some little trouble in keeping them off the boats. They were most disorderly, and inclined to be quarrelsome, one Kakhyen drawing his *dah* when pushed off the boat by my peon. In return for the presents they brought, consisting of grain and yams, they begged opium and gunpowder, and were most importunate in their requests; but I declined to give either, saying I had none; ultimately they were satisfied with an addition of some beads and red cloth.

217. The river now becomes most tortuous in its course, and is cut up into narrow channels—not exceeding fifty yards wide—by enormous rocks, some of which stand thirty feet above water. The rapidity of the current through these gorges is terrific in the extreme, and required the combined strength of our three crews to tow the boats, one by one, through the hazardous openings. The eddies and whirlpools caused by the position of the rocks rendered the boats at the time almost unmanageable, and it was with difficulty they could be kept from dashing up against them. I contemplated an awkward return voyage. The first two rocks are crowned with pagodas; the former is in a good state of repair, and surrounded by a rubble parapet; but the latter is all in ruins and overgrown with jungle, which tends to add to its romantic appearance. The three largest rocks are known as the elephant, cow, and granary; but the origin of these names I could never trace—certainly they bear no resemblance to their namesakes.

218. Reached the hamlet of *Lek-mot* at 5 P.M.; it numbers fifteen Shan and Pwon houses, and is named after an adjacent rock, said to

represent a thumb, which the word signifies. Mango, jack, cocoanut, areca, *Bixa orellana*, *Crotalaria*, and *Jatropa* are common about the village. Disturbed at night by shouts and reports of guns, which turned out to be the villagers in pursuit of a tiger that had just carried off a child. This caused a great panic amongst my people, who begged to be allowed a shot at the crowd, imagining they were Kakhyens running off with plunder. Slight shower of rain at 9 A.M.

219. *Wednesday, 14th January 1874.*—Thermometer 55° at 6 A.M.; dense fog up to 7 A.M., when we started. Pulled up at 9 A.M. on the right bank for quarter of an hour, to have a chat with the *Pwons* of *Kowmea*. They were remarkably civil, frank, and open in their conversation. Their cultivation is conducted on the *toungya* system. The Burmese authorities demand from them a house-tax of Rs. 10 per annum, and the Kakhyens levy blackmail in proportion to their profits, which resolves itself into an unlimited demand. The acts of the Burmese authorities are spoken of as unjust and oppressive, and even more dreaded than the raids of the wild mountaineers. During the rains, I am told, the roar from the mountain torrents on either side is deafening, and the river often rises in a night forty feet, but the floods are not of long duration. This is quite probable, when the difference in width of the defile and open river is contemplated. My breechloader and revolver were objects of admiration and wonderment, especially the *six-shooter*, which I discharged at their request, and surprised them still more by saying the process could be kept up *ad infinitum!* This variation from facts must be pardoned and accepted as a *diplomatic official romance*. The interior of a Pwon's house is remarkably tidy and clean, considering the style of life the poor wretches lead. It is entirely a bamboo building raised six feet off the ground, a notched piece of timber serving as steps. The walls and flooring are of split bamboos, the roof is thatched with a *saccharum*, and semicircular gables serve as a covering to the balcony in front and rear of the house. This type of building is peculiarly Shan. Never more than one family occupies a house : in this respect the *Pwons* notedly differ from the Kakhyens and other mountaineers. Later on in the day, I visited some Shan hamlets. The female costume of the people is that of a Burman woman's, with the addition of a cloth round the head, and a girdle ; the men, however, wear loose white trousers down to the knee, a huge brimmed straw hat (some of which are remarkably fine and costly), and are tatooed from the ankle up to the waist, and very often up to the breast. They are a remarkably fair race, with broad flat features,

thick lips, and the narrow oblique-set eye of the Chinese. Their general expression is good-natured and pleasing, and some of the young girls approach on prettiness. After marriage, the women blacken their teeth, which is a great disfigurement, and their mouths are distorted to an unnatural shape by the perpetual habit of chewing *pán suparee*, the discoloured saliva trickling down either side as they talk, in a most disgusting manner. I was the first European they had ever seen; and men, women, and children flocked round me in curious amazement. My musical box was a source of great amusement, and the self-revolution of the barrel attributed to a supernatural power. The sleight-of-hand tricks I displayed seemed to strike them dumb, and when I changed the little pebbles they kept handing me, into two and four-anna bits, there was a dead silence for a few minutes and a horror-stricken expression written on their faces; then followed a burst of applause, and they all *sheekoed* (bowed in obeisance) proclaiming me a great *nât*, and begged I would remain until they could collect offerings worthy of my acceptance, but I declined, and took my departure.

220. Made fast at *Myintha* for the night. The defile ends here, and the river widens out considerably; the hills also recede rapidly to the west, but more gradually decline to the east, and the country has a general flat, though well-wooded, appearance. This is a village of considerable size and importance, inhabited by Shans and Pwons. It is strongly stockaded, and each house within, protected by a substantial log barricade. The streets are only wide enough to admit of a single head of cattle passing at a time, with an object to prevent the place being unexpectedly stormed and overrun by Kakhyens. Around, and within the enclosure, grow *Ficus elastica* (three) averaging six feet high, said to have been grown from cuttings brought last year from Mogoung. Limes, oranges, pine-apples, plantains, areca, cocoanut, papaw, and jatropa were also cultivated. The following indigenous trees and shrubs were likewise noted: *Shorea robusta*, which is tapped for the gum that exudes from it; *Erythrina, Cæsalpinia, Nauclea, Bauhinia, Urena, Calamus*, and a wild jasmine, the leaves of which the Kakhyens use as a substitute for *phan*. *Podostemon* and *Lohit campanula* common on rocks. Small patches of *Sinapis* are cultivated here and there on the river-bank, the tops serving as a substitute for greens. It had been bitterly cold all day; the sun had not once appeared—north-easterly wind, and drizzle towards evening; thermometer never rose above 69° Fahrenheit.

221. The scenery throughout this defile is sublimely grand and picturesque, but in places awful to contemplate as one stands watching the trackers encouraging one another by fiendish yells that echo

through the woods, and straining every muscle to gain ground as the boat sluggishly quivers through the fierce rapids now running flush with the boat's gunwale : all now depends on the trueness of the towing-line—that gone, and we are lost, for the best and strongest swimmer could not live in such places; fortunately, there are times when there is little to apprehend, and one can serenely contemplate the beauties of this wild yawning of the mountains, clad on either side to the water's edge, with a diversity of foliage, rendered more brilliant by the undulating hills that rise one above another, casting their tall shadows around with softening tints. Here and there, too, on either bank, in the solitary haunts may be be seen a few Pwon and Shan huts, set in *toungya* clearings peeping through these dense woodlands, while the angular masses of rock that project into the stream, and render navigation so dangerous, are generally crowned with some emblem of religious ideal.

222. *Thursday, 15th January 1874.*—Thermometer 54° at 6 A.M. Make a short excursion inland to the west. Visited by two Burmans, who represent themselves to be officials, and as having received instructions from the Governor of Bhamo to offer me every assistance. My suspicion is aroused by their overanxiety to prove their royal lineage and the ancestral claim they had on the appointment. I did not avail myself of their services. The country explored was densely wooded, but extensive clearings have been made for paddy cultivation : the staple tree is *Shorea robusta*. Woodlands rich in ferns and orchids; many of the latter are in flower, and present a brilliant show. Passed through the Shan hamlets of Nauphia, Pindone, and Nabay, each strongly stockaded. The accounts of this part of the country once having been well inhabited, but since depopulated by the repeated raids of the Kakhyens, which remained unpunished by the Burmese Government, are in a measure supported by the vast tracts of paddy-land that now lie idle and overgrown with wild grasses; nor is proof wanting up to the present day of how brigandage remains unpunished : the very weapons with which these people perpetrate their most desperate deeds, are sold, and manufactured to their fancy in Bhamo, Mogoung, or some other Burmese village. Unquestionably, the country suffers materially from this insecurity of property, and yields but a tithe of the revenue it would, were life and property safe; but this alone is attributable to the absence of a well-organized Government, which the people would hail with delight. I do not believe the Kakhyens are the blood-thirsty, ungovernable savages they are generally represented to be ; they are no worse, I venture to say, than those around us would be, but for the dread

of our laws, whips, prisons, and gallows; all their greatest atrocities are committed under the influence of liquor, and actuated, in the first instance, either by a spirit of revenge, or by absolute want. In their sober senses, I have always found them civil, remarkably hospitable, and both intelligent and ingenious; under the present Government, however, they are the dread and curse of the country, and there is hardly a lowlander who would not rejoice to hear of their extermination; one old Shan, who saw my revolver, remarked— "Ah! that is the sort of thing we want, to polish off these Kakhyens; something that will kill them by twenties," and on being reasoned with, as to the probability of these people being less malicious if honestly dealt with, he continued, " no, we have tried to purchase safety, but the bribe only kindled the jealousy of the other tribes, and we cannot afford to pay every one; they are a treacherous set, and can only be likened to a dog's tail which alone keeps straight when spliced to a stick." Though this animus exists between the Shans and Kakhyens, nevertheless they are dependent on one another for their daily wants; and carry on a brisk system of barter, the former exchanging with the latter salt, *gnapee*, &c., for cotton, yams, paddy, pigs, &c.

223. A large quantity of paddy is exported yearly from here to Bhamo. An annual tax of Rs. 10 per house is levied by the Burmese authorities, but the people complain bitterly of the extortion practiced by the tax-collector.

224. Shot a barking deer (*Cervus muntjak*), two *Grus antigone* (both females), painted partridge, quail (small button), and peacock. Noted, *Zanclostomus tristis, Hydrocessa albirostris, Halcyon pileata, plotus melanogaster*, and *Passer indicus* very common.

225. Vegetation: *Dillenia, Nauclea, Hopea, Terminalia, Fici pentaptera, Gordonia, Grislea, Grewia, Phyllanthus, Rosa, Thunbergia, Calamus, Daphne, Jasminum, Saccharum*, and *cynodon dactylon*; sugarcane is also cultivated (the red variety).

226. Started for Tsimbo at 3 P.M., reached there by 7 P.M.; water remarkably strong. There was a rise of one foot in the river last night.

227. *Friday, 16th January 1874.*—Tsimbo, a Shan and Shan-Burmese hamlet of fifty-five houses, enclosed in a double stockade, occupying a rising site on the right bank. Heavy fog up to 8 A.M. Thermometer 53° at 6 A. M., a rise of three feet in the water during last night. The river here is about five hundred yards across, but encumbered with shoals and sand-banks. *Sesamum indicum* is cultivated to some extent, and oil expressed in the ordinary mill of the country. Started to examine the poisonous spring

situated in the heart of a forest about seven miles due west from here. Our course lay through a dense jungle of *Inga xylocarpa, Schleichera trijuga, Blackwellia tomentosa, Nauclea,* teak (limited and stunted), *Dipterocarpus, Erythrina,* and an undergrowth of *Calamus,* plantain, *Daphne, Jasminum, Phyllanthus,* and *Zingiberaceæ*.

228. I found, besides the principal spring, there were two others, all situated in the bed of the same water-course that drain the neigbouring undulations, and is overgrown on either side by a *Licuala peltata*. Round the pools I collected the following dead animals : three rats (perfect), nine butterflies, three sparrows (decomposed), a parrot (comparatively fresh), and the bones of various animals I could not distinguish.

229. Nearing the principal place, our guide told us that if we approached it quietly, we would find the water perfectly calm, and that it would continue to foam in proportion to the echo raised in the forest. This was an exaggeration of a truth. The water certainly became more agitated as we neared the spot, but this can be accounted for by the nature of the surrounding soil which consisted of moist red sand, from which the water continues to exude by pressure. Tradition, however, traces the origin of this place to a wrathful *nât*, who was wrecked here in his golden craft, and cursed the place ! The cause of the death of the animals is sufficiently accounted for in the subjoined extract of a letter from the Chemical Examiner to Government :—

" I have the honour to forward the result of the analysis of water forwarded with your letter No. 2825, of the 24th July 1874. The water is supersaturated with carbonic acid gas, like ordinary " soda water." If such a water found its way to the surface of the earth, under such circumstances as would allow this gas to accumulate, as in the poisonous hollows in the Solfatena near Naples, any animal going to drink, or sleeping near the place, might be poisoned by breathing this gas. All the solid matters were separated from the water and carefully tested for poison ; but no poisonous substance existed in them. The total amount of solid matter was so unusually small, *viz.,* one hundred and twenty parts per million." * * * *

230. A few hundred yards beyond the springs, are some fine specimens of *Ficus glomerata*, known to the people as the *borde bain,* or *Ficus elastica*, and said to have been planted by the Poongyees as votive offerings at the wreck of the craft. The trees bore marks of excessive and recent tapping. The coagulated juice of this tree, has no elasticity, but rather attains the consistency of *gutta-percha* when quite dry. Continuing a westerly course, in the direction of the

hills, which are a continuation of those through which the river has forced its way, we passed, *en route*, vast deserted paddy-clearings, and the ruins of three Shan hamlets plundered by the Kakhyens last year ; the inhabitants had to re-establish themselves on the banks of the river near Tsimbo. Proceeding northwards, we followed the water-shed (elevation four hundred and twenty-five feet) for a few miles, and commenced the descent a little before sunset. Our guide now showed symptons of uncertainty as to the direction he should take, and it was soon apparent we had lost our way. Continued due east, which brought us to the river by midnight, where we bivouaced till morning being too tired to proceed any further. Reached Tsimbo by 9 A.M. the next day, having overreached the place last night by about ten miles. Additional plants collected : *Broussonetia papyrifera, Ruellia indica, Anodendron paniculatum, Santalacea* (climber), *Vallaris solanacea, Spathodia stipulata, Eleusine, Asclepiadea, Grislea, Pladera justiciordea, Dicksonia,* and *Polypoddium wallichianum ; Saccharum* and *Arundo* common.

231. Shot a smooth-skinned bear, *Urus malayanus,* a civet-cat, a mungoose, some painted partrigdes, and two varieties of pheasants—*Polyplectron albo-ocellatum,* and *Phasianus fasciatus.*

232. *Saturday, 17th January 1874.*—Fog ; thermometer, 49° at 6 A.M.; river fallen two feet overnight; start at 7-30. (There is a tolerably good road from here to Mogoung, which can be reached in eight days easily I am told.) The Shan-Burmese villages of Tangarzoo, Pugan, Wagza, and Nahbho are the first passed ; the two former situated on the right bank, and the others on the left, all stockaded, but none of them exceeding twelve houses. The river here is divided by an island some five miles in length ; apparently a disconnected portion of the main land, judging by the age of the arborescent growth and course of the river. Trees, defoliated ; and tobacco cultivated on the more recent disgorgements : the quality of the plant is pronounced excellent by the natives ; but the leaf seemed too coarse to me. We took the western channel, which varies in breadth from one hundred to three hundred yards, with an average depth of seven feet of water, but little charged with silt. Continued to pass groups of Shan and Burman huts on either bank, with plots of tobacco culture on the river-frontage. Hailed His Majesty's *dâk* boat with royal mails from Mogoung to Bhamo ; but the current was too rapid to allow of the boat stopping to take my letters. The white flag with red peacock in the centre was the only distinguishing Government mark. The two channels unite opposite the Shan-Burmese hamlet of Noung-sa-yah : country to the east continues undulating, and tolerably wooded, with

mountains at no considerable distance ; to the west, vast tracts of saccharum and scrub arborescent growth alternately line the banks. Another two miles and a reef of serpentine rocks crops up in the centre of the river, and at this season are eighteen inches above water, the beach becomes pebbly, and the banks are of a stiff clay full of angular stones of convex form, and many now dry, and filled with a layer of coarse gravel. Here we came on a band of Kakhyens encamped on an island washing for gold; the sand was of a quartzy nature with iron. At first they lined the shore to look at us, the attraction no doubt being my cabin-boat and the British ensign, but immediately I was seen, there was a general bolt, and an attempt at concealment in their huts. I went ashore, but it was with difficulty I gained their confidence, and got them to answer my questions, and initiate me in their art of gold-washing.

233. The method is simple, and not very dissimilar to that practised in Hungary; which is, washing on inclined tables. A plank about four feet long, fourteen inches wide, and two inches thick is employed, with a number of transverse grooves cut in its surface. This is supported in an inclined position. An open workbasket is then secured to the top of the plank, and filled with sand which, by a repeated succession of washings, passes through the perforation in the basket, leaving the gold with a certain per-centage of sand in the furrows of the board. This mixture is removed into a flat wooden basin, and by a peculiar movement of the hand, the gold is entirely separated from the sand. A family of five earn about Rs. 2-4 per diem. I purchased two annas (in weight) of the gold dust for Rs. 2-11. Under a better process, gold-washing here, would doubtless be a remunerative occupation.

234. The velocity of the current increases considerably, and it is with difficulty the boatmen can find a firm hold for their poles ; the pebbles below are constantly playing false, and the men kept tumbling into the river, much to the amusement of their companions ; fortunately, they can all swim, so no harm results from a capsize. Made fast at a sandbank a little south of Mogoung *choung*, there being no village any where near.

235. *Sunday, 18th January 1874.*—Heavy fog. Thermometer 48° at 6 A.M. Start at 8. 30. A.M. The mouth of the Mogoung river is much obstructed by snags, it does not exceed two hundred yards in width, and only a portion of that, contains water. The remains of a tolerably large village destroyed by fire is situated at its junction with the Irrawaddy. The main range of hills, here threw off, at right-angles to the river, a low spur, which reaches

to the water's edge, and known as the Pah-tin range. *Hopea* and *Dipterocarpus* preponderate. Shot *Nettapus, Coromandelica, Herodias gaizetta, Pophyrio neglectus*, and *Pelargopsis amanropterus*. Crabs (*Thelphus*) common. The river now spreads out to about 500 yards; the right bank maintains its undulating character, and is covered with low scrub jungle, but to the west, the country is a continuous flat, extending to the far distant hills, and traversed by two small streams, the latter being known as the Nan-sha-choung. Came on a group of twenty Paloung huts stockaded, and situated on the right bank. The inhabitants were recent settlers from Bhamo, though originally from a district south of that place. Their occupation entirely consists in the manufacture of *dahs*, and curing fish by a process of smoking—both thriving trades apparently; they return to their homes early in April. The fish we purchased from them were two species of *Cyprinus*. My peon killed a snake, *(Dipsas monticola)* one foot nine inches long. What money could not secure, empty pint hock bottles did; for four of these I got eleven eggs, and a brood of jungle-fowl chickens.

236. The Paloungs can but be regarded as a section of the Shan race, a dialect of whose tongue they speak. The two people intermarry, and their costumes assimilate, though physically, perhaps, the *bonâ fide* Shan carries off the palm. They have the repute of being good agriculturists, though the poppy was the only plant to which they had turned their attention here, and of this they had about two acres under cultivation. The plant is cultivated for the seed (they say), which is used in the manufacture of sweetmeats, and not for extraction of opium as I at first imagined.

237. *Assah* is the next Shan-Burmese village we came on; it comprises twenty-seven houses surrounded by a strong bamboo palisade; the inhabitants were chiefly engaged in felling and exporting teak to Bhamo. Bearing north-east, towering above all the other mountains appeared to-day, for the first time, a sugar-loaf-shaped peak which will doubtless serve as a land-mark for some days to come. Made fast for the night at an island with pebbly beach; the rocks here are a few feet above the water's surface, and the rapids are heard for some distance. Much pestered by a *Tipula* (*daddy long legs*) while writing up my journal.

238. *Monday, 19th January 1874.*—Detained starting till 9 A.M. by dense fog. Thermometer, 48° at 6 A.M. *Bixa orellana* common, and cultivated for the dye the seed yields: also a *Calamus* lines the banks. The low range of hills to the west continues to hug the shore. Reached Ahyane-da-mah by noon: the river here is a shallow, placid stream of about three hundred yards wide, the navi-

gable channel not exceeding nine feet in the deepest part: the water is clear, and the pebbly-bottom perceptible. Ahyane-damah contains both a Shan-Burman and Kakhyen population, but that portion of the hamlet inhabited by the former is stockaded, and separated from the latter by a narrow gully or ravine. This amalgamation was brought about, by the Shan-Burmans seeking the protection of the Kakhyens, for which they pay an annual tax. I was fortunate in arriving here a few hours after the death of a Kakhyen woman, and witnessed the peculiar customs these people have of dealing with their corpse. At first, I was regarded an intruder, and angry words arose, accompanied by a threat of murder—all the male community having drawn their swords. Order was soon restored, however, by blending the *suaviter in modo* in due proportion with the *fortiter in re;* and after the distribution of a few trifling presents, and a little display of *legerdemain*, I was acknowledged an object of reverence and fear, and had it all pretty well my own way. Just before leaving, my power of witchcraft was put to a severe test by my being asked to restore the woman to life; however, I soon disengaged myself from the entanglement by explaining that it would not be to *their* benefit that I should interfere with the ruling of the *Atropos* of their faith; fortunately, the excuse was accepted, and I maintained my reputation as a great *nat!* I was then conducted to the ground selected for the last resting-place of the poor woman, and begged to express an opinion as to the propitiousness of the site; I pronounced it favourable in all respects!

239. Immediately the soul takes flight, the corpse is laid out straight with the head to the west, and lashed round with a white bandage from the feet to the waist, the arms are also straightened out on either side in the case of men and married women, but with unmarried girls (though they may be mothers) they rest crossed on the bosom with a hand on either breast. The body is dressed in a new suit of clothes, but all ornaments are removed, and it is covered from head to foot with a new blue and white striped cloth. During the operation of laying out, which is always performed by the sex of the corpse, all evil-spirits are supposed to be expelled the house by a deafening beating of gongs, the discharge of all guns available, and other unearthly noises produced by the inmates. Revelry now commences, neighbouring friends are invited,* and feasting and drinking is kept up from two to ten days, according to the position of the relatives of the deceased. For two days the corpse is open to

---

* The mode of invitation among these people is peculiar. The cooked flesh of a sacrificed buffaloe is made into small packets in plantain leaves, and circulated among those whose company is requested; the appointed time for assembling being regulated by the number of cane bands round each packet.

the inspection of friends and relations, after which it is fastened up in a coffin (generally of mango wood) and buried the third day. The period that elapses between the death and burial greatly depends, however, on the circumstances of interested survivors : in some instances the body is embalmed, and not buried for twelve months perhaps, but a lapse of this length seldom occurs, except in the case of Tswabwas or other chiefs. During these bacchanalian gatherings the most obscene scenes transpire, and often quarrels arise resulting in bloodshed. Myself and followers were asked to join in the dance round the corpse, which we did, much to the satisfaction of the father of the deceased. The dance was simply a *walk-round* in slow time, at each step, the knee being raised as near the shoulder as possible, and time kept to the music, (which consisted of a drum and three gongs) on short sticks with which we were all provided. The gesticulations were barbarously indecent, and unmistakably suggestive; but the viler the joke, the better it was appreciated by men, women, and children. On occasions of this sort the usual etiquette of leaving by the same door entered at, is suspended, and all are allowed to enter and depart as they please, it not being an uncommon practice for visitors to cut their way through the mat walls. At the four corners of the burial ground were erected offerings to the *nāt* of the forest, consisting of bamboo crosses, with a gilded bamboo mat shield suspended to one end, and a wooden gilded *dah* to the other. Here I also noticed a peculiar pellet-bow, with a single cane for the string, the cradle for the pellet being formed by a slit in the cane which is kept apart by a couple of small props.

240. Shortly after leaving *Ahyane-da-mah*, we met the daughter of the Kantee Tswabwa on her way to Mandalay, where she was to have been presented in marriage to the king;—vassalage perhaps would have been a more *apropos* term. These people are, I believe, a branch of the Mauroo clan, and the women are celebrated for their long hair and beauty, but I was not allowed an opportunity of judging for myself. The party were comfortably housed on a bamboo raft, boats not being obtainable much north of Talo. Reached Hokah by 6 P.M. The river had varied little in width throughout the day, and the water had remained clear, displaying a pebbly bottom; rocks crop up here and there, rendering navigation difficult, and reducing the main channel to about seventy yards wide. Disturbed over-night by the trumpeting of elephants that had come down from the hill to feed on the sugarcane.

241. *Tuesday, 20th January 1874.*—Thermometer 43° at 6 A.M., a clear crisp morning. Went for a ramble on shore, and visited

the head-men of Hokah, a village principally inhabited by Kakhyens, though a few Shan-Burmese occupy a semi-detached portion enclosed by a bamboo palisade. The Kakhyens at this early hour were all sober, and welcomed me with all civility : liquor was handed round after the usual fashion, and pressing offers made for me to partake of food, which I declined under the plea of want of time. Their mode of life differs but little from that of their highland brothers, with whom they are in constant communication, and join in their wild raids when called upon. The Shan-Burmese had here again placed themselves under the protection of the Kakhyens, who are reputed never to betray the confidence placed in them, though they regard it no breach of honour to plunder the village under their protection, provided the inhabitants are warned of their intention : action in such cases soon follows the alarm, and the result is uncontested pillage.

242. They spoke of themselves as one great tribe known as Thainbows, with various ramifications, each branch taking its name from the clan it represented ; they denied there being any distinct division between the mountaineers of either bank, and explained that the *Singphos* were merely a separate clan, who, by intermarriage with Shans and lowlanders, had in a measure adopted their costume, and in other respects also lost their identity. The Mauroos they gave as their clan, and the Marains, Murrils, Lesses, and Labines as their sub-clans. Another interesting feature in the social laws of these people, is, that each class is governed by *Homa*, whose sway is absolute in all matters of importance : the sub-clans are under the immediate rule of a Tswabwa, who assisted by a *Pomine* (generally elected by the people) exercises entire control over the village he represents.

243. I was surprised at the general frankness of these people, and their willingness to give information ; certainly the liquor had been round twice, which, perhaps, may have had something to do with their candour. They seemed most anxious to visit Rangoon, and learn more about us, but had evidently been intimidated by false reports circulated at Bhamo. The disinclination of the people of the plains to deal fairly with them was given as an excuse for their depredations, and instances were cited in which unquestionably they had been manifestly cheated.

244. This colony had only temporarily settled on the river's bank to collect salt and *ngapee*, and it is encampments of this nature that petty traders dread. Before leaving, I distributed a few presents, with which all seemed greatly pleased, and the last words of the Tswabwa's wife were—as she put some hard-boiled eggs into

my hands,—" when you go to Pakoo on the other side of the river ask for my sister Mooroorah ; she is young, and will make you very comfortable." Some of the children had English rupees strung round their necks, which, I was told, served both as an ornament and charm against the evil eye, the Burman coin, however, is merely appreciated for its intrinsic value. As a specimen of the workmanship, I purchased a bamboo basket here for two annas, the texture was remarkably fine, though not nearly so good as one that was refused me as belonging to a woman who prized it, in remembrance of her deceased mother. There is only one bamboo they say that can be utilized for such purposes ; it is called by the Kakhyens *messangye*. Shot two peacock-pheasants, painted partridge, and a hare. Round the village were cultivated yams, plantains, limes, chillies, pumpkin, poppy, and *Lablab vulgare* and sugarcane. Buffalo hides were being collected here for some merchant trader, and realized one Rupee each. Mogoung can be reached from here by land in a day and a half, the route being through a flat country.

245. Continued northwards, reaching Talo by 3 P.M. opposite is the Shan-Burman village of Khoung-phoo. The river had gradually narrowed to about one hundred and fifty yards, but in other respects the stream had remained unaltered. The country to the west is undulating to the water's edge, but to the east the hills are far distant, and the plains wooded principally with a *Shorea*, from which the gum is collected and exported in large quantities to Mandalay. Clearings of considerable size for paddy culture have been common. *En route* met a party of Kakhyens washing for gold. Shot an otter, a pelican, a *Brahmini* duck and a fine *Ketupa ceylonensis* that had just captured a fish (*Oreinus*) weighing eight pounds, off which my people made a hearty meal. Talo not long since was a place of great importance, but, owing to the disturbed state of the country, the trade with western China *via* this route has ceased, depriving the Kakhyens of the handsome revenue they derived as guides and escorts, and reducing them to a great state of poverty. They are alive to their loss, and had now guaranteed protection to Talo and all traders who came there : they had also presented the Governor of Mogoung with a pair of elephant tusks in hopes that he will assist in re-establishing the western trade. This move on the part of the Nangsingtoung Kakhyens had caused much jealousy among the neighbouring mountaineers, who threatened to burn down Talo and the adjacent villages. In the evening I called on the royal phoongyee, a young man of about twenty-seven : he was courteous, but reticent in public ; and accepted the presents placed before him,

with an air of indifference; but I soon found they had the desired effect, and that to have gone empty-handed would have been fatal to my object. Elsewhere I have explained, this rank is only bestowed on the more cunning of the priesthood, who are calculated to make good spies, and all royal mandates of a confidential nature are issued through this channel. Talo contains fifty-two houses and a large *koung* built of *sal*, the posts being twenty feet above the ground, and 2·25 feet in diameter. It has a mixed population of Shan-Burmans and Kakhyens, who in this instance are allowed to live within the stockade, and are well paid for their protection. The phoongyee spoke of the aversion these mountaineers have to water, and corroborated what I had previously heard regarding their waging war with this element, whenever one of the tribe is drowned—a ceremony already spoken of. There are four *Ficus elastica* trees here, each twenty years old; they are annually tapped, and the caoutchouc sent to Mandalay. No reliable information could be obtained regarding the yield. The juice is collected by driving pen-shaped bamboos into the extremity of the diagonal cuts which extend to the depth of the *mesophlœum*: the vessels filled; coalescence is brought about by exposing the liquid to the direct rays of the sun, or more commonly, by placing it in an earthen pot over a slow fire; neither of these processes, however, unassisted by pressure gives good results, for the coagulum is seldom free from small cells which retain a portion of the aqueous solution, resulting in rapid decomposition of the rubber, and materially decreases its market value. I am told by the phoongyee, that the *Ficus elastica* flowers here towards the end of March, and the seeds ripen in May. He also gives as his experience that seedlings will not grow beneath the parent trees, and that the most successful way of rearing plants is by throwing the seeds on some old thatched house, or in the recess of a *Platycerium wallichii*. Obtained the phoongyee's permission to make an excursion into the Kakhyen hills to the west, and received the promise of a Kakhyen Tswabwa as a guide, a few of the same tribe as coolies, and a guarantee of protection for my boats during my absence. Arranged to start the next morning at 10 A.M. About midnight I was awoke by my interpreter, with a message from the phoongyee, saying he wished to see us alone! It was a strange hour to ask for an interview, and I apprehended treachery, but determining to face the danger, whatever it might be, I buckled on my revolver under my coat, and met the priest with disguised suspicion. He was quite alone, and seated in a distant corner of the monastery lighted by a dimly-burning oil lamp; we were motioned to be seated, a profound silence of a few minutes then followed, when he beckoned my interpreter near him, and the conversation was carried on, in a whisper. From what he said, it appeared he regarded it unwise to say all he wanted before the large crowd that had assembled, when I called during the day, fearing the conversation might reach His Majesty's hearing. He now, however, told us he had received instructions that I was not to be allowed to take away any *Ficus elastica* plant, nor receive any information about them, but that as I had assured him the chief object of my mission was to collect these trees for a good purpose, and that they were eventually to be planted in and about the *vicinity* of the *Shwe-de-gyee* pagoda, he would, on a promise of secrecy, assist me to the utmost, and even add a few plants to my collection. I accepted his offer with thanks, and expressed a hope that I might at some future date be in a position to display my gratitude. The conversation now took a political turn, and I was questioned regarding the strength of the British force in Burma, and the ultimate object we had in view; though cautious in my replies, I was equally careful to display no want of confidence. A few words of information now in respect to the habits and customs of the mountaineers among whom I was going, and advice as to the action I should take in case of difficulties, ended the meeting, and I got back to my boat at 2 A.M. Before closing this day's diary, I must mention that two Kakhyen slaves were exposed for sale here—a boy and a girl of about eighteen and thirteen years respectively, the former having been valued at Rs. 80, and the latter at Rs. 60: evidently they were Shan-Burmese that had been captured when mere infants at some raid; they seemed happy and contented, and were equally well dressed with the rest of the party.

246. *Wednesday, 21st January 1874.*—Fog less dense than usual. Thermometer 47° at 6 A.M. Started at 10 A.M., after a good deal of trouble in getting the people together. My party mustered thirteen men, of whom five were Kakhyen coolies, the sixth, the *Pomine* of Kowkar—who acted as guide—and the remainder, my peons, and interpreters. All carried arms, embracing swords, spears, crossbows, and muskets. Following a southerly course we soon came in sight of Hokah, and although on looking at the map, this appears rather an indirect line, yet it is considered the most practical, being the nearest to the old trade route to China, which lay in the direction we intended taking. From about opposite Hokah, we struck off due east, passing through a continuous forest of *Shorea*, which had been cleared for the culture of paddy and *Sessamum indicum*, with some regard to system, the intermediate belts of trees having been left to demarcate the different holdings. The soil is a black loam. Came on the fresh dung and prints of elephants, and shortly

afterwards met a party of twenty Kakhyens tracking up the herd; we joined them by invitation. After about two hours I got a shot at a fine young tusker, and lodged a ball behind his ear—this brought him on his knees; and immediately a volley was fired by the whole party, which finally disposed of the huge brute. The Kakhyens were wild with excitement, and we all joined hands and danced round our victim, shouting and capering like savages. A portion of the flesh was brought away for an evening meal, but I confess I had not the pluck to taste the stew, much to the surprise of my Burmans, who assured me it was capital, and that the trunk and feet were the greatest delicacy imaginable. There was no time to wait for the tusks to be cut out, nor was there a spare hand to carry them; my guide, however, promised that they should be made over to me on our return to Talo, as the whole party were relations of his, and he could vouch for their honesty. We hurried on, and *en route* I bagged a few snipe, a *bittern*, and a *Grus antigone*: the disposal of the first established my fame as a marksman, and raised me immensely in the estimation of the Kakhyens, who looked with wonderment at the rise and fall of the birds. But a short distance from the foot of the hills,—which I roughly estimate to be seven miles from Talo,—we diverged a point leaving the trade route to our right. The ascent was commenced about sun-set, and by 8 P.M., after a stiff climb, the highest peak of the first step of this range or spur was reached, and glad enough were we all. Here we rested for the night.

247. The first thing I was conducted to the Tswabwa's house, and received a hearty welcome. He apologized for the smallness of his abode, which necessitated some of my party being accommodated under a seperate roof. The unfinished state of the houses was accounted for, by the whole village having recently been burnt down, during an engagement with a neighbouring tribe, who had been repulsed with great loss. Trespass was the origin of the engagement—people of this Tswabwaship having shot an elephant out of bounds, and refused to conform to the established law in such cases; now the quarrel had taken the form of a blood-feud, and animosity will continue to smoulder until opportunity offers a good opening for revenge, or the ransom demanded is paid.*

---

* The sporting laws of these people are peculiar, though not altogether unreasonable. The exact limits of each estate or holding, though but defined by natural boundaries, are universally known to the Kakhyens. Game shot beyond bounds is the entire property of the proprietor on whose land the criminal happens to be killed, and the poacher has to pay a fine of one female buffalo. Animals wounded within bounds and killed beyond, are equally divided between the sportsman and owner of the holding where the animal finally falls. The law chiefly relates to large game, though trespassers are very summarily dealt with, if they cannot give a satisfactory account of themselves.

The Tswabwa expected to be re-attacked at any moment, and had surrounded his village with a substantial double-walled bamboo stockade— a precaution only taken by mountaineers when at war with one another.

248. It would be a waste of time describing the class of architecture or arrangement of this village, for it was identical with that at *Ronelein* spoken of at page 116. Acheenoung, for that was the name of our guide, was most attentive, and insisted on our having something to eat—a compliment I reluctantly accepted—for the result of the last Kakhyen meal was still fresh in my memory. It was long past midnight before the party broke up, and although there had been a good deal of liquor consumed, all were tolerably sober. Unquestionably, the Kakhyens are dangerous when drunk, and should be avoided in their cup; but " *in vino veritas ;*" and if the desirable medium between *drunk* and *happy* can be maintained, it is the time when the most reliable and valuable information can be gained from these people. Until the liquor had taken effect, the Tswabwa was most reticent, and left the whole of the conversation to his *Pomine*, Acheenoung, but immediately he became slightly inebriated, than he threw off all reserve, and was as loquacious as the rest. I chatted with them on various topics, and was surprised at the intelligence displayed, in their questions and answers. They appeared to take quite as great an interest in our manners, customs, and religion, as we do in theirs. The *nâts*, *I* believed in, was one of the subjects I was asked to explain, and although it was difficult to enlighten them on this point through an interpreter, yet they seemed to accept my explanation, and endeavoured to assimilate their belief with ours, the Tswabwa remarking that " though there was a difference in our colour, we were of the same flesh and blood." This conversation confirms me in the opinion that, though like the early Greeks, these people are firm in the belief that the universe is pervaded by spirits; yet they are equally satisfied of the existence of a Supreme Being, who they supplicate through the medium of certain recognized spirits, that have been handed down from the earliest teachings of Thales as objects of reverence. Their mythology teaches them that each handiwork of God's, has its special guardian spirit, whether it be the moon, the sun, the forest, the ocean, the workman's axe, the elements, or the least important of His creation, and that in time of need or tribulation, they should invoke the divinity who presides over, and is co-existent with, the object they desire to accomplish. They spoke once of having had a written language and religion, but that these have been lost to them ever since a hungry Kakhyen ate up their bible, which was inscribed

on leather. They have no priests, but each village elects its *mcetway* or soothsayer, who is supposed to be gifted with superhuman power, and in the confidence of the *nâts*. On occasions when matters of importance are referred to him for final decision, he retires towards dusk, to the corner of the house set apart to the *nâts*, and begins a solemn wail, which increases towards midnight; he then shows symptoms of madness, throwing himself into all sorts of contortions; at this stage, the *nâts* are supposed to communicate their rulings, and, after some *little* consolation from the surrounding inmates, he reveals the secret, which generally agrees with the wishes of the people.

249. The information gained here, regarding the manners and customs of this tribe, corresponds with that gathered at Hokah, and noted in my diary of the 20th current. This is very satisfactory. They spoke of having been at one time, subjects of the Burmese Government, but now glory in their freedom, and declare their right to levy black-mail on all who pass through their country. This, however, is but partially correct, and only applicable to those tribes whose homes are in the far distant mountains; those near Bhamo still continue to pay tribute, though it can hardly be said that they are under the control of the Burmese authorities. They have no systematic form of government of their own, and only acknowledge the authorities noted in my diary of yesterday. The *Homa* and *Tswabwa* are supported by the people, but the *Pomine* is dependent on the latter. The two former claim a portion of every animal slaughtered, a measure of every brew of liquor, and a basket of paddy per head per annum from every male adult in their holding. They also cultivate on their own account, claiming gratis from their subjects a day's labour for clearing, one for preparing and sowing the land, and one for reaping, besides which they utilize their slaves and menials as agriculturists. In consideration of these privileges, both are expected to entertain guests and assist those in distress. Acts of oppression on the part of the Chiefs are not tolerated and lead to open rebelion, generally resulting in the murder of the unpopular ruler.

250. Those women who had joined us in our cups, were if anything, more curious than the men regarding our habits; but their inquisitiveness took a different turn, and they wanted to be told something about our women, their costume, the use we put them to, and the number of wives we were allowed, substantive and officiating. Other suggestively naughty enquiries followed, which brought forth peals of laughter, especially from the young girls who had now gathered round me, and were playfully familiar in

their attentions. To preach morality under present circumstances, would have been a mere waste of breath, so I accepted their chaff all in good part; though no doubt the phlegmatic disposition I evinced, lowered me considerably in their estimation; for their uncivilized life teaches them to disbelieve in celibacy and continence, and in early life, even to condemn the practice as unnatural; yet, strange to say, a breach of the VII. commandment in their sight, is an unpardonable offence and punishable by death.* Polyandry is unknown among them, and polygamy rare. It is difficult to describe how utterly devoid these people are, of all sense of modesty or even decency, responding to the cravings of nature regardless of time, place, or seclusion.

251. Before turning in, the *Tswabwa* wanted to know if I would stand by him in case of an attack to night; and, after being assured that I would, he retired to the family apartment, which is partitioned off from the guest-room by a mat walling. It was now for the first time I became aware of the absurd objection these people have, to strangers leaving a house by any other door than that by which they enter. Having occasion to go outside, I proceeded by the back-door, but I was stopped by a tipsy Kakhyen who drew his sword, and refused to let me pass; the mistake was soon explained; but so spasmodic and unexpected was the action of the man, that I am only surprised I did not shoot the fellow in self-defence. Towards morning, a band of Kakhyens arrived and established themselves at the lower end of the apartment we occupied. They kindled a fire and commenced smoking opium. Evidently from their boisterous talk and excited state, they were under the influence of liquor.

252. *Thursday, 22nd January 1874.*—Bitterly cold, north-easterly wind. Thermometer 40°. My people looked the picture of misery, and appeared quite torpid. All was silent till sunrise, when the women commenced to turn out and busy themselves with their domestic duties. The old women were engaged feeding the pigs on boiled paddy bran, and tending to the wants of the cattle generally; while the young girls were occupied fetching water from a spring some fifty feet below. It is surprising to see the loads they can carry. I noticed one girl climbing a steep slope with no less than seven bamboos of water, each two feet long and five inches in diameter: they were supported on the back by a shoulder strap, and another band that passed round the forehead on which a portion of

---

* Yan Sing *alias* Johnson suggests that this law might be extended to more civilized countries with a good effect. He even goes still further, and would have a *Vehme Secret Society*;—a body, I believe, who exclusively applied itself to the preservation of female purity, and the punishment of incontinence, especially that of unmarried girls.

the weight rested. Others were again engaged husking paddy by pounding it in a wooden mortar, and preparing dough from the flour of a sort of *millet* which is cultivated in these hills, I am told. I did not see the standing crop; but, judging from the seed, it is the *ragee* of the Deccan. The process of kneading was peculiar. The flour is first mixed with *til* oil in a mortar and worked into the consistency of paste, the lump of dough is then hurled with some considerable force against a post erected for the purpose, and pulled out in a long roll on the opposite side, this is coiled up again, and the process continued until the required homogeneity has been attained. A little *jaggery* is sometimes added, and the bread is not at all unpalatable. By 9 A.M. the men commenced to make their appearance, but the old Tswabwa slept on undisturbed. For the last two hours I had been roaming about within and without the stockade, adding to my collection of plants and insects, some of which were known to me, and others not. I was now challenged by a young fellow to shoot against him, he having been told by Acheenoung that I was the better shot, which he did not believe. The mark selected was the stem of a young *Bombax* about fifty yards off. He requested that I take the first shot, which I did and missed, my ball striking a tree nearly in line, but a yard or two behind the right one. This delighted the lad immensely, and he prepared for his turn. First discharging his gun in the air, which he said had been loaded some days, and could not be depended on, he re-loaded with great care, then resting the barrel on the stump of a tree, after an aim of some three minutes, fired, and hit; springing to his feet he danced in and out of the crowd, brandishing his gun over their heads, and challenging the world! This firing brought Acheenoung out, and hearing of my defeat, pluckily backed me again for a charge of powder and bullet: this time I was victor, which led to a quarrel and the drawing of swords, for the boy was so disappointed that he lost all control of his temper, and commenced to abuse Acheenoung, who wrenched the gun from his hands and threatened to shoot him with his own weapon; men, women, and children now joined in the dispute, which was ultimately settled by us both having to contest for the palm a third time. I endeavoured to miss, and as for my opponent, he was far too excited to go anywhere near the mark; thus peace was soon restored, and the crowd who, but a few minutes before, were ready to have committed blood-shed, were now all good humour and smiles, chaffing us both immensely for our bad shooting.*

---

* The Kakhyens manufacture their own gunpowder, and always give a preference to the wood of trees yielding an open grain; this is exactly the reverse of our ideas, the closer-grained and more woody trees being preferred in England, especially the *Salix* family.

253. On returning to the house, I found the Tswabwa seated by himself, smoking a pipe, and watching the party who turned up early this morning. He asked Yan Sing (my Burman interpreter) for a *sali*,* but expressed disgust at being handed the balance of a lighted one: he was soon satisfied, however, by a new one being substituted with an explanation that among the Burmese, it is customary to pass round a lighted cheroot.

254. Breakfast was now served, and the old lady of the house placing mine before me, with a smack of the tongue and a knowing grin, drew attention to one dish in particular; this turned out to be the elephant stew; what effect hunger might have had in dispelling fancies is hard to say, but want of appetite, and the novelty of the dish rather set me against the delicacy. There is no reason why elephant flesh should not be good, for the animal is a remarkably clean feeder; I dare say the meat is rather coarse and sinewy, but that is no draw back to a Burman, who has good molars and the digestion of an ostrich. The fact is, I had been feeling rather squeamish from the effect of last night's dinner, which was the most indigestible meal I ever made; under an unimpaired appetite, I have in my day tasted far more revolting dishes than elephant stew, and enjoyed them too, *e. g.*, porcupine chops, camel curry, and locusts cooked in oil. The meal over, which had been provided exclusively for the benefit of the Tswabwa, my followers, and self, liquor was handed round after the usual fashion, no distinction being made in this mark of hospitality, all present receiving a like share of the flowing bowl, which was apportioned by the females who took particular care to see that no one's cup remained empty for long.†

255. The Tswabwa, struck with the aroma of my tobacco, asked permission to have a whiff, and in this instance did not object to my pipe being handed over lighted to him. My old and faithful *briar-wood*, spliced in three places, and valued for old acquaintance

---

* A Burman cigar.

† The Kakhyens brew two descriptions of liquor—one from fermented rice, and the other from the husk, both are sweetened, and if consumed in any large quantities have an intoxicating effect. The brew is manufactured in a bamboo, with an arrangement that admits of clear liquor being drawn off. In the centre of the fermenting mass, a small hollow bamboo is lodged, pierced with holes (sufficiently small to exclude the grain) at the lower extremity to a height of three inches, into this fits loosely a hollow bamboo *plunger*, which is left a foot higher than either of the other bamboos, and by placing the thumb on a small hole—about the size of a pea—bored three inches from the head of the plunger, the desired quantity of clear liquor can always be obtained. Though this contrivance seems simple to us, one would hardly have expected to find it in use among these wild mountaineers. Another ingenious contrivance these people have is for striking fire. Imagine a child's pop-gun with one end closed, and an air-tight fitting ram-rod, the extremity of which is a cavity to contain the tinder,—generally the silk cotton of the *bombax*. Fire is produced by rapidly plunging and withdrawing the ram-rod, which generates, by a process of friction and compression, the requisite heat to produce combustion.

sake, to be polluted by a filthy Kakhyen! bah! the idea was far more disgusting than elephant stew—the sacrifice, however, had to be made, and I had to resume my smoke; but, after all, the idea was worse than the reality, and I dare say had I not witnessed the operation, I should have been none the wiser.

> "Tell me where is fancy bred,
> Or in the heart, or in the head?
> How begot, how nourished?
> It is engender'd in the eye,
> With gazing fed; and Fancy dies
> In the cradle where it lies."

256. The *Tswabwa* having accomplished his desire, which resulted in a sneezing fit, he handed on the pipe to his *Pomine*, who tried the same experiment with similar results, and I was once more possessor of my old friend. The cavendish was condemned by both parties, as bitter and suffocating.

257. With the distribution of presents, my visit at Kowkar was brought to an end. Some little judgment had to be exercised in this matter, or jealousy and ill-feeling would have resulted. It was necessary that the gifts be divided into three classes, and that each class should correspond not merely in quality and value, but even in size and colour. The best allotment falls to the *Tswabwa* and his family, the next in quality the *Pomine* and his family are entitled to, and the remainder is equally shared among the people of the village. I noticed the party that arrived early this morning were not introduced as being entitled to consideration, and on asking the reason, I was told that they were merely a band of highland bandits, who had rested here on their way from an engagement with a neighbouring tribe: they had been defeated, five of their party killed, and three of those present wounded, two in the arms, and one in the thigh. Finding I was willing to give some small return for any curiosity, I was deluged with all sorts of rubbish, among other things produced was the seed of a *trapa bicornis* that they endeavoured to palm off on me as the horns of a small deer brought from China. I received a cordial farewell, and just before leaving, the *Tswabwa* presented me with sword, and a complete suit of male and female attire, for which he refused to accept any equivalent; he wished me good speed, and expressed himself my humble servant, and one who would at all times be ready to fight for me or assist me through to China if needed. The women expressed their appreciation of my visit, by presents of flowers, hard-boiled eggs, and some of the sweet cake I had witnessed them making in the morning. I invited the whole of this village to a return party at Talo on the 25th instant.

258. We left Kowkar at half-past eleven A.M., and continued in a E.S.E. direction, passing through a densely wooded mountainous country, where the toon forms a prominent feature in the arborescent vegetation, and the wild rose and yellow raspberry everywhere abound: parasitical air-plants were also common, including *Orides, Oberonia*, and *Vanda*. En route, a few minutes were spent watching a party of Kakhyen men and girls winnowing paddy. In an enclosure that had been cleared of all weeds, levelled and coated with mud plaster, the grain previously trodden out by buffaloes was formed into a series of small heaps each of about two feet high; round these, parties of men and girls armed with circular fans (made from the stalk and sheath of the bamboo) dance to a merry song, and with each downward motion of the fan, a peculiar sort of back kick is given, by which process the chaff is thrown without the circle of dancers and the corn remains within. Liquor is freely consumed at these gatherings, and towards evening most of the party are drunk and riotous; it is during such festivities, our guide told us, scenes of the most obscene nature are committed, neither mothers, daughters, nor sisters being safe from violation and insult. The expense of these gatherings is always borne by the party to whom the crop belongs.

259. The ascent of the second step of the spur we crossed was far more steep than the one just accomplished, and my people begged for a halt of a few minutes at very short intervals,—they were so utterly blown. Half way up, a resting-place has been erected by the Kakhyens, where they have built a few neatly-constructed bamboo-seats, much after the pattern of our garden chairs. From here we had a capital bird's-eye view of the low country and the hills we had ascended. Looking west, the amphitheatre of hills mantled throughout in one impenetrable dark forest, and dotted here and there with a few Kakhyen hamlets, with their terraced system of cultivation, was very grand. My barometer read 2,900 feet, and there was a crisp bracing feeling in the atmosphere, not only most exhilarating, but very favourable to views. The sky was bright and sunny, but just sufficient haze to mellow the picture and preserve the objects in true perspective. We were on the tramp again in ten minutes; but, with the exception of Yan Sing, who was plucky to the last, all my people of the plains started with a heavy sigh, and disconsolate glance at one another. The Kakhyens, however, shoulder their loads in a cheerful manner, and with the short elastic step of a mountaineer, jogged merrily along.

260. As we proceeded, our guide, continued to draw attention to certain knolls and fells, which at one time or another had been scenes of blood-shed, and in every instance he led us to believe his

clan had been victorious. Slabs of sand-stone set on edge here and there (besmeared with the blood of some animal) he told us were in memory of the tigers that had been killed : thus far I counted five of these marks, the blood-stains on the last still being fresh. Acheenoung was a capital companion, and full of anecdote and information. Now he pointed to a craig in the far distance occupied by the Kakhyen hamlet of Kyoungtoung, which we presently came to, and found to comprise nine houses of the usual type. It was approached by a *cul-de-sac :* we halted here a few minutes beneath a *zizyphus* tree, the fruit of which all commenced to gather. The place was almost deserted, the inhabitants being out harvesting. At a distance of some two miles further on, we left to our west a small group of buildings known as Kottar, inhabited by recent settlers, who were still busy clearing and constructing terraces for cultivation. Mantat, the next Kakhyen village, met *en route*, is one of considerable size and importance. We were detained here some little time, while our guide called on the *Tswabwa* to demand the tusks of an elephant his clan had wounded within his limits some months ago, and ultimately tracked up and killed within the Kowkar Tswabwaship last week. This placed us in rather an awkward position, for it was probable that we might have been drawn into the dispute, and indeed it almost appeared as though Acheenoung had brought us this way for the express purpose of assistance. Fortunately, the *Tswabwa* was not at home, and although his wife, family, and *Pomine* were present, and the elephant's tusks rested against the posts of the verandah, yet it not being customary with these people during an unsettled dispute to enter one another's houses in the absence of the male proprietor, I was glad to find the matter had to lie over for future discussion. Mantat was once the seat of the *Ayandoomar* clan, who, after a blood-feud extending over three years, were finally defeated and ousted ; they have since established themselves on the banks of the river in a village bearing the name of the clan. Certainly, Mantat is the largest and most flourishing Kakhyen village I had yet seen : it numbers some forty substantially built houses, and allowing each house contained thirty inhabitants, the population would have amounted to 1,200. Besides the usual ornamentation in the form of animals' skulls and trophies of a similar nature, the *Tswabwa's* house was decorated with bamboo appointments. At the four corners of the building were carved open-work bamboo bells, suspended by a chain of the same material cut out of a single culm, and finished off with a sort of coronet and fibrous fringe also of bamboo. The day was fast drawing to a close, and our guide proposed taking a short cut, which meant proceeding in a straight line up the face of a very steep ascent; this brought us to the head waters of the Mansah-choung, and continuing our course in a north-easterly direction along the main water-shed of the mountains just ascended, Mansing village was reached : it is situated on a bluff at an elevation of 3,300 feet. Here I noticed a pretty little Kakhyen girl dyeing some home-spun thread blue, with a decoction of equal parts of the leaves of *Ruellia indigafera* and *chavannesia esculenta*. The ladle with which she baled out the dye was the section of a bottle-gourd (*Lgenaria vulgaris*) cultivated as a vegetable ; this she very good-naturedly gave me in return for the bead necklet I had presented her with. Both the plants use for dyeing are common in these mountains, and now for the first time I learnt from Yan Sing, that the latter is not only common in the forests of British Burma, but that it is likewise cultivated for its fruit, which has an agreeable acid taste, and is used by the Burmans for culinary purposes.* On the out skirts of Kantsat, where we remained for the night, there was a Kakhyen burial ground, the graves were marked by mounds of earth, and the tombs of those still fresh in the memory of their friends had a roof put over them, and decorated with bamboo ornaments. The cemetery was overgrown with plants of the *zingiberaceæ* order—they being the only class the leaves of which can be utilized for votive offerings. Kantsat at the time of our arrival was in a most disturbed state ; there were two disputes pending settlement,—one, on account of a wife that had not been paid for, and the other, connected with the deaths of three of this clan who had recently been shot in an engagement with some other tribe. Further, I was now informed for the first time that we were beyond the Koukwar Tswabwa's limits, and that in visiting Kantsat without previous warning, we were looked upon as trespassers and intruders. Although myself and party had been taken to the *Tswabwa's* house, and had received a cordial welcome from the womenfolk, yet the *Tswabwa* not only declined to see me, but sent word to say that I could have come with no good object in view, and that none of us should leave the village alive : his old mother, however, tried to smooth matters by assuring us that there was nothing to be feared, that her son was merely under the influence of liquor, but that when sober he would relent of his rudeness, and only be too glad to form our acquaintance. This was all very well, but I was not at all certain what outrage he might commit in his drunken fit, neither were we strong enough to defend ourselves. My Burman peons suggested an immediate retreat and concealment in the jungles for the night ;

---

* For the further uses to which this plant is put, I must refer the reader to my Note on *Caoutchouc*.

this, however, I would not hear of, and gave them clearly to understand that, if things came to the worst, and we had to fight for our lives, I should unhesitatingly shoot the first man who showed the white feather. Dinner was now placed before us, and for the first time my people were off their feed, it was quite evidently the fate that awaited us if attacked, for the cowardly curs were simply paralyzed with fear, and their voices trembled as they spoke. Both Yan Sing and myself endeavoured to cheer them up; but it was in vain, they would not be fortified, and only replied " what is the use of stopping here to risk our lives?" The whole village was by this time a regular pandemonium, and the forest echoed again with the wild shouts of the drunken crowd, as they kept chasing one another about with lighted torches; beating drums and gongs in every direction, and discharging guns recklessly: two bullets passed through the house we occupied, and one unpleasantly near to where I sat. About midnight, our guide came and told us that the *Tswabwa* had directed the *Meetway* to consult the *nâts* regarding our final disposal, and that we had better leave our things and bolt without delay. Such a move I saw was simply impracticable, for the house was surrounded by men mad with drink, and to have attempted to run the gauntlet must have resulted in the massacre of us all; so I resolved to brave it out to the last.

261. About an hour later on, the maniacal cries and writhing of the *Metway* could be distinctly heard, but fortunately the *Tswabwa* by this time was dead drunk, and the rest of the party too inebriated to take any part in restoring the soothsayer to his right senses, so he was left to bring himself round, and retain, for his exclusive benefit, the decision revealed by the *nâts*. Things now gradually cemmenced to quiet down, and by early dawn, peace reigned supreme—thus terminated one of the most anxious nights I had ever spent.

262. *Friday, 23rd January 1874.*—Day dawned to find us still awake: the thermometer read 39°, and my peons were huddled round the embers of last night's fire; while Yan Sing and myself sat nose and knees together waiting for results. Truly time hung heavily for the last few hours; but I must be thankful that I am alive to chronicle events. As the sun rose, our prospects appeared to brighten; the little warblers gladdened us with their merry notes, the womenfolk proceeded with their domestic duties, and even my disconsolate peons cracked a joke at last night's misfortune. At eight o'clock I ventured to go outside to look around me; and, following some women on their way to fetch water, reached a mountain stream where I refreshed myself with a wash. The girls were not scared by my presence, but rather regarded me a desirable acquaint-

ance, and assisted in the collection of some *Podostemon* and *Lohit campanula*, for which we had to climb steep rocks : they also gathered some *Thunbergia laurifolia* and *Clematis*, both now in flower, with the slender stems and graceful foliage of which they decorated my hat on their descent. Returning to the village, I found Yan Sing in a great state of distress ; for I had left the house with the intention of returning in a few minutes, and my long absence led him to imagine I had been killed.

263. Acheenoung now put in, an appearance smiling from ear to ear, and looking none the worse for his last night's debauch : he patted me familiarly on the back, and remarked all was right ; the *Tswabwa* and his sons intended calling, but I was not to refer to last night's affair, but receive them in a friendly manner. Regarding the presents I proposed to distribute, he suggested I be silent, as he would refer to them when explaining the object of our visit: accordingly, when the *Tswabwa* and his sons arrived, I was all smiles and politeness ; the former apologized for his conduct of last night, and explained that he was much annoyed with Acheenoung bringing us here uninvited, and that, being under the influence of liquor, he did not know what he was doing. Now that he had learnt from our guide I was not evilly disposed towards Kakhyens, and would not bring about their destruction by cursing the ground on which I trod as my relations had done years ago,* he was glad to make my acquaintance and secure my friendship. The usual eating and drinking part of the entertainment being over, I distributed a few presents, and invited the Chief and his villagers to the proposed entertainment at Talo.

264. He accepted, but said all his clan could not be present, as they were busy getting in their crops, though he would bring with him as many as could be spared. Curiosity now led me to enquire the contents of the silver tinselled box in the corner of the room we occupied, and to my disgust, I found it contained the corpse of the *Tswabwa's* brother, who had died three months ago : this amply accounted for the unpleasant scent I had noticed on first entering the house. Accompanied by the *Tswabwa*, his sons, and a few other of the male community, I took a walk round the village to note the different crops cultivated ; in some instances, they had been reaped, but in every case there were sufficient traces left to identify them. There was paddy, wheat, maize, cotton, roselle, chillies, poppies, egg-plant, gourds, beans, and potatoes,

---

* This is the second time allusion has been made to the land-slips spoken of by Dr. Anderson at page 366 of his report of the *Expedition to Western Yunan*.

the latter having been grown from tubers obtained from Mogoung which were about twice the size of walnuts. The poppy is grown solely for its narcotic principle : it was flowering now, and the capsules are operated on with a *dah* a month or so later. The flowering annuals, the seeds of which must, at one time or another, have been imported, were—*Iberis, Odorata, Althæa, Gomphrena glabbosa, Impatiens balsamina, Amaranthus, Celosia cristata, Datura alba,* and *Tagetes erecta.* In honour of the deceased brother of the Tswabwa, we were asked to fire a *feu de joie* before parting ; this terminated the interview, but the Chief insisted on his two sons accompanying us to Talo. The younger, a lad of about ten years old, was a charming little fellow ; we became great friends, and he expressed a wish to be allowed to remain with me. Following the mountain ridge for another six miles, we commenced to descend in a westerly direction; all declivities were covered at a most rapid pace, resulting in many a fall. Once on the trot, and the pace gradually increased to full speed, until we found we could only stop ourselves by laying hold of some tree, round which we unavoidably swung with the impetus of the pace. Some of the cliffs it was impossible to descend on foot, and these we slipped down on our hams. After five hours' hard walking over hills and precipitous ravines, we reached the summit of the last hill we had to descend. It was too dark to continue on, so we lighted fires and bivouaced here. There was a heavy dew throughout the night, and at 3 A.M. the thermometer stood at 42°.

265. *Saturday, 24th January 1874.*—Started at 6 A.M.; thermometer 41° ; spent a miserable night, for it was too cold to sleep, and the irritation caused by the long awns and husked seed of the spear-grass, that had worked its way through my trowsers and stockings, was horridly annoying. *En route,* a nest of earth-bees was dug up, and specimens of the wax and insects collected. The Kakhyens put this to various uses, and, among others, it serves as a protection to the flash-pan of their match-lock in rain. Acheenoung here drew the attention of one of my peons to an *Urtica,* who unsuspiciously plucked some leaves, and, Burman-like, at once tasted and smelt them, when the practical joke was soon rendered apparent by the stinging microscopic hairs of this nettle, and the Kakhyens had a good laugh at his ignorance. In little over an hour, we had reached the foot of the hill and followed a track that runs parallel with the Nan-ma-lee *choung* which disgorges itself at Talo. Judging from its breadth at the mouth, this appears a tributary of considerable size ; yet it is nothing more than a mountain torrent and unnavigable, excepting in the height of the rains, when I am told it can be ascended for some thirty to forty

miles by boats of ordinary size. The valley is identical with that described at the set-out of our journey.

266. The burning of grass in the plains had already commenced, and it is anything but agreeable walking through the smoky atmosphere loaded with charred particles; not only do the eyes suffer, but fits of sneezing or coughing are brought on, which are most tiresome. Before reaching Talo, a narrow *nullah* of about 30 feet had to be crossed, on a single bamboo pole propped up in three places. The Kakhyens and my people went over bare-footed with no difficulty, but to me the feat did not seem so easy, and, as I expected I lost my balance half way, and tippled over into five feet of water,—this was grand fun for my followers; however, I was not long in scrambling up the opposite bank, and joining in the laugh at myself. We got back to our boats about 3 P.M., and found the river-bank lined with over a hundred Kakhyens, who had come to the entertainment promised them. It was too late to prepare a meal to night, so the dinner was postponed until the next day. On registering the exact number, I found there were a hundred and thirty-three men, women, and children; none of these had come empty-handed, in fact, it was a case of a sprat to catch a salmon. An old half-witted Shan-Burman woman of Talo now forced her way into my presence, and, in a most excited state, begged that I would not confine my charity to the Kakhyens, but remember herself and family, who were poor and in need of assistance. A few silver bits soon quieted the old thing, and we got rid of her. Although my little ramble for the last four days had been attended with difficulties and privations, yet I thoroughly enjoyed myself; indeed, a tramp through the gloomy mountain homes of these aboriginal people, cannot fail to leave its impression, and increase one's stock of knowledge, though the intellects of those among whom we roam be inferior to our own. The Kakhyens are in some respects but one remove from the savage, yet in others they display an intelligence which more than counterbalances their ignorance.

267. My limited experience leads to the belief that they are by no means so low in the scale of humanity as they are generally classed. In all dealings I had with them, they were honest, and when in their sober senses, cheerful, kind, and hospitable, displaying also other desirable characteristics, which go to prove that, with a very little trouble, this tribe might be moulded into a rational, well-conducted people. Strange to say, I did not see a single pony east of the Irrawaddy after leaving Talo, all inland traffic at this season being carried on with mules, bullocks, or buffaloes. The

latter are also employed for all agricultural purposes, their natural habits better suiting them for the work than bullocks, who knock up ploughing through fields knee-deep in slush and mud. In the hills, I have come across some most noble specimens of the domestic buffalo far larger even than those magnificent animals found with the Todas of the Neilgherries; they have to be avoided however, for their forest life preserves them almost in a wild state. The class of cart used in the plains corresponds with the solid-wheeled vehicle met with in British territory. The following is a list of that portion of my collection of trees, shrubs, ferns, and grasses with which I was familiar, the remainder were unknown to me, and must be published at some future time when they can be identified—*Quercus, Castanea, Acanthaceæ, Kaulfussia, Alsophila, Pentaptera, Magnolia, Fici* (exclusive of *Ficus elastica*), *Begonia laurine, Dicksonia, Cedrela toona, Dipterocarpus, Gordonia, Elæocarpus, Guttiferæ, Megola, Smithea, Careya, Phyllanthus, Dillenia, Emblica, Arbutus, Hoya, Shorea, Davallia, Büttneria, Podostemon, Smilax, Brakes* (some seven feet high), *Calami, Viola patrinii, Musa, Phrygnium, Ixora, Poederia, Panicum, Plantago, Daphne, Rubus* (near villages), *Strutheoloides, Arum, Grewia* (two varieties), and *Urtica nivea; Saccharum officinarum* was also common. My diet of the last few days brought on an attack of dysentery, for which the stewed chillies were to blame I believe, for I remember Captain Strover cautioned me against eating many of them as being conducive to this disease.

268. *Sunday, 25th January 1874.*—Rose at 6 A.M.; thermometer, 45°. Took a constitutional, and bagged some painted partridge, jungle fowl, and *Carpophaga sylvatica*; also saw numbers of ducks and geese, but could not get a shot. On my return, found a snake (*Calamaria monticola*) had been killed in my cabin, which measured two feet four inches. The next few hours were spent in receiving and making presents. The same precedence had to be observed in entertaining the Kakhyens, and accepting their gifts as was followed when visiting them. It was no easy matter to keep these inquisitive people from swamping my boat altogether, for, eager to see the interior arrangement of my cabin, they pressed on in such numbers that I clearly saw that, unless I received them on land, there would be an accident; accordingly, I established myself on the bank beneath a large umbrella, and the Tswabwas sat beside me. The business of giving and receiving presents being at an end, I returned to my boat for breakfast; but even then I was not left alone, and was compelled at last to satisfy their curiosity by turning the boat bow on to shore, and throw open the front door for their general edification. Returning to my umbrella, where large supplies of *pán-suparee*, lime, and tobacco had already been laid out on plantain leaves for

public use, I astonished my guests with a musical-box, galvanic battery, and sleight-of-hand tricks.

269. The musical-box seemed to please them very much, and several attempts were made to feel the teeth on the barrel, when I opened the glass cover to give a better idea of the rapidity with which the fly-wheel revolved. The galvanic shocks, however, had rather an intimidating effect, especially when I put on extra power for the benefit of a young fellow, who pluckily came forward to show that he was proof against the influence of the *nât*; a couple of shocks soon made him cry *peccavi*, and I was asked never again to use it. They begged that on no account I open the box for fear of the *nât* escaping and doing them some bodily injury. I made no attempt to remove the delusion, as I thought perhaps it might rather have a beneficial effect than otherwise. Next came the *legerdemain* part of the performance; this crowned my fame, and the crowd prostrated themselves at my feet: had I been so disposed, I might have even eclipsed Brigham Young in vice, for both mothers and fathers were anxious to present me with a daughter as a votive offering, and gain my blessing in return; the former offer I declined, but their latter desire I bountifully contributed to. Another and very important part of the entertainment had now to be seen to—the circulation of liquor. There was some difficulty in meeting the demand, for although the whole of the liquor that had been presented me had been carefully stored up for this occasion, yet there was not sufficient for more than a third of the party; the deficiency had therefore to be made up after a prescription of my own, consisting of twice the quantity in water of their own brew, beer six bottles, brandy one, gin one, spirits of wine one, painkiller one, and one of essence of ginger. The combination proved a success, and the *Tswabwas* pronounced it excellent, and asked for a few bottles to take away with them. The poorer of the party were arranged in line; and dinner, consisting of boiled rice and pork curry, served out to them on plaintain leaves: the *Tswabwas* and their relations were seated separately on mats, and allowed plates to feed off; with this the entertainment ended.

270. I now visited the hpoongyee; he expressed delight at my safe return, and after a long conversation about the mountaineers, and the probability of the re-opening of the old trade route to Western China from here, he desired Yan Sing to ask me to call again later on in the evening. I went over about 11 P.M., and found him seated alone counting his beads. He cautioned me to be very careful after leaving this, saying he had received information that there were a party of Kakhyens determined on revenge, for having been fired at by the late Mr. Graham, and that it was just as likely as not,

they would avenge themselves on me instead. From enquiry I found the band consisted of the gold-washers I met a little above the Mogoung river, some of whom Mr. Graham fired at and wounded with large shot imagining they were dacoits.

271. After being asked to send him from Rangoon a musical-box, a pair of white rabbits, some yellow cloth, and a pair of gaiters, I wished him good-bye, and expressed my obligation for his polite attention, and especially for the young *Ficus elastica* tree he had presented me with.

272. Purchased three peacock-pheasants (alive) for two rupees; this bird is common in these latitudes, and easily snared with a decoy bird, which most of the Kakhyens keep. Talo exports south annually in considerable quantities *indway*,* *pwaingyet*,† paddy, til-seed, and cotton.

273. *Monday, 26th January 1874.*—At 6 A.M. thermometer, 46°. Just as I was about to start, the hpoongyee sent for me, to obtain my name and address in writing. The monastery was crowded with Kakhyens, so I took the opportunity of asking the names of the *Tswabwas* and their *Pomines*, with a view to testing the truthfulness of the information already supplied me. These people have a great aversion to giving their names or address, for various suspicious reasons; but apparently I had gained their confidence, for they had given me theirs correctly in the first instance. As a parting gift I gave each *Tswabwa* a warm coat of mine, and their *Pomines* a coloured flannel shirt a-piece. I left Talo at 9 A.M., the bank was lined with crowds of Kakhyens to see me off, and much to my surprise as we were leaving our moorings they fired a *feu de joie*, which we returned. About 2 P.M. there was a heavy shower of rain accompanied by thunder. Passing the Nan-ma-lee *choung* either side of the river presented a pebbly beach, and the valley retained the character noted below Talo.

274. The Nantabet *choung* is the next tributary on the left bank met with; at its junction with the Irrawaddy is situated the village of Nyoungbintha, partly inhabited by Shan-Burmans and partly by Kakhyens; the houses of the former are enclosed within a bamboo palisade, and separated from the latter by a narrow ravine; here we made fast for the night. The guide provided by the Go-vernor brought down word to say, that the Kakhyens had only returned from a pillaging expedition night before last, and expected to be attacked themselves to-night; and suggested the advisability of anchoring some little distance from the bank,

---

* *Indway* is the gum that exudes from the *Shorea* (*robusta* ?).
† *Pwaingyet* is the wax of the bee *Trigona læviceps*, that builds in the hollows of *Shorea* (*robusta* ?).

which we did. I had not laid down many minutes when a volley of stones were thrown at my boat; some struck the wall of my cabin, and others fell short and dropped into the water. This awoke Yan Sing, who came and warned me to be prepared for action, and then went to awake the people in the other boats, reminding them of the instructions I had already issued; which were, that no one was to expose himself above the gunwale of the boats, nor fire a shot until the word of command had been passed by me. Three shots were now fired from the bank, the bullets striking into the water some few yards beyond Yan Sing, who foolishly stood at the bow of the boat with a bull's eye lantern in his hand. The next shot passed through my cabin, smashing the lantern on the table, where but a few minutes before I had stood arranging my cartridges; the following three shots appeared to have been directed at Yan Sing, for a bamboo, which was within a few inches of him, was struck in two places, and the third bullet whizzed by sufficiently near, to make him drop his lantern as though he had been killed. It was evident now that they were bent on mischief, for the repeated warnings we gave through the Kakhyen interpreters were received with jeers and laughter. I fired six shots, at intervals of a minute or so in the direction of the village, for it was too dark to see the enemy; after my third shot two were returned without effect, but my next three silenced them; and this ended the affair. No one was killed on either side, I am glad to say. After order had been restored, for, perhaps, ten minutes or more, I noticed my boat being canted; this, together with the splashing of water alongside, at once led to the idea that an attempt was being made to board us, and seeing a man wringing wet endeavouring to clamber over the side, there seemed little reason to doubt who he was; another second, and our old guide would have been no more had he not that very instant given his name. Poor old fellow, fright had suggested this novel idea as the safest mode of retreat during the skirmish. Immediately the first shot had been fired, he jumped into the water and lay alongside that part of the boat furthest from the shore, supporting himself by one hand on the gunwale. He remained the butt of our party ever since.

275. *Tuesday, 27th January 1874.*—At 6 A.M., a dense fog; thermometer, 47°. Still at Nyoungbintha, waiting for Moung Gynet, who had been despatched from Talo across country to a village some twenty miles up the Nantabet *choung*, where it had been reported there were numbers of *Ficus elastica* growing. It was my intention to have proceeded there by boat; but on arrival here I found there was not sufficient water. The *choung* at the mouth, though a hundred and fifty yards wide, merely contains two feet of water.

During the rains, it is reported navigable for large boats to a distance of ninety miles, and is the route by which the interior is transported to the Irrawaddy.

276. Either bank is populated both by Kakhyens and Shans, who cultivate, to some considerable extent, *til*-seed, paddy, and cotton. At 10 P.M., I went up into the village, accompanied by my guide, a Kakhyen interpreter, and Yan Sing, to inquire into the reason of the attack last night. I was informed that the assault was not committed by any of the villagers, but by the Kazar Kakhyens who had come to wage war with them : it was prudent here to make a virtue of a necessity, and accept their explanation, but I gave them to understand that a repetition of such conduct would result in my storming and burning down their village.

277. My people amused themselves by making pipe-bowls, little utensils of sorts, and statuette caricatures of my guide Moung Oung from a blue clay that forms a strata of the river-bank here. The Burmese are very natty with their fingers, and, like the Chinese, their organs of imitation and colour are strongly developed, but they are wanting in originality. A peon, I picked up at Myanoung, proved to be a skilful carver, and his idle hours were spent in carving cocoanut-shells for me. The designs represented a combination of the vegetable and animal kingdom ; the signs of the zodiac forming a belt round the centre, and the whole finished off with a silver rim and neat little pedestal ; these vessels answer a number of purposes, among other they can either be used as sugar-bowls or salt cellars, a difference in the depth of the shell only being required. The open carved ones, lined with silver, have also a very pretty effect. Samples of tea said to be grown by the Ḳakhyens, west of the Irrawaddy, were brought me to-day ; the leaves appeared smaller and of a better quality than those I saw at Bhamo ; but I am a poor judge in such matters, never having seen what really constitutes a good specimen of this plant. The green leaves, I was told, undergo no proper system of curing, they are simply dried and compressed in hollow bamboos, from which a slice is cut off when required, the wall peeled off, and the beverage prepared in the usual manner. Heard that the Kakhyens had sacrificed a fowl, and directed their Meetway to place himself in communication with the spirits to ascertain the future safety of the village. The *nâts* declared an evilly-disposed person was amongst them, and that the further immolation of a pig was necessary for their welfare: it was whispered, I was the evil genius. Moung Gnet returned in a canoe, accompanied by the Pomine and four other Kakhyens of Lakwah village. They had been sent by the Tswabwa in charge of presents, consisting of a tiger-skin, some vegetables, and liquor, and a request to visit him, and

assist in the protection of his village, which had been threatened with an attack from the powerful Oolone clan to the north. I declined the invitation, under an excuse of want of time, but reciprocated his expressions of friendship, and sent him a few pieces of cloth in return for his presents. Moung Gnet stated that things had already assumed a most warlike aspect, Lakwah had been enclosed by a treble bamboo stockade, and that a hundred men (thirty Shans and seventy Kakhyens) had arrived from Thanay, a village to the south, to assist in the engagement; he further added every preparation had been made for my reception, and in token of his esteem and good feeling, the Tswabwa had bound himself to sacrifice a buffalo on my arrival, and drink a portion of the blood with me after washing our swords in the gore. This peculiar system of sealing friendship is common with these mountaineers.

278. The enmity between these people extended over five years, the *casus belli* being the non-fulfilment of a monetary obligation undertaken by the Oolone Tswabwa, but the exact nature of the transaction I could not clearly ascertain. It appears that I had been misinformed regarding the existence of *Ficus elastica* anywhere down this *choung*; the tree is not even known to the people in this vicinity. The shooting here was capital; painted partridge, peacock, jungle-fowl, peacock-pheasants, and hares being common in the cotton-fields; and up a backwater I bagged a *Spatula clypeata, Querquedula crecca, Ceryle rudis, Dendrocygna arcuata,* and *Plotus melanogaster.* *Urocissa occipitalis* continued to be seen, but I spared him, having already three specimens of this lovely magpie, and he was no use for the pot. I also shot a porcupine, a leopard-cat, and an elk (*Russa hippelaphus.*) In the fields I noted *Oxalis corniculata, Corchorus capsularis, Triumfetta, Melochia, Corchorifolia,* and *Pintapetes phœnicca;* the poppy is also extensively cultivated. I presented the Tswabwa of Nyoungbintha and his son, and the Pomine and his son, with white and red *goung-boungs* respectively. To the head-man of the Shan portion of the community, I gave a piece of white cloth. The night passed off quietly.

279. *Wednesday, 28th January 1874.*—At 6 A.M. thermometer 47°; up to 8 A.M. a dense fog, when we left our moorings. For the next few miles, the banks are of alternate layers of yellow and blue clay, the hills continue to run parallel with the stream at a distance of some miles, the water is beautifully clear, and the bed of the river covered with pebbles of all shades and colours, the current increasing in strength, and the channel narrowing to a hundred feet. We were now hailed by a band of some fifty Kakhyens asking if we had any goods to barter, but we took no notice of them, and passed on. A little further on, is a group of Shan

houses, where my people exchanged salt for some sun-dried venison To the west, the mountains give off a spur known as the *Natsay* hills reaching to the water's edge, and running parallel with the stream, which now takes a north-east and south-west course.

280. They bear the sterile aspect of the undulating country in the vicinity of the earth-oil wells at Yenanjaum, the plants of the *Euphorbiaceæ cactaceæ*, and *Capparidaceæ* orders being the most common : a few fossils were collected. The barren appearance of these hills is rendered more conspicuous by the densely-wooded country by which they are surrounded. There is a legend attached to that portion of the spur which sends up two conically-shaped little hills, called Moung-na-mar, signifying brother and sister. It is supposed that these two committed a felony, and were then and there converted into stone. This account savours somewhat of the fate that befell Lot and his wife. The wild rose and raspberry still gladdened us with their presence, and the low alluvial banks are over-grown with *Calamus*, *Cæsalpinia Sepiaria*, and *Saccharum spontaneum*; the arborescent growth being represented by *Bombax*, *Shorea*, and *Terminalia*. Shot some *Chalcophaps indica* and *Carpophaga sylvatica* ; snippet, ouzel, brahminee-duck, and *mina* are common. Made fast for the night at a sand-bank.

281. *Thursday, 29th January 1874.*—At 6 A. M., thermometer 48° ; dense fog up to 8-30 A.M., when we started. Passed a group of Kakhyen houses on the left bank, established below a magnificent *Ficus glomerata* ;́ the hills to the west are gradually nearing the river's bank, and continue to be mantled densely with trees. Hailed a fisherman's boat and bartered quarter of a pound of tobacco for four large *gobio* (red-eyed gudgeon). The fishermen were Shan-Burmese, and were also prepared to exchange their fish for pieces of silver : the price fixed being equivalent to about an anna a viss ; their scales are on the principle of the steel-yard—a bamboo graduated by notches substituting the *steel-yard;* on this slides a stone suspended by a string which registers the weight ; just below the indicator is suspended a basket for the convenience of the article to be weighed. Kakhyen houses in twos and threes along the bank were becoming more common, and the numerous scars and sword-cuts that disfigure the men were sufficiently on the increase to attract attention, and pointed to the disturbed state of the country. A range of mountains sending up a sugar-loafed peak, which had hitherto served as a land mark, became more apparent to-day, and a second peak was now distinguishable ; but from the sinuosity of the river it was difficult to say on which bank they were. Made fast for the night at the Kakhyen village of Sankah. There was a dispute going on here between these people and a party of mountaineers from the Mogoung Districts. The quarrel was about the Shan por-

tion of this community having left their homes on the right bank, and sought the protection of this village. The reason for their flight was that they had been robbed of all their buffaloes, and a heavier black-mail levied than they could meet. The Kakhyens from Mogoung demanded their immediate return, but the Tswabwa of Sankah declined to give them up, stating that war would be declared at once if the buffaloes were not returned. With those familiar with these people, however, the popular opinion was that the matter would eventually be decided by arbitration, and the spoil divided between the two mountain tribes and the Shans. Heard that the day after we had passed Shweyin a trader had been robbed, his boat destroyed, the boatmen killed, and he himself compelled to swim for his life.

282. *Friday, 30th January 1874.*—A beautiful, clear, fresh morning; started at 6 A. M.; thermometer, 43°. Some two miles further up, stopped for a few minutes at a sand-bank: the fresh dung and pugs of tigers were seen, but nothing of the animals. This formed the apex of a permanent island over a mile long and densely wooded with large trees. Gold-washing is also carried on here, and it is generally understood that the Kakhyens learnt this process from the Chinese, with whom they traded in jade long before the Burmese knew the value of the stone. A specimen of *Agathis loranthifolia* was brought me, for which I presented a bottle. The wood is so hard, that it can be substituted for nails, and it is supposed to possess some charm which wards off harm from the happy possessor; even among the Burmans in British territory, it is driven into house posts to avert the evil eye. Arrived at Katcho at 2·30 P.M.: this is a large Shan-Burman and Shan-taloke village, numbering a hundred and fifty houses enclosed in a double bamboo stockade and situated on the river-bank which is fourteen feet high, ascended by a ladder consisting of a log of wood notched for steps; beneath is a shelving, pebbly shore. The inhabitants said they do not fear the Kakhyens, and have repulsed them on every occasion a raid has been committed: opposite is the island of Zeeghoon, where Moung Sain, an *amat* of the Mogoung District resides. I was told that he is a nobleman by birth, and that his appointment is hereditary. I sent Yan Sing to call on him and show His Majesty's order to the Governor of Mogoung, sanctioning my travelling through his district: I also expressed a hope of seeing the *amat*. Received a verbal reply, saying he would call on me the next to day. Found that Mr. Graham had established two brokers here, and provided them with cloth, twist, thread, &c., to barter for rubber, amber, ivory, jade, and so on. The channel that separates Zeeghoon from Katcho is about a hundred yards wide, and the highest rise up to date

had not exceeded twelve feet. To the north-east of the village, without the stockade there are seven fine specimens of *Ficus elastica* and two of *F. glomerata*. They were the most healthy specimens I had yet come across; mainly accountable to their never having been tapped; orders, however, had this year been received from the capital to collect the juice. Cocoanuts are grown to some extent both on the main land and island; they are reported to fruit abundantly. Katcho evidently is of some antiquity, but no reliable information can be gathered as to the exact date when it was founded; nor is any substantial data forthcoming regarding the *Ficus elastica*; some say that they are self-sown, and others, that they were planted here as offerings to the *náts* some seventy years ago, when Katcho was first established. The type of buildings is identical with the present class of architecture, and is therefore valueless for any chronological purpose. The following measurement represents the dimensions of the three finest specimens:—

No. 1.—Height ... ... 130 feet.
Circumference of space occupied by crown ... 750 ,,
Ditto trunk ... ... 95 ,,
Ditto inclusive of aërial roots ... 139 ,,
No. 2.—Height ... ... 118 ,,
Circumference of space occupied by crown ... 697 ,,
Ditto trunk ... ... 89 ,,
Ditto inclusive of aërial roots ... 127 ,,
No. 3.—Height ... ... 115 ,,
Circumference of space occupied by crown ... 639 ,,
Ditto trunk ... ... 81 ,,
Ditto inclusive of aërial roots ... 135 ,,

283. *Katcho.—Saturday, 31st January 1874.* Thermometer 42° at 6 A.M. Cold, north-easterly wind throughout the day, accompanied by passing showers. The *amat* called, and presented me with a dish of betel-leaf and *suparee*-nuts; and in return I gave him a piece of muslin, some matches, and scent; he asked also for some gunpowder, which I added to his presents. He is a fine, tall, athletic man, though remarkably dark for a Burman; his general conversation, mode of expression, and manners lead to the idea that he is a shrewd, intelligent man of business; he speaks of the tribes within his district as being treacherous, deceitful, and troublesome; but says, he finds that kindness, blended with firmness, is the form of government best suited to them. The overland route to Mogoung he gives as follows:—

From here to Archay, one day ... ... 10 miles.
Archay to Tapau, ditto ... ... 25 ,,
Tapau to Thapone, ditto ... ... 18 ,,
Thapone to Mogoung, ditto ... ... 10 ,,

According to this, I found our charts wrong: the Mogoung river takes a more easterly course, and the Irrawaddy lies more to the west. The physical characteristics of the country through which this line passes is described as mountainous, intersected by valleys cultivated with paddy and *til*, and peopled by a tribe of mountaineers known as the Kantee Kakhyens. I gave him a sketch of my plans, and begged his assistance in procuring coolies and a guarantee of a safe through route, both of which he promptly promised, adding that I will find no difficulty in accomplishing the journey, as the road is practicable, the country in a settled state, and nothing of importance to impede progress. Amber can be procured in abundance at Minenah, he gave me to understand, and that the Kakhyens in the hills pay an annual tribute to the King, consisting of slaves, amber, and ivory, but that the inhabitants of the plains pay tax at twelve Rupees per house a year which is collected by himself and subordinates without any trouble. In the evening took a stroll along the pebbly beach and shot three floriken (*Sypheotides aurititus*), which I found among the tamarisk bushes and wild roses. On my return, I found an antelope had been brought for sale; it was shot in the hills to the east, where they are said to abound. The horns are supposed to possess some medicinal property; and ground down with water, are used as a salve in cases of *ophthalmia*—a disease prevalent in these parts. A single horn sells for five Rupees. As a substitute for earthen water-pots, hollow bamboos are used, four feet long; in the bottom is fixed a small wheel of about four inches diameter, which ingenious contrivance enables children of about six years old to fetch water; and it is amusing to see the little things dragging these heavy weights, riding cock-horse fashion to their homes, thus combining pleasure with labour.

284. *Sunday, 1st February 1874.*—A bleak, north-easterly wind still continued, and the thermometer read 45° at 6 A.M.; my boatmen were too doubled up with cold to start before 8 A.M. The character of the river and features of the country from here begin perceptibly to change: the current increases in rapidity, and the channel is blocked up here and there with white granite rocks over which the water rushes with a loud roar. Low, alluvial banks still continue, fronted by the dry, stony bed of the river, and the mountains were fast closing in on either side of us: cultivation was nowhere to be seen, and the stray hamlets met with were made up of groups of two or three huts occupied by Kakhyen squatters. Stopped at Mokelway for a few hours, and took a Kakhyen guide to explore the interior. The country is undulating and the base of the main mountain range at a rough guess I estimated to be twenty miles, the spurs, however, thrown off by it were less distant. The *Shorea* still continued to be the staple forest tree, but oaks

Mangolias, chestnuts, and *Toon* were likewise common; I also noticed *Broussonetia papyrifera*, *Daphne*, and a *Dodonæa*. The forest is likewise rich in *Epiphytical archideæ* and ferns, of which I made a large collection: bamboo of medium growth is also common. In the depth of this forest I came on the ruins of two old pagodas, but they were in too dilapidated a state to admit of any conclusion being drawn as to their original design; the brick and mortar, however, of such parts as still remain in tact are capital. On one of the bricks in the basement we made out, by the aid of my magnifying glass, "1167, 13th *Kussone*," but it is probable this brick had been planted, when repairing the pagoda some years after its erection. Here, for the first time, I may say, since my arrival in the province, I shot a jungle-cock with speckles on the neck and crop—an old, familiar friend of India. I also got a long shot at a tiger, but missed, much to the disgust of my guide. After making a few presents to the Kakhyens I started again, reaching Thagahya by 6 P.M. This is a Shan-Taloke village, situated at the mouth of a creek of the same name, spanned by a wooden bridge consisting of two planks of *sal* with hand-rails. Thagahya is enclosed by a double bamboo stockade, and numbers forty houses and a monastery occupied by three Shan-Burman phoongyees, who teach the boys reading and writing: situated at the back of the latter is a large *Ficus elastica*, which is now partly defoliated; it was planted by the original inhabitants of this village, who, two years ago, were plundered by the Kakhyens, and compelled to retreat across the river, and seek the protection of the mountaineers of that bank. The river here narrowing to about one hundred and fifty yards, overlaps its banks during the floods, and inundates the village, which has necessitated the construction of a viaduct raised three feet off the ground and running the entire length of the stockade, which is two hundred and thirty feet. To the east, large clearings have been effected for paddy and *til* cultivation. Here cabined bamboo rafts serve the purpose of boats where the women and children sleep at night, anchored in the middle of the river from dread of the Kakhyens, who come down in large bands and plunder and burn the villages, carrying off what human beings they can. Before turning in for the night, the headman of the village sent down word to say that I need not be alarmed at the report of guns throughout the night, as this was only a precautionary measure to show the Kakhyens that they were on the alert.

285. *Monday, 2nd February 1874.*—Thagahya and Winemew cloudy, and much warmer; thermometer, 55°. The *amat* from Zeeghoon arrived and informed us he had heard that the trader who

was robbed on his way up river, had been cautioned not to proceed on, as there was a band of dacoits lying in wait for a rich merchant, who was coming up from Bhamo with three boats of valuables. They evidently referred to myself and party. The love for gain, however, induced the trader to push forward, which resulted in the loss of both life and property.

286. I here had a most providential escape: as it was only by my boatmen refusing to hug the right bank on account of the rapidity of the current that we were not drawn into an engagement, for just after crossing to the opposite shore, I noticed a gang of some fifty men emerge from the jungle, but they did not engage further attention. The only matter of surprise is that these Kakhyens do not commit greater depredations, considering they have no one to fear. Cases of plunder and even murder, when reported to the Woon, are simply disposed of by a demand for blood-money from the Tswabwa of the offending tribe, who, on the other hand, sets forth a counterplea that his people were merely paying off an old grudge, eventually making what settlement he thinks fit. It had been my intention to diverge here and visit the hills to the east; but my guide, Moung Oung, refused to give his consent, owing to the disturbed state of the country, and the head-man of Thagahya having declined either to countenance the journey or furnish me with coolies or a guide. Started my boat at 10 A.M. for Winemew, proceeding myself by land, the distance not exceeding a mile and a half, though the route by water, owing to the tortuous windings of the river, is quadrupled. Here I was told Winemew is the last Shan-Burman village met with, and the most northerly point to which traders venture. The names of other hamlets were mentioned, but they are insignificant in size, and peopled by the Lapee tribes, who fear neither God nor man, and gain a livelihood by their swords. Winemew, which comprised some thirty houses, is protected by a strong barricade of stout timber, eight feet high, planted firmly in the ground, and a double outer walling of bamboos. It is situated on a high bank of yellow clay fronting the river, which does not exceed a hundred yards from shore to shore, while the expansive water at this season is not over a third of that breadth. To the west is a densely-wooded alluvial plain, extending to the base of the mountain, which is about two miles distant. Representatives of Mogul and Suratee firms of Bhamo are here to be seen, living on bamboo-rafts, with a small supply of chintze, twists, thread, beads, opium, and salt, which they barter for ivory, jade, rubber, amber, hides, and silver. The insecurity of their position is admitted; but the handsome profits they realize, seem a sufficient inducement to

make them risk their lives. They are tolerably strong in number, and well armed; and, as a further protection, pay black-mail to the chiefs of the more dangerous tribes for their safety. On the other hand, they say that the mountaineers also find it advantageous leaving them alone, thereby securing articles they are in need of, in exchange for their mountain produce. The late Mr. Graham, spoken of in my previous diaries, I found, had also appointed a broker here; and a Suratee merchant stated he had left instructions that rubber is hereafter to be regarded as a State monopoly, and that none but his broker is at liberty to purchase it. This order not only gave rise to ill-feeling and dissatisfaction, but likewise considerably enhanced the value of the staple. Strange to say that, although the inhabitants of this village have taken the precaution of securing to themselves safety from the attacks of highland bandits, by the erection of a substantial stockade, yet they have failed to clear the dense forest around them, which reaches to the very wall of the enclosure, over the top of which even some of the branches extend : yet at a distance of a mile further inland, clearings have been made for paddy and *til* culture, stretching almost to the base of the mountains, some four miles off. Another matter which points to the want of forethought on the part of these people is the presence of a tribe of Leesaws within the village, who are engaged in the manufacture of arms which are sold to the Kakhyens. These people seem to be a sub-branch of a Shan tribe whom they closely resemble in appearance, and whose customs, costume, and a dialect of their language they adopt. I note at page 136 of Dr. Anderson's report of the expedition to Western Yunan in 1866, he writes, regarding the Leesaws,—" *the most interesting circumstance connected with the Leesaws is the strong affinity of their language to the Burmese.*" This leads me to believe we are speaking of different people, as there was not the faintest trace of any similarity in their dialect to that of the Burmese. My Burmans could not trace a single word that resembled their mother-tongue.

287. To-day a message was brought me by a *panthay*, purporting to be from Hajee Syed Ebraham, a chief of this tribe, who had been compelled to retreat from Momein during the recent massacre, and was now encamped about two days' journey from here in a north-easterly direction. He was reported to have gained the assistance of the Kakhyens and Shan-talokes about him, and by whom he and the fragment of his army, numbering some hundred and fifty men, were gratuitously supported. The messenger stated that it was the intention of the chief, immediately he had sufficiently recruited his force with Shan-Talokes and Kakhyens, to march once again towards the scene of action, and re-establish himself, if possible.

288. I was further informed that Hajee Syed Ebrahim visited England with the embassy in 1872, and that he is a cousin of Tussacone, who befriended the expedition in 1868, in return for whose services he requested my presence and assistance, both of which I was forced to refuse.

289. News reached us this evening of the King's *dak* boat having been attacked at the mouth of the Mogoung river, but that the rebels were repelled, losing their guns and other arms; also that Hokah had been attacked and plundered with a loss of twenty lives, the dacoits only having lost one man. A reference to my diary of the 19th January 1874 shows that this village was not stockaded, the people having placed themselves under the protection of the Kakhyens;—the Tswabwa, in consideration of certain grants allowed him, having guaranteed to them safety. It now turned out, however, that the outrage was committed at the suggestion of the Tswabwa himself. This corroborates the practice referred to in my diary of the 20th January 1874.

290. The hot bed of disturbance at present appeared to be in the Moohaian District, where the Thainbows are reported to be a most uncontrollable lot. I had received no royal pass-port to travel through this district, though eventually I had to explore parts of it, as anticipated.

291. To the east of Winemew, and quarter of a mile beyond the stockade, are ten *Ficus elastica*, growing among the other forest trees at some distance apart. In size, and luxuriance of growth they rival even those noted at Katcho. This year for the first time they were to be tapped. No information was forthcoming regarding the origin or date of their birth, but it had been satisfactorily proved that all the rubber purchased here comes from the western forests, and that the tree is not known to the people of this side of the river. Defoliation had commenced. The peach likewise thrives here, and produces fruit plentifully, which the people eat, though it is not much in favour. From description it is of a flat variety, and the seed was first introduced by traders from the East. Here, also, I noticed an improvement in the canine tribe: the *pariah* of the village is not the sorry, miserable-looking beast hitherto met with, but a fine, noble, shaggy-haired dog, taking somewhat after the St. Bernard, though not quite so tall. I offered Rs. 30 for one, but the owner would not part with him. Here again, the river presents a floating village for the accommodation of women and children at night; firing is also kept up till early dawn, but with little good effect, considering that five buffaloes were reported to have been stolen last night from within the stockade. My followers ran short of rice, and although every effort had been

made to purchase some, the people refused to sell. They had, inconsequence, to make shift with the natural products of the forests, until a fresh supply of grain was obtained from Zeegoon.

292. *Tuesday, 3rd February 1874.*—Left Winemew at 9 A.M., cutting north-easterly wind; thermometer 43° at 6 A.M. There had been a rise in the river of two feet overnight. Morning spent in writing official and private letters, which I despatched to Bhamo by a Mahomedan trader. Tigers are very common in the vicinity. Their pugs are everywhere to be seen, and it is not at all uncommon to find fresh droppings round about the stockade of a morning. The Kakhyens shoot them for their flesh, which they eat, using their teeth as ornaments to their sword-belts or as charms; their claws they dispose of to Chinamen, who, I believe, also consider they possess some spell. Three miles above is Tahay which consists of three Kakhyen houses. The river is divided by the island of Noung Talo, partly overgrown by trees, among which I noted two cocoanuts. The stream to the right is about fifty yards wide, but too shallow even to admit of my boats passing up; that to the left is double the breadth, with six feet of water in the deepest part. We were now sufficiently near to fix the position of the two mountain peaks mentioned in my diary of the 29th January 1874. They lie in a North North-East direction, and the altitude has been fixed at 3,800 feet. The voice of the rapids are distinctly to be heard, and it was with difficulty we could make any way against the stream, which was now hourly increasing in strength. Mine-nah was made by dusk, and here we stopped for the night.

293. *Wednesday, 4th February 1874.*—Thermometer 40° at 6 A.M.; a dense fog continued to rise from off the water up to 8 A.M., when we left Mine-nah,—a Lapee hamlet situated on a high cliff overhanging the stream. Opposite are also a few houses known as Myet-kyee-nah, inhabited by the same tribe. The river increases in tortuosity, and the spurs of the great chain of mountains richly clad in forest growth reach to the water's edge. We now found ourselves passing up a noble gorge, whose romantic beauty cannot be surpassed, even in the annals of poetry itself. The hills echoed forth the wild cries of my boatmen, cheering one another on as they endeavoured to stem the fierce current, now purling over the rocky bed casting its spray on either side in wild delight, and washing our boats from stem to stern. Our progress was slow, and the pace continued to decrease, until the crew found it was hopeless any longer depending on their poles. They jumped overboard with their towing ropes, and renewed the struggle;—poor fellows, bent nearly double, and straining every muscle, it was as much as they could do, to creep along; Moung Oung, the Governor's man, suggested we halt

and return, but no—there was yet a little further distance to be accomplished, and I stimulated the boatmen by a promise of an extra day's pay all round. This had a good effect, and they buckled to their task with double vigour. Another couple of hours' labour brought us to Muntgoung; and here their troubles were at an end. Here the river divides into two great arms,—that to the east being considerably the larger, but the rapids forbid further progress, though for boats of lighter draft, I believe, the channel is navigable for miles further north. I found that Muntgoung and the last three hamlets were mere temporary abodes, having preserved the names of their permanent homes in the mountains. The Lapees are a clan of the Manloo branch of the great Thainbow tribe. In costume, customs, and mode of living, they are identical with the clan; but evidently they are poorer and much more filthy in their person, neither men nor women ever seemed to have combed their hair, which is cut square over the forehead, and at the back, allowed to hang in clotted masses about the shoulders. None of the women we met had jewellery of any sort, their adornments consisted of wood and grass ornaments manufactured by themselves. A marked peculiarity about this clan is that the women are tatooed in bands from the ankle to the knee; but not the men. The few hamlets we had noticed on the river's banks, were occupied by parties who had come to catch fish, which they smoke—dry, and take back to their homes. They both spear and net the fish, the former operation being performed at night by torch-light, which attracts the fish in large numbers, and render them easy prey; the netting process consists in holding a net (made from the twine of *urtica nivea*, which is common about here) across a portion of the rapid and temporarily damming up the remaining half with stones, which is also guarded by men with spears, who harpoon any fine specimen that attempts to fly the barricade in its struggles. Our boats had hardly been made fast when the whole of Mount Toung, armed up to the teeth, came to the river-bank; they seated themselves in a line, and remained perfectly quiet, apparently awaiting to see what would be our next move. They were not kept long in suspense, for I ordered a huge bonfire, round which we all sat chatting up to a very late hour: this I considered the wisest plan to divert their attention from mischief, for they looked ugly customers, and I should not have been surprised, had they troubled us before morning; at present they were all civility, and sent for nuts of a *castanea* for me, which they said grow within a stone's throw of us. They spoke of their homes as being three days' journey from here in a north-east direction, and described the climate as colder throughout the year than what it was here at this season, but they made no mention of snow, which perhaps may be attributable to our enquiries on this subject not being sufficiently intelligible to them. The next day, I arranged to take a trip into the interior, at which they seemed delighted, and promised me guides and coolies; however, as I purposed meeting my boats again, by evening, there was no necessity for the latter. It was reported that two men had been killed yesterday, when after a tiger, and that there was every probability of my getting a shot at more than one to-morrow; this conclusion was, no doubt, arrived at from the havoc committed by these beasts.

294. *Thursday, 5th February 1874.*—We were enveloped in fog up to 8 A.M., when the mist gradually cleared off; thermometer 44° at 6 A.M. I was anxious to watch the result of my boats shooting the most dangerous part of the rapids, and arranged to meet the *Lapces* at Minenah. The contrivance my boatmen adopted to prevent the boats descending with too great velocity was novel, but effectual. Midships, either side, they fastened long ropes to the boat with heavy boulders attached; these acted as a drag, and two men at the stern and two at the bow with bamboo poles regulated the course; but, although this ingenious precaution materially slackened the speed, yet we accomplished in fifteen minutes what took us yesterday over seven hours to perform against stream. I had to wait some little time at Minenah for my guides, but eventually they turned up, and I started on my inland excursion at 10·30 A.M. We proceeded in a southerly direction, until abreast of Winemew, then struck due west for that village, where I had arranged to meet my boats. There was no beaten track, but we continued in a zigzag manner over hills and valleys; the climbing in places was most difficult and fatiguing, and in many places we had to cut our way through the cane thickets. The vegetation remained unchanged; but, in addition to previous collections, I added many other specimens unknown to me. Here, also, I came across a quantity of the bamboo spoken of at page 14 as the Prince of Wales' feather*. My guides told me this variety extends high up in the hills to the east, and seemed curious to know why I was collecting some of the leaves and stems of such a common thing. At about one o'clock, as we were silently ascending the side of a hill, I felt a smart pull at my coat, and my attention was directed to a clump of bamboos on a small ridge some forty yards to our left: not a word was spoken, but my guide, in a bent attitude, pointed to the spot, where I saw just the head of a magnificent tiger resting on his fore-paws, steadily looking down on us. I took a shot, and the thud, and deep growl of the beast told me he was wounded,

---

* This bamboo, from my description, has been identified by Dr. Brandis as *Bamboosa regia*, from which all royal umbrella-handles are made.

though the crushing through the forest sounded like his retreat, and I gave up all hopes of the skin, for I had determined not to track the brute up, having once before, in India, been badly mauled by foolishly following up a wounded tiger on foot. The Lapaees, however, rushed off in a body before I could stop them, and in about ten minutes, returned with the tail of the animal, saying he lay dead but a short distance from where I fired ; I was glad he had been found, but it was very vexing the tail had been cut off, for it spoiled the value of the skin. He measured from tip to tip eleven feet two inches, and had a rich glossy coat of a deeper yellow than any I have shot in India. The operation of skinning detained us a couple of hours, and it was long after dark before I got back to my boats. I presented the four Lapaees, with new red *goung-boungs*, some shot and powder, and three Rupees each, with which they seemed well satisfied, and said if I would stop a few days and go up to their village, they would show me plenty of large game sport.

295. *Friday, 6th February 1874.*—Thermometer, 6 A.M., 49°. Left Winemew at 7, reaching Katcho by 8 A.M., where we remained engaged all day cutting slips of *Ficus elastica*, and planting them in little open-work bamboo baskets, filled with sand and leaf mould, which were sent down to Bhamo on a bamboo raft in charge of Moung Gnet. The raft cost five Rupees ; and I was told the bamboos would realize twenty Rupees in Bhamo, which was far in excess of the amount expended on the transport of the plants. I questioned whether the consignment would reach Rangoon alive, but the experiment was worth while trying. My attention was here drawn to a Shan-Burman woman carrying a white child, of about two years old, with blue eyes and red hair ; she proved to be the mother ; and the father, I was given to understand, is a Burman, who had recently been transported to Mogoung. The complexion of the child would not have struck me as anything uncommon two hundred miles further south, but in these latitudes the little fellow seemed rather a *rara avis*, and I was led to make careful enquiries as to the mother's antecedents, for it appeared probable the child might have been kidnapped ; her life, however, at Mandalay, from where she had recently come, sufficiently accounted for her son's European type of physiognomy. It had drizzled throughout the day, but this had not interfered with the cremation of a Shan-Burman on the island of Zeeghoon, opposite ; evidently the deceased was of a poor family, for the ceremony was not attended with any distinction. The corpse was simply packed in a pile of wood, round which his friends and relations stood until the pyre had been reduced to ashes. I sent word to the *Amat* that I intended crossing over to Zeeghoon the next day, and arrange

with him for my overland journey to Mogoung. Received some letters by a native trader, that had been sent me by the Assistant Resident of Bhamo.

296. *Saturday, 7th February 1874.*—Heavy thunder-storm and rain towards early morning; everything in my cabin got drenched, for the roof was only of bamboo matting; thermometer at 6 A.M., 48°. Towards midnight my boat was pelted with stones. I knew that this was the precursor of an attack, and on coming out of my cabin I could distinctly see figures standing on the bank: this time I determined to test what the effect of taking the initiative would be, and fired in the direction of the men; the result was capital, for the gang dispersed at once, and troubled me no more. Later on, we heard heavy firing at Moung-way,—a village about a mile and a half from where we were anchored; the shouts and cries of the people for assistance could also be distinctly heard, and in the morning we learnt that the village had been attacked, but the Kakhyens repelled, with the loss of one of their party, who was shot dead through the heart. The people from Katcho had made an attempt to assist their neighbours, but the bridle-path between the two villages had been spiked with poisoned pieces of bamboo, which prevented them carrying out their good intentions. This is a precaution the Kakhyens always take, when they want to avoid pursuit, or prevent villagers assisting one another in the case of an attack, and I found that even along the bank to which we were moored, the same system had been carried out, evidently with the view to stop us going to the rescue of the assaulted village. Crossed over to Zeeghoon, and called on the *Amat*, who took me to visit an old phoongyee of eighty years of age, and very feeble; apparently he was not expected to live much longer, for beneath the monastery his coffin was being hewn out of a single log of toon; the lid had already been completed, and was gorgeously decorated with gold and silver tinsel. The old man expressed his regret at my going among the Kakhyens, who, he said, should be avoided as much as possible, for they are without religion, and therefore merely on a par with wild beasts. Here I met the phoongyee of Talloo, on a visit to this old patriarch, who, I was told, had educated most of the priests from Talloo northwards, and seemed to be held in great respect by all. My musical box, and sleight-of-hand abilities were now referred to, and I was asked to send to my boat, for the instrument and perform some tricks, which afforded great amusement to the large crowd of men, old women, and children assembled in the monastery. On returning to my boat with the *Amat* I proceed to arrange about my trip; and was surprised to find him inclined to be obstructive; he seemed to have

changed his views, altogether, giving as a reason the disturbed and unhealthy state of the country. I took the opportunity to point out the very short interval, that had elapsed since he first told me that there was nothing to prevent my accomplishing the journey, in peace and safety; but, Burmanlike, ever ready with a lying rejoinder, he remarked that it takes less time for the Kakhyens to rise in arms, or for a disease to appear, than to kindle a fire; finding, however, I was inflexible, and determined on taking the route originally selected by him, he put forth a claim for twenty-five Rupees to secure a guarantee from the Kantee Tswabwa for the safety of myself and people. I felt I was being imposed on, but endeavoured to outwit the rascal, by stating my funds were limited, and that I was not prepared to meet such an exorbitant demand; ultimately, I agreed to pay twenty Rupees, which terms were accepted, and the money paid. The escort and coolies were promised to be in readiness by ten o'clock the next day. Being now out of the Bhamo district, I discharged Moung Oung, the guide provided by the Governor, presenting him with twenty Rupees, a silk handkerchief, and a certificate reporting favourably on his behaviour.

297. *Sunday, 8th February 1874*—Thermometer, 50° at 6 A.M., took a walk round the Island and found the peach and *areca catechu* growing side by side; also noticed two fine specimens of *Ficus elastica* held in sacred reverence, and not allowed to be tapped; they were planted twenty years ago, I am told, and measured as below :—

No. 1.—Height	62	feet.
Circumference of space occupied by crown	420	,,
Ditto trunk	41	,,
Ditto including aërial roots	69	,,
No. 2.—Height	59	,,
Circumference of space occupied by crown	390	,,
Ditto trunk	37	,,
Ditto including aërial roots	47	,,

N. B.—In both these specimens the aërial roots were scant. Shot six *Carpophaga sylvatica, Centropus eurycercus,* : also noticed *Caracias affinis, Alcedo asiatica, Upupa longirostris, Palæornis magnirostris,* and *Urocissi occiptalis.* On returning to my boat I found no signs of the coolies, so proceeded at once to the Amat's house, to enquire the reason. He stated that the men refused to go unless paid in advance, and he fixed their wages at Rs. 5 per head, limiting the journey to five days. The advance was made, and I started for Ah-chay at 3 P.M., where the Amat promised to join me with the escort and coolies before dark. The old hpoongyee now sent word to say he wished to see me before my departure; he had only a few kind words of advice to offer, cautioning me to avoid the Kakhyens as much as possible, and make a friend of the royal hpoongyee at Mogoung, who was a pupil of his, and a man of greater influence even than the Governor; in proof of which he stated that the royal postal boat cannot be despatched from Mogoung without his consent. As a parting gift he presented me with a musk-sack, which is greatly prized by all Orientals; the pouch is obtained from the male musk-deer, and is found near the navel of the animal. Reached Ah-chay, a Kakhyen hamlet of half-a-dozen houses embedded in a dense forest situated on a high bank of yellow clay, by 7 P.M. where we made fast for the night. I did not like the appearance of the place at all in the present disturbed state of the country, for nothing could have been easier than for the people to have potted us from above without endangering themselves. Here we found a party of Shan-Burmans bivouacing on the river-bank; they had come down by raft from a village seventy miles north, where they had been robbed of everything, and their village burnt down by the Kakhyens. They were on their way to British territory, but had been stopped here by order of the Amat, their raft cut adrift, and themselves directed to return at once by land to Zeeghoon. The poor people presented a most miserable appearance, and asked me to intercede, on their behalf, but I told them that that would be of no use, for I had no authority, here. This is no solitary instance in which emigration from Burma Proper has been prohibited. The Amat arrived long after dark, without any coolies or guard for me. I was most vexed, but he faithfully promised all the men would be forthcoming early tomorrow morning.

298. *Monday, 9th February 1874.*—Thermometer, 52° at 6 A.M. Sent off for the Amat, who, after a couple of hours' delay, appeared with eight armed men as an escort carrying guns, swords, and spears, and four women to carry my things. I had everything in readiness for a start, and bade adieu to Ah-chay at 9 A.M., having first despatched my boats for Mogoung, with instructions to delay nowhere on the road. We were now bound for Tapaw, and followed a very zig-zag course; the country we passed through may be described as hilly, though the greatest altitude reached did not exceed 900 feet; the formation is lime-stone, resting on dark clay. The vegetation is prolific in growth, and made up of *Fici, Magnolia, Acacia catechu, Cedrela toona, Quercus, Bombax malabaricum, Begonia, Lagerstræmia grandiflora* (few and stunted), *Gordonia arborea, Gmélia arborea, Careya arborea, Phyllanthus, Melanorhœa usitatissima* (a few of the trees were tapped for the black varnish it yields), *Pentaptera glabera, Dillenia pentagyna, Nauclea, cordifolia diversifolia,* teak (sparse and poor specimens), *Dodonœa burmanniana calami,* plantains, bamboos (of two varieties), *Araccœ* (wild), *suparee* and plants of the *Zingiberaceœ*

order. Besides which were numerous other plants unknown to me, but form part of my collection. The valleys presented large paddy clearings, the soil was black and cracked to a depth of a foot or so, reminding me of the fields met with in Berar and other parts of India, where this class of soil is thought peculiarly adapted to the growth of cotton. Tapaw (over twenty miles from Ah-chay), the village fixed by the Amat for us to sleep at, was reached by 8 P.M., but I found we were not expected and the people not only refused us shelter, but declined allowing us to encamp anywhere near them; not even did they make an exception to the Kakhyens of our party. I was greatly put out at this piece of rascality on the part of the Amat, for all my followers were knocked up with the hard day's march, and the women threw down their loads and declined to move another step. Hesitation was out of the question, for the Kakhyens were in a very excited state, brandishing their swords about in the most wild manner, and threatening our lives in case we did not leave at once; any attempt at resistance must have resulted in bloodshed, and fortunately my Burman peons, seeing the danger of opposition, shouldered the loads themselves and marched off with them at a much brisker pace than even I had wished; for anything like a retreat from fear, I thought, might stimulate the Kakhyens to put their threat into execution. I tried in vain, however, to establish self-possession and order, but the further we got from the village the more rapid the pace became, until I found a general bolt was contemplated, and had to bring the leader to the halt by a threat of a bullet in his back if he did not stop. Our escort had already deserted us, and apparently had come to terms with the people of Tapaw; we had to bivouac for the night in the forest, and miserable enough we were; it poured in torrents till early morn, so that it was impossible even to light fires to keep ourselves warm, nor had we a dry thing to put on, when the rain ceased.

299. *Tuesday, 10th February 1874.*—Thermometer 54° at 6 A.M.; at early dawn I served brandy all round, and took a strong nip myself, which did us all a deal of good no doubt; we found ourselves covered with blood from leech bites, and some of the beasts were still adhering to us; there were two varieties of the anelides,—the small black one, and the larger sort with yellow stripes on either side. It had often occurred to me that murrain may be produced by these animals which, perhaps, are swallowed by the cattle when grazing. All attempts to kindle a fire—(now that the rain had ceased)—to dry our kit proved unsuccessful, for the wood was too wet. Just as we were preparing to start, and had divided the four loads amongst six of us,—for I had arranged to carry my own collections,—our escort and female coolies, accompanied by some men and women of

Tapaw tracked us up, the former begging me return to their village, which I positively declined to do. The guard explained their absence during the night by saying they had missed us; and the villagers accounted for their strange behaviour under the plea that they had received no intimation from the Amat that we were coming, and that our unexpected arrival led them to believe we had come to plunder the village; they further added that they were not of the Kantee clan, nor did they acknowledge the Tswabwa of that tribe: from further enquiry I also found that, throughout my journey to Mogoung, I should nowhere meet with Kantees, so that it is evident the charge of twenty rupees made by the Amat was a gross imposition. Continued our march westward, following the top of a range of hills, which course we preserved, and descended in an east-south-easterly direction until reaching the foot, when our route passed through an undulating country, up to the Shan-Burman village of Tahpoon, situated on the banks of the Mogoung river, The physical features of the country remained unaltered; neither was there a perceptible change in the nature of the vegetation; teak, however, became more common, though it is not the magnificent tree met with further south, and I noticed some of the finest specimens of *Bombax malabaricum* I have ever seen: one tree measured 33.5 feet in circumference, and was a hundred and twenty feet high. The population seemed exceedingly scant, yet the deserted *toungyas* in the hills and plains leaves the impression that this part of the country must once have been more densely peopled than it is at present. During the whole day's journey we did not come across a single hamlet of any sort, though parties of Kakhyens were often met. The fresh prints and dung of elephants were also of common occurrence. By 9 P.M., we encamped for the night on the banks of the Mogoung river, opposite the village of Tahpoon, as there was no one to ferry us across.

300. *Wednesday, 11th February 1874.*—Thermometer, 55° at 6 A.M. Crossed over to Tahpoon in small canoes: this is a Shan-Burman village, numbering thirty-five houses and three monasteries built of teak, situated in a grove of jack-fruit and mango trees, with a bamboo stockade on all sides but that fronting the river: without and to the south of the palisade is a settlement of Kakhyens. We were allowed to occupy a deserted shed, without any walls, on the sloping bank of the river. I called on the head hpoongyee, who mentioned having once visited Moulmein and intimated his intention of shortly returning to British territory, as he was dissatisfied with the insecurity of life and property here. Within the last two years it appeared this village had been burnt and plundered, and

that during the last raid, two young women and three children had been carried off by the mountaineers. The small colony of Kakhyens outside this village had established themselves here, much against the will of the people, who are too weak to offer resistance, nor can they look to their Government for protection from the outrages these freebooters commit. After starting Yan Sing for Mogoung, (accompanied by two of my own peons and a guard of four Shan-Burmans from this village), with a letter to the Governor, presenting my royal passport and asking him to kindly arrange about a house for myself and party, I visited the Kakhyens, and was surprised to find that they had adopted the Shan-Burman style of house; they had no cattle, nor even pigs; but appeared mainly dependent on the proceeds of their plunder, which is carried on in conjunction with the rest of the clan located in the hills: they also cultivate paddy in the plains, and extract teak timber which is bartered for any other article they require. Here I managed to pick up a specimen of a Kakhyen fiddle, a most primitive invention. It consisted of the section of a club-gourd *(Trichosanthea anguina)* common about here, with neck, pegs, and tail-piece of bamboo: the belly was of the sheath of the bamboo, and the bridge, of bone; it had three strings of twisted horse-hair, and the bow was a bent piece of stick and horse-hair; as a substitute for rosin, saliva was used and the sound produced can better be imagined than described. This and a bamboo flute with four holes as notes, and blown on the principle of a penny-whistle were the only instruments besides the gong and drum, that I met with, among the highlanders of either bank. Their idea of tune—which gives perception of harmony and discord in music—is singularly wanting; yet they are capital timeists, as is noticeable when they are dancing or singing to music. I took a stroll in the evening, and shot some painted partridge and junglefowl *(Gallus ferrugineus)*. I observed that the carts of this country had no wheels, but were on the principle of sleigh dragged by buffaloes; they are peculiarly adapted for passing over swampy land. Two of my peons showed symptoms of fever towards night—the result no doubt of over-fatigue. I served them with quinine, and a threat that they would be left behind if not quite well the following day; the latter remedy was given as a stimulant, for I knew they would, indeed, have had to be very bad to consent to separation from the rest of the party. I was not in a position to show sympathy to any one, or should never have got on.

301. *Thursday, 12th February 1874.*—Thermometer, 57° at 6 A.M. I was awoke in the middle of the night by a rush of water down the slope where I was sleeping, on the ground. I was too knock-

ed up, however, to become conscious of my position until everything was wet through : my followers were similarly situated, but they were not disturbed until I awoke them, even the man placed on sentry was peacefully slumbering with his musket between his legs, and not a dry stitch of clothes on, nevertheless he had the cheek, after being shaken into his senses, to say he was not asleep, but merely shamming, with a view to shoot the first Kakhyen that dared to enter! We shifted our position, and got into a drier place, but were too tired for wet beds to interfere with rest. Just before I fell asleep, the man on duty gave the alarm of a snake, but this was the last I heard of it until morning, when the brute was found coiled up under the blanket of my peons who were all sleeping huddled together. It was a *Dipsas monticola*, measuring two feet four inches long, and evidently it had crawled up from the river-bank. Started for Mogoung at 8 A.M. The first part of the journey was through paddy-fields of black soil which rather tried our legs, for the whole valley we were crossing was a sheet of slush and mud in places nearly knee-deep,—so heavy had the rain been here lately. At the base of the hills we had to cross, before reaching Mogoung, was the Kakhyen hamlet of Poonkan, and a little further north, likewise at the foot of the range, was an extensive grove of palmyra (*Barrassus flabelliformis*) and cocoanuts, from both of which were suspended fruit. *Duabenya grandiflora* were also common on the slopes. Here Yan Sing turned up, and reported that a house in the village had been rented for me at Rupee a day. Reached the summit of the hill (altitude six hundred and fifty feet), by 2 P.M., from where, there is a commanding view of Mogoung and the surrounding villages, studded over a vast sea of paddy-fields, and embowered in clumps of bamboos situated at distances, averaging quarter of a mile apart. A mile from Mogoung, we passed through a Kakhyen village, the inhabitants being Buddhist converts, and adopting the Burmese costume ; many of the boys had been taught to read and write, in their own monastery, which was built by a Tsawbwa, named Swablow, a man of considerable means and influence ; but how he had acquired his wealth I had been unable to ascertain. He had also built a small pagoda on the rising ground to the east of Mogoung, called Pawsoung, and a second monastery at Mogoung ; the priests, who are Burmans, are supported by the Kakhyen converts. Before passing up the main street that led to my residence, Yan Sing begged I would divest myself of the different feathers and flowering creepers with which I had decorated my hat, for fear the people might imagine I was insane; his next move was to get the stragglers into something like order; the procession was then headed by my Burman peon, carrying the three old Brown Bess followed by myself, Yau Sing bringing up the rear-guard, consisting of the women coolies and Kakhyen escort. The first thing on arrival, I sent to the Governor for a guard of six men to escort my boats up the Mogoung river, the country through which they had to pass being in a state of rebellion. I received a verbal reply that the men would be in readiness next morning, but that they would have to be supplied with ammunition, and paid at the rate of twelve annas per diem.

302. *Friday, 13th February 1874.*—I did not awake till 7 A.M.; whenI found the sun well up, and the thermometer at 69° : there was a marked change in the temperature of this place and the country I had just passed through. It was 11 A.M., before the escort were ready to start : they expected to reach the mouth of the Mogoung river, they said, in two days ; but I had my doubts of this ; for, although it was a flat country they had before them, yet I feared daily wages would have had a bad effect. Before calling on the Governor, I sent over a present of carpets, some pieces of muslin and scent, asking him to appoint a time when it would be most convenient for him to see me : in a few minutes I received a message, saying he would be glad to make my acquaintance at once. He was a fine, gentlemanly old man, about sixty years of age ; his house was enclosed by a bamboo mat wall on all sides but that facing the river, and was situated about the middle of the town ; the building was throughout of bamboo with the exception of the posts, which were of teak ; but, nevertheless, had a very neat appearance—indeed, far more tidy than is usual to find even with Burmese officials of his rank : at the bottom of the steps that led up to the reception-hall, which was raised five feet off the ground, were four old pieces of ordnance pointing towards the river. Facing the entrance was a raised platform of teak, fifteen by twelve feet square, fronted by a verandah with a trellis-work railing that ran the whole front length of the building. The platform was surrounded by a handsomely-carved railing, and at the back was a stand of well-cleaned arms, including guns, spears, swords and pistols, arranged with some regard to order ; on either side of the little gate, that communicated with the passage leading to his private apartment, were a pair of the finest elephant tusks I had ever seen : these were apparently those that were presented to him, by the Kakhyens of Nansingtoung with a view to the re-establishment of the old route to Western Yunan : the dais was carpeted and furnished with chairs and tables : the whole presenting a striking contrast with the reception-hall of the Governor of Bhamo. Immediately I arrived, the Governor, who had hitherto been seated on the carpet, rose to receive me, and taking both my hands in his, seated me in a chair opposite to the one he

now took. Evidently he was unaccustomed to the position, for immediately the first formality began to wear off, he cocked up his legs, and adopted the position he would have done if squatted on the floor. Fruit, tea, and sweets were now placed on a little table between us, and after filling his mouth with *pán-suparee*, he pressingly invited me to partake of the refreshments; but as I was suffering from a severe attack of neuralgia, I was not in the humour to eat, and explained my reason for partaking so sparingly his good things: he expressed his regret at my indisposition, and sent the eatables over to my house. His son, who had been to England with Mr. Edmund Jones, was now sent for; and had it not been that I was prepared, I should have taken the man for a menial: he was so remarkably black, and had nothing on but a greasy, dirty silk *loongyee* which he could not have changed or washed since the day he put it on: his knowledge of English extended to "yes" and " no,"— generally misusing the words, not knowing what was said to him: he had inveigled his old father into the belief however that he knew the language thoroughly. A pair of binoculars the son had purchased in Paris were now produced for my opinion; of course, I pronounced them the best; a photographic album was next brought forth, containing the most extraordinary collection possible to imagine, made up of some of the *deme mounde*, the royal family, the Burmans, and Mr. E. Jones, &c., and it was rather amusing to listen to the adventures the son stated he had with certain of the parties; then was exhibited a stereoscope, with French slides of a most lascivious character, and which the old man said he delighted feasting on, in his idle hours. Having listened to all his nonsense for some time, and humoured his fancies, I ventured to sound him on the probable success of my tour in his district; he spoke of the Kakhyens as a most debased lot, whom he had no more commpunction in hanging than dogs, and affirmed he had just ordered the execution of a chief, whose tribe had recently plundered some boats on their way up here from Bhamo; but that the sentence had been suspended on a guarantee from the royal hpoongyee that the property would be returned. My travels, he added, would be attended with great danger, nor could he vouch for my safety. In respect to the climate, he told me that the sun is only seen here for three months, and for the rest of the year it rains, from which circumstance the place has been called Mogoung, signifying "place of rain." I now took my departure, and at his request promised to let him know my future plans in a day or so. Chinamen, I am told, are not allowed to visit the jade mines, and that all the best specimens of this stone are sent to the capital; ivory and india-rubber are likewise regarded a royal monopoly, the latter selling here at Rs. 50 per 100 viss. Much risk attends the jade trade, which appears to me a mere speculation; not only must you have a most accurate eye for colour, to judge the exact tint of green that realizes the highest price, but it also requires great experience in determining the precious from valueless *ophite*. Rather a gross piece of injustice on the part of the Governor had been brought to my notice to-day. A block of serpentine, valued at Rs. 300, had been exposed for sale for some days, and eventually a speculative chinaman closed with the owner for Rs. 275; it turned out a prize, and he was offered Rs. 7,000 for it. This reaching the Governor's ears, he demanded the block at the price paid, and sent it down to Mandalay. There were all sorts of rumours rife regarding the object of my visit; among others, it was supposed I was exploring with a view to ascertain the feasibility of taking the country in revenge for various sleights that had been shown us. In the evening, I visited the royal hpoongyee, who, strange to say, is an Arakanese by descent; his monastery was situated to the extreme west of the town. He told me that he visited Calcutta with the embassy in 1865, and that all other members of the mission had been promoted to Governors; but as he could not accept that honour, he was appointed to his present office by the King, with instructions to report direct to the capital, everything that went on here; the dismissal of the last Governor was, he boastingly added, on his report. As a mark of distinction he had been presented with a gilt bedstead—an honour alone conferred on royal priests. He now produced some of his treasures, among which were two fine large crystals presented by his Kakhyen disciples living on the high mountains to the west, and a pipe that had been given him by a Mr. Henri, who resided in his monastery, for many months, when working the jade mines and india-rubber for the King. He threw out hints that the Governor would place every obstacle in my way, not wishing the wealth and prosperity of his district to be known to foreigners, but that I was not to be daunted, as I might depend on him for assistance. It is strange that though a Buddhist, this hpoongyee believes in the existence and influence of *nâts*, impressing on me that I could alone hope for success by sending an offering in the form of cocoanuts, rice, and plantains to the spirit of the forests, who resides beneath a wide spreading *Ficus* on the slope of the high mountain opposite. Superstition is another marked feature in this priest's character, for he believed that the direction from which forthcoming changes and events arise are predicted by the roaring of a tiger throughout the night. The following interesting circumstances he related regarding the origin of the india-rubber trade in Upper

Burma. It appears that, some years back, when Mr. Henri was sent here to work the serpentine mines, the gutta-percha tubing of the pumps (used to get rid of the water that filled the excavations) got out of order, and that he was about to return them to Mandalay for repair, when, noticing the little baskets used by the people for baling were covered with a thin film of a material he thought might answer his purpose, he inquired what it was, and was shown the tree that yielded the substance; this proved to be a *Ficus elastica*, which circumstance was reported to the palace, and the European merchants of Mandalay were not slow in introducing the article into the market, for which there was now a large demand. Before taking my departure, an old English kettle-drum bearing the royal arms was produced, which had been brought by the hpoongyee from Arakan : this I was asked to send to Rangoon for repairs, but I postponed the commission until my downward voyage, by which time I hoped the matter would have been forgotten. All matters of importance are decided by a committee, I learnt, composed of the Governor, the royal priest, and the old hpoongyee of the town, which latter canonically ranks superior to my new acquaintance.

303. *Saturday, 14th February 1874.*—Thermometer, 65° at 6 A.M. Mogoung is the penal settlement of Burma Proper, and the centre of the jade and amber trade. It numbers 600 houses, exclusive of the thirty-three small hamlets surrounding it, and which serve as outposts in room of a stockade. Though now deserving but the name of a village, it is a place of great antiquity, and intimately linked with the ancient history of this province; and, if the records of the past may be depended on, it was proclaimed the capital of the Pong Kingdom in 1337 A.D. by Queen Soognampha. It is questionable whether this is the original site ; I was told not, and that ancient Mogoung is higher up the river.

304. The village is irregular in shape, being widest in the middle ; it is divided into squares by a main street paved with burnt bricks set on edge, running the entire length, and intersected again by cross-roads at intervals of from 200 to 300 yards apart. The bulk of the population are convicts, principally Burmans and Shan-Burmans, undergoing different terms of transportation : those who can give security that they will not abscond are regarded ticket-of-leave men, and form part of the village police ; but all others are heavily ironed, kept to hard labour, and put in the stocks at night, there being no prison : for food and clothing they are dependent on their relations and charity. There is a small colony of Chinese engaged in the ivory and amber trade; jade and rubber being included when opportunity offers. They invest largely in opium, imported

from the Shan states, which is sent to Bhamo, and thence reaches the capital; the manufacture of *shamshoo* is likewise a source of considerable profit to them, the liquor being largely consumed both by the inhabitants of Mogoung and the mountaineers. The remainder of the community is made up of Burman traders from Bhamo and Mandalay, with a sprinkling of Mahomedan and Suratee pedlars, who bring piece goods and an *olla podrida* collection from Mandalay, which they barter for whatever there is a demand, far south of this. The place is kept remarkably clean, the system of sanitation being that in force at Bhamo. Every precaution is taken to guard against fire, though, nevertheless, this place is in flames once a year. At 9 P.M., a patrol goes round with a drum to remind the people of the Governor's order, and the punishment that awaits the party who is found with a light or fire in his house after the mandate has been proclaimed. The roads are well-avenued with fruit trees, principally mango (now commencing to flower), jack, and tamarind: around the monasteries and private buildings, limes, oranges, guavas, papaw, and plaintains are common. Once a week, a market is held in the main street between the hours of 7 and 9 A.M., when the neighbouring villages send in for sale, grain and native vegetables, chiefly consisting of wild roots and herbs; sun-dried venison is also common, but the system of curing makes it unpalatable to Europeans. The people of Mogoung also expose for sale, on these days, *ngapee, lapet*, salt, sugar, candles, thread, needles, *tamines, loongyees*, piece-goods, beads, and endless tawdry, which sell well among the Kakhyens and other tribes that flock in here, on market days. The stalls are generally kept by women, who are remarkably shrewd and businesslike, both in the art of buying and selling.

305. The rupee is the only recognized coin, and that merely realizes ten annas; purchases of smaller value are paid for in bits of silver at the current rates, so that it becomes necessary for both vendors and buyers to be provided with scales and weights. It is a tiresome process of exchange and a most wasteful one, a loss in chipping off *wee* pieces of silver from the larger block to equalize the balance, being unavoidable. The trades are represented by carpenters, silversmiths, and blacksmiths; the first are skilled workmen, and find plenty of employment in the construction of the ecclesiastical buildings now greatly on the increase here; the silversmiths are principally occupied in alloying silver for the market,[*] but they are by no means good jewellers; and the blacksmiths— who are Shans, and but temporary residents—do a good business in

---

[*] For further information on this subject, *vide* page 76.

the manufacture of swords, which they sell to the Kakhyens at from Rs. 2-8 to Rs. 5 per blade. Weaving is also carried on, but chiefly for home consumption, though the owner is generally open to a good offer. Squatters are taxed at Rs. 2-8 per head, and permanent residents at Rs. 12 per annum per house.

306. *Sunday, 15th February 1874.*—Thermometer, 69° at 6 A.M.; rain overnight; my house leaked like a sieve. So entirely has the surrounding country, to the base of the hills, been denuded of timber to make room for paddy cultivation, that I actually found firewood selling here at Rs. 2 per stack of 65·5 cubit feet. Yan Sing had an interview with the royal hpoongyee to-day, who sent word to say that I was to report secretly to him any order I received from the Governor.

307. *Monday, 16th February 1874.*—Thermometer, 71° at 6 A.M.; dense fog up to 11. Royal *dák* boat arrived, bringing letters from the Resident of Mandalay, dated up to 24th January. An order was issued by the Governor that I was not to go out shooting, as the report of a gun would excite the Kakhyens, and probably bring about a disturbance; I was most vexed at this, being chiefly dependent on my gun for the pot, and besides which the order interfered with my collection of birds. The *dák* boat leaving for Mandalay to-morrow, the remainder of the day was spent in writing letters. I had been suffering greatly from an attack of neuralgia, and a return of dysentery; the last time it troubled me I cured myself in four days, simply dieting and using tepid claret-and-water injections.

308. *Tuesday, 17th February 1874.*—Thermometer, 71° at 6 A.M.; dense fog up to 10 A.M.; sent my packet of letters over to the Governor for despatch. I was too unwell to leave my house to-day.

309. *Wednesday, 18th February 1874.*—Thermometer, 72° at 6 A.M.; dense fog up to 9 A.M.; still confined to my house; a native doctor called and offered to cure me: I too gladly accepted his services at any figure, but his remedy only increased the pain which now extended down the whole of my left side, and I was unable to leave my bed: by way of consolation, the wretched ninny told me this was part of the cure, and that in a few days I would be quite well. It is needless to add that I did not give him a chance of experimentalizing any further on me.

310. *Thursday, 19th February 1874.*—Thermometer, 69° at 6 A.M.; fog, less dense. I found the greatest difficulty in procuring anything to eat, the people would not part with their fowls without an order from the Governor, and that could not be obtained. After great trouble I managed to purchase for one rupee an old

blind fighting-cock, no longer fit for the ring : this, cooked with rice and native vegetables served me for three days ; fortunately I was not inclined to eat much, neither was the dish calculated to promote my appetite. Numerous visitors came to see me more from curiosity than sympathy, and I gained much information—valuable information—from them. It appears that when a husband is absent whose turn it is for picket duty, the wife has to take his place, and in cases where the party is not a married man, a male or female relation is given as a substitute.

311. *Friday, 20th February 1874.*—Thermometer, 72° at 6 A.M. ; a fine, bright sunny morning. I was still confined to my house.

312. *Saturday, 21st February 1874.*—Thermometer, 71° at 6 A.M. ; slight shower of rain overnight : heavy fog up to 10 A.M., which penetrated my room, the walling merely being of bamboo-matting, and in a very dilapidated state. In the forenoon, I took a stroll to the end of the town, and with the permission of the royal Hpoongyee, extracted a soda-water bottle full of juice from a *Ficus elastica* growing at the back of the royal monastery. Half of the exudation I condensed by direct exposure to the sun, and the remainder,—with an equal bulk of water,—I consolidated by evaporation over a slow fire in an iron vessel. Besides these two systems, which are practised by the Kakhyens, they adopt two other processes,—one is to allow the milk to coagulate as it exudes from the tree, winding the dried substance into a ball ; and the other is to pour the milk in a very thin layer—not thicker than the eighth of an inch—on a fine mat placed out in the sun, and surrounded by a moulding of clay an inch high ; this soon coalesces, and is then removed, and likewise made into a ball. I had endeavoured to find out the process adopted by Mr. Henri, to utilize caoutchouc in the form of a cement for repairing the gutta-percha tubing of his pumps, but no reliable information could be obtained. One account was that he boiled ten tickals of caoutchouc with two and-a-half tickals of *kunnion* oil, but this is most improbable. Hearing that a party of thirty-three Singphos from the amber mines had arrived with their yearly tribute, consisting of four pair of elephant tusks, a pair of amber idols, five spears, some slaves, a stuffed musk-deer, and two golden cocks, I requested to be allowed to see the last two named, which the Governor very kindly sent over. The golden cock, I found, was a pheasant, closely resembling in plumage our European *golden pheasant*. This bird is considered exceedingly rare, and not found beyond the limits of the mountains to the extreme north of the *Pendwine* district, lat. 26° : neither is the musk-deer met with fur-

ther south, I am informed: it was about the size of a roebuck, with a grey coat of coarse fur, and short horns, and two projecting teeth in the lower jaw; the sack of musk had been allowed to remain untouched. Last year these highlanders killed a Burman officer, who had been sent to the amber mines, to ascertain the reason for the annual tribute and vassalage not having been paid, but a reconciliation had recently been brought about by the intercession of the hpoongyees. The Kakhyens, Singphos, or Thainbows as they are called, to the west of the Irrawaddy, differ greatly in appearance and costume from their kinsmen of the opposite bank. They are shorter and more square built, with a fairer complexion, flatter features, and less hair about the body generally; indeed, had I not been told who they were, I should have mistaken them for a Shan tribe,—so much more civilized are they to look at than the wild mountaineer of the eastern range. Both men and women dress their hair *âla* Burmese; the cloth the men wear round their loins is of a blue ground, with narrow green lines forming checks; the women adopt a coloured *loongyee*, which extends from under the arms, covering the breasts, to below the knees, but on neither sex did I notice cane garters, or girdles, or *cowrie* ornaments in any form. Their jewellery was more after the Burmese fashion; neither was the ear bored in any place but the lobe, which was occupied by an ordinary amber tube. By repute they are the most blood-thirsty and dangerous of any of the highland tribes, but that they are in a stage of transition is apparent from the fact that numbers of them have become Buddhist converts, and all, as a rule, respect the hpoongyees, abide by their decisions, and exempt them from assault or plunder. The foregoing remarks more particularly refer to the clans of the Hokum Valley and that vicinity, the tribes of the Moohinyin district being almost identical in appearance, costume, and habits with those to the east.

313. Two reports reached the Governor to-day,—one, was that sixty-five Thainbows of the *karko* tribe had assembled on the Nanyah *choung*, which takes its rise in the vicinity of the serpentine mines, and that they threatened the lives of all who passed up that way. This disturbance originated in a native of India having run away with a lump of Jade unpaid for; the other report was that three Shan-Talokes had been killed during an engagement, near the Endawgyee lake, three days ago.

314. *Sunday, 22nd February 1874.*—Thermometer, 71° at 6 A.M.; fine morning; my boats arrived at 3 P.M., having taken eight days to perform the journey between this and the mouth of the Mogoung river. In places the water was described as so shallow,

that the three crews had to unite their strength to drag the boats one by one over the shoals.

315. *Monday, 23rd February 1874.*—Thermometer, 73° at 6 A.M.; I called, and had a chat with the royal hpoongyee to-day, and presented him with a carpet, some pieces of muslin, candles, and scent: he sent for some leaves of different plants for me to name, amongst which were peppermint, *Poinsettia pulcherrima*, *Jatropha multifida*, *Granadilla (Passiflora edulis)*, the fruit of which the Burmans eat, he stated : *Iberis odorata*, *Celosia cristata*, *Tegetes erecta*, and some roses *(tea)*, all of which excepting the latter, had been cultivated from seeds presented by Mr. Henri. I was also shown a root of a tree, the Kakhyens are said to poison their spears with ; he did not know the name, but gave me a specimen. I tried the effect on dogs; it was very slow in its action, though death ensued within three days causing great pain to the poor animal, for the first four hours after the poison was inserted. I next called on the head hpoongyee, who resided at the opposite end of the town, and gave him a few presents; his monastery was crowded with the *Kantee* mountaineers from the amber mines that had come down with their annual tribute, and among whom, white muslin *gong bongs* were being distributed. They amused themselves watching the machinery of an eight-day clock, from which the face had been removed as being useless. The old hpoongyee was remarkably reticent, so that I did not trouble him very long.

316. *Tuesday, 24th February 1874.*—Thermometer, 72° at 6 A.M.; thunder-storm overnight, accompanied by rain. I sent Yan Sing to the Governor, requesting the favour of an interview; but the reply was, he would not be visible until the next day, and that arrangements had already been made for a guide to accompany me. In the evening he sent over a present of sweets and two spears, and begged I would allow him to see my revolver, breech-loader, and other fire-arms, which I did. Made all arrangements for a start the next day.

317. *Wednesday, 25th February 1874.*—Thermometer, 72° at 6 A.M.; heavy fog up to 10 A.M. I called on the Governor according to appointment, and was introduced to my future *chaperon;* certainly, he had not a prepossessing appearance. By request, I stated the route I proposed to take which was up to Kamine, thence to the amber mines through the Hokong Valley, round south by the serpentine mines and back to Mogoung *viâ* the Endawgyee Lake and *choung* of the same name. The Governor at once put his *veto* on my proceeding to the amber mines, stating he did not consider the country in that vicinity had sufficiently settled down since the recent rebellion, to warrant my going there with any degree safety.

In respect to the remaining portion of my programme, he said, the matter must be left to the discretion of my guide, who would better be able to regulate my movements as we progressed; on leaving, he took my hand in both of his, and with a tremulous voice and extra squeeze wished me good-bye, but appeared too agitated and overcome to say more : the old fox played his part admirably; I am sure he must have once been educated for the stage. I failed lamentably in doing justice to the scene; the warning was too short, though the by-standers endeavoured to elicit my sympathy by drawing attention to the leaky condition of the Governor's eyes. Yan Sing suggested that I should produce my handkerchief, and trumpet in it; but this would have overpoised the gravity I had hitherto been able to preserve, and I should, I am afraid, have but too clearly shown that I regarded the whole thing a farce. I left Mogoung at 4 P.M.; the first creek passed was the *Nanmyne*, which forms the western boundary of Mogoung, and takes its rise in the hills to the south-west. I made fast for the night at *Nanpoung*, a Shan stockaded hamlet of seven houses. The country on either bank thus far is flat, and covered with high grasses and a few *Salix*.

318. *Thursday, 26th February 1874.*—Thermometer, 69° at 6 A.M.; heavy dew overnight; I heard to-day for the first time that Shan children take the names of their fathers, and wives that of their husbands. Old Mogoung we passed by 2 P.M.; nothing more remains to mark the site of the old village but a long square slab of sandstone on the right bank of the river.* Here and there I diverged to explore some little way inland. The country we were passing through was very uninteresting; a low range of hills on either side, with a few stunted teak trees here and there, and the banks overgrown with *Saccharum* and *Arundo* grasses, was all that was seen throughout the day. I collected specimens of a giant creeper unknown to me. Made fast for the night at a sand bank about two miles above old Mogoung. The cry of jungle fowl was everywhere to be heard, but I did not get a shot.

319. *Friday, 27th February 1874.*—Thermometer, 72° at 6 A.M. It was cloudy throughout the day : portions of the creek were walled in by banks of sandstone formation, and here the current was exceedingly strong. I gave my boatmen a rest at *Nansoukir* on the right bank, a hamlet of eighteen houses enclosed in a bamboo stockade : nearly all the male population had left by order of the Governor to attack a party of Kakhyens that had committed a raid, on a village south, a few days back. Heavy firing from the direction in which the men had gone could be

* I am inclined to think it was here that queen Soognampha, in 1337 A.D., established the capital of the Pong Kingdom.

distinctly heard. I stopped for the night at Nang-haing, a Shan-Taloke village, on the right bank, consisting of nine stockaded houses situated on a creek twenty-two yards wide at the mouth, taking its rise in the mountains to the west. Here the banks are less overgrown with grass, and the *Salix* is on the increase.

320. *Saturday, 28th February 1874.*—Thermometer, 61° at 6 A.M. There was a thunder-storm, accompanied by rain, overnight. I left my boats at Nang-haing, and explored the country for about six miles inland, joining them again at new Kamine. It was cloudy throughout the day. The horn-bill (*Hydrocissa albirostris*) we were constantly coming on. Moung Oolah, for that was the name of the guide provided by the Governor, was much opposed to this excursion, endeavouring to make me believe that there were no *Ficus elastica* anywhere in this vicinity; but plenty of wild highlanders, who would not lose the opportunity of killing myself and party. This statement about the Kakhyens I accepted for what it was worth; but, regarding the non-existence in this locality of the tree I was in search of, I knew better, having already gained information on this subject during my stay at Mogoung. It was here that Mr. Henri first collected india-rubber by order of the King, and I came across the *Shantees*, which himself and party occupied while the operation was going on. The huts were situated on a mountain stream that discharges itself into the Mogoung river, about half-way between Kamine and Nang-haing. A Shan from the latter village, who had worked with Mr. Henri, accompanied me, and described the method in which the trees were tapped. Incisions were made in the stems and roots with a *dah*, regardless of method, apparently, for the cuts were at irregular distances apart—some vertical, others oblique—while those on the roots were cross-ways; and from two to four feet distant; at the lower end of the inscisions in the trunk were driven hollow bamboos, shaped in the form of a pen into which the juice poured; and the exudation from the roots was allowed to coagulate round about the wound, and subsequently collected and formed into a ball. According to the Shan, a full-grown tree yielded from thirty to forty-five viss, which was collected in the space of a month. The rains were said to have been the season when the operations were carried on, but what the strength of the establishment was, I could not ascertain : some days Mr. Henri was said to have had thirty men, others twenty, others ten, and so on ; but there is one thing certain, *viz.*, that the labour was forced ; and, I was told he committed great oppression, which one day led to his being very roughly handled by some of the highland coolies. The *Ficus elastica*, I saw, were growing on side slopes of hills of foliated lime-

stone, but nowhere did I notice them on the *plateaux*. The trees were, without exception, epiphytical in habit, growing at great disstances apart, perhaps a quarter of a mile or more, in an evergreen forest reeking with moisture: the vegetation being generally made up of *Dipterocarpus tuberculatus, Fici, Lagerstraœmia grandiflora, Careya arborea, Magnolia, Pentaptera paniculata, Begonia, Gordonia, Bombax malabaricum, Nauclea, Strychnos Nux-vomica, Bauhinia, Diospyros, Phyllanthus, musa, Calami,* Bamboo, tree ferns, *araceœ, Broussonetia papyrifera, Agathis Loranthifolia,* and bordering on the streams *Breedelia uptusa,* also the wild rose. The following measurements represent four of the finest *Ficus elastica* met with during the day :—

No. I.—Height	... ...	... 118	feet.
Circumference of space occupied by crown		... 709	,,
Ditto trunk	... ...	... 83	.,
Ditto including aërial roots	...	... 119	,,
No. II.—Height	... ...	... 102	,,
Circumference of space occupied by crown		... 715	,,
Ditto trunk	... ...	... 87	,,
Ditto including aërial roots	...	... 123	,,
No. III.—Height	... ...	... 94	,,
Circumference of space occupied by crown		... 690	,,
Ditto trunk	... ...	... 81	,,
Ditto including aërial roots	...	... 114	,,
No. IV.—Height	... ...	... 85	,,
Circumference of space occupied by crown		... 695	,,
Ditto trunk	... ...	... 84	,,
Ditto including aërial roots	...	... 130	,,

321. In no instance did I observe reproduction below the parent tree, but examples were not wanting of the seed having germinated in the *Polypodium wallichianum*, growing on *Bombax*, and other giant trees, from which the aërial roots of the *Ficus elastica* descended, giving a strange appearance: these in later years, by a process of inosculation, unite into one, forming the huge stem for which these trees are noted. In trees that have reached maturity, the lateral roots keep close to the surface, and, in many instances, are more than half exposed, that part above ground representing logs of three feet circumference, gradually tapering away as they descend the hill in search of moisture from the stream below; such trees I also found to have thrown down roots from the wide-spreading branches in the same manner as the *Banian* tree, and evidently intended by nature as supports for their bulky limbs. On returning to my boats, late in the evening, some Shan-Talokes from the serpentine mines, reported having met two gangs of Kakhyens, at the mouth of the Nanghaing *choung*, but that they bolted on being fired at. This was evidently the party we had heard of at Mogoung. Kamine is situated on the right bank, at the confluence of the Nanghaing *choung*, which takes its rise in the mountains to the north, and during the rains is navigable for small boats within

a short distance of the amber mines. It numbers thirty-five Shan houses enclosed within a stockade, and a custom-house, where all duty on amber and jade is levied; the inhabitants, though professing the Buddhistic faith, are nevertheless believers in demonology, as was apparent from the votive offerings everywhere to be met with about the village. Scenes of a most indecent nature were witnessed daily: the men and women bathed naked, exposing their *hoc genus omne* in a most bare-faced manner.

322. *Sunday, 1st March 1874.*—Thermometer, 73° at 6 A.M.; heavy dew last night. The river here commenced to narrow, and was obstructed by snags; the course was sufficiently winding to admit of an inland excursion, at different times, without impeding progress. The banks on either side are low, and extend to the base of the hills, which vary in distance from half a mile to one mile: a little further on, we came to a small pagoda on the right bank, situated on a slight elevation of red clay: it is known as the *Saithma Pyah*, signifying *Doctor's Tank*, the idea being that, no matter what the disease, all are cured who bathe in it. Here again we are carried back to scriptural teachings, and reminded of the healing properties of the waters of the pool of Siloam.

323. The building was in a good state of repair, and apparently reverenced by the mountain tribes, as well as others: just about this building, I collected some *Ficus elastica* seedlings growing in the fern previously mentioned and attached to a *Bombax* forty feet off the ground; fortunately, I had some good climbers with me, who were always ready to risk their lives for a few annas. I shot some heron, a peacock, and a vulture; the latter was seated in its nest of sticks with a lining of grass built on the summit of a high tree; before I fired, it swooped down on us three times in a most determined manner, once nearly carrying away the steersman's *go̅ung boung*. I found two unfledged birds in the nest. Made fast for the night at old Kamine.

324. *Monday, 2nd March 1874.*—Thermometer, 73° at 6 A. M.; dense fog; heavy fall of dew overnight. The first part of the morning was employed planting the *Ficus* seedlings, of yesterday's collection, in small open-work bamboo baskets, containing one part of sand, and two, of vegetable mould. This was the original site of the village of the same name lower down; but a misunderstanding between the people brought about the division. In a straight line the two villages are not over three miles apart, but they are separated by the tail end of a low spur of hills. The character of the stream remains unaltered, though, perhaps, it has decreased in breadth; the vegetation continues unchanged. I added *Antidesma paniculata* to my collection, with numerous other specimens unknown

to me. My stock of *Ficus* seedlings continued to multiply: my people, knowing that every plant brought me represented four annas, exerted their energies; but at the end of a day's collection, I had to be careful, for I found a considerable number of *Ficus lucifera* presented for payment in lieu of the genuine tree. We were constantly coming on elephant-paths to the water, the tall grass through which they passed having been trodden down and formed into regular lanes, which materially facilitated my inspection of the forest. Immediately on making fast for the night, where there was no village, I made a man ascend the highest tree at hand and see whether he could detect smoke anywhere, as the Kakhyens, (now that the crops were gathered in), generally go about the country in gangs, plundering whoever they can, and, of course, it was necessary for us to be prepared for all emergencies. Moored at a sand bank for the night.

325. *Tuesday, 3rd March 1874.*—Thermometer 68° at 6 A.M.; heavy dew overnight. The hills were growing closer, and the river less obstructive by fallen trees, but more blocked up by large serpentine boulders, reducing the channel in places to a width of thirty feet, where the water was very rapid, and great difficulty experienced in clearing the gates. I ascended the highest hill, of the left bank, which was 900 feet. The surrounding country, as far as the eye could reach from west to north-east, was made up of a level country intersected by low hills. The .high Shwe-dong peak, which is opposite to Mogoung, bearing east-north-east, was conspicuous. Teak of small growth was distinguishable here and there by its flowering crown, but nowhere did I come on any fine specimen. The *Ficus elastica*, however, continued everywhere to be seen, but still it retained its solitary habit. A little higher up the river, I noticed extensive *toungya* clearings on the range to the west, and situated on a bluff: in the midst of the cultivation was the Kakhyen hamlet, of *Thakhow*, which takes its name from the range. *Dillenia aurea* now became more common, and my people gathered the fruit which, with the addition of a little salt, they appeared to relish. Stopped for a few minutes at some Shan huts on the left bank known as Suckhore; round the group of buildings was growing *Cajanus indica, Castor oil, Baigon,* and cotton; the gatherings from the last cotton crop had been made, and the the people were carding it on the principle followed in India. The bow used for this purpose, was suspended from the roof by a string, and consisted of a buffalo-horn and cat-gut. The current increased in velocity as far as Nantain *choung*, which takes its rise in the hills to the west, and that part of the Mogoung stream, south of the confluence, is known as the Endow *choung*. A mile before reaching this point, the river was

blocked up by a weir reaching from bank to bank. There was a small colony of Kakhyens here, who leave their homes from February to the end of March to catch fish, which they smoke-dry and take down to Mogoung for sale, whence they are imported to the capital by itinerant traders. Our guide now told us it would be necessary to send for the Tswabwa of this settlement, who resided at Mahmine, seven miles to the east, and seek his protection. This would have caused great delay, and I was much opposed to the move : fortunately, the Chief just then arrived, and after a long conversation, and the receipt of few presents, he guaranteed us safety to the limit of his district, which extended only a few miles from here : beyond that, he said it would not be safe for us to venture, as the neighbouring clan was lying in wait for any trader that passed, against whom they had vowed vengeance, in consequence of some one having recently taken away a piece of jade unpaid for; however, I was determined to run the gauntlet. The weir is formed by throwing a wicker-work barricade across the river, with an opening of seven feet in the centre, which then takes the form of a V. In this, the fish, principally *Opsarius gracelus* and *Barbels*, are captured in hundreds, simply by closing a gate when the trap is sufficiently full. The curing process consists, first, in gutting the fish and then laying them on a bamboo bench with bars six inches apart, beneath which a fire of damp wood is kindled, which completes the operation. Before we were allowed to pass, the usual black mail of two rupees per boat was demanded and had to be paid. Here, for the first time, I collected thirty young *Ficus elastica* seedlings growing among the rubbish, on the site occupied by these people last year : these were claimed as private property, and I had to pay eight annas each for them. For this I was not sorry, as it stimulated the people to collect for me ; and I was promised a number more on my return. Made fast for the night some way up the Endow *choung*.

326. *Wednesday, 4th March 1874.*—Thermometer, 69° at 6 A.M. Endow *choung* winds through low marshy land covered with tall grasses, and a stray salix here and there ; during the monsoon, I was informed the Endawgyee lake overflows its banks, and the whole of this country is one sheet of water. I had plenty of shooting here, consisting in *Halcyon pileata, Ceryle rudis, Lobivanellus atromichalis, Porphyrio neglectus, Nettapus coromandelica, Dendrocygna arcuata, Plotus melanogaster,* and *Spatula clypenla.* Made fast for the night along side of the bank.

327. *Thursday, 5th March 1874.*—Thermometer, 63° at 6 A.M. Last night, I was awoke by the trumpeting of elephants ; they were close by, and the echo through the hills had a most peculiar effect, each animal having a distinct note. In my drowsy state, I was at

first at a loss to understand what the noise was, never having heard so many trumpeting at the same time: for the moment, I imagined it was the shouts of hundreds of Kakhyens bearing down upon us, but the delusion was not for long. Towards evening it came on to thunder, and rain, and two of my boats remained behind. The tortuous windings of the *choung* separated us by water some considerable distance, though in a direct line we were within hail of one another, and I found that the boatmen declined to come on in the storm; but a threat of an unpleasant nature, if I was compelled to return, soon brought them to their senses, and we all made fast together for the night.

328. *Friday, 6th March 1874.*—Thermometer, 62° at 6 A.M. Dense fog up to 9 A.M. From where we made fast last night, the Endow *choung* widens out considerably, and there is a gradual fall in the country, towards the Endawgyee lake, which we entered by 2 P.M. Here the Endawshwe Toung-gyee range gives off a low spur reaching to the water's edge; it is capped by a small pagoda, where my people asked permission to make offerings for our future safety. Continued to skirt the western bank, until reaching the Nanpatoung *choung*, where we remained for the night. We had not made fast over quarter of an hour, when a band of mountaineers from Nansay came to inquire if we had met a boat with four *Kullars*, natives of India, anywhere on this side of the fishing weir of the Mahwine tribe; finding we had not, they left us. The hills here present a barren, inhospitable appearance, and are principally covered with grass which had been recently burnt. I took a ramble over the hills, and found iron cropping up everywhere, and the party that accompanied me picked up iron pyrites cubically crystallized, mistaking them for gold. As usual, before turning in for the night a peon was sent to the top of a *Ficus*, some three hundred yards further up the lake, to get a view of the surrounding country; he reported that there was an encampment of a hundred Kakhyens seated round a fire, on the hills to the N. N. W.; for my own satisfaction, I climbed the tree, and found, as I had expected, facts were exaggerated; there was an encampment in the direction indicated, but with the aid of my night glass, I could not distingnish more than twenty men gathered round a blazing fire. I descended, and made arrangements for reliefs to be perched on the tree, throughout the night, to watch the movements of these men.

329. *Saturday, 7th March 1874.*—Thermometer, 62° at 6 A.M. Heavy mist, which had a charming effect as it gradually ascended from the lake, and unveiled the surrounding mountain scenery. Started my boats to Winelone, a Shan stockaded village on the banks of the lake: I followed up by land. The country is of a rolling

nature, the intersecting valleys being cultivated with paddy and *til*, and the side slopes of the hills, dotted with *toungya* clearings; round about the village was grown castor oil, *Bixa orellana*, tobacco, plantains, limes, Jatropha, cotton, or poppy; the natural growth was represented by wild strawberries, raspberries, and roses on the bank beyond the influence of the overlap of the lake : arborescent vegetation was sparse and made up of teak, *Eurya, Acacia catechu, Grewia, Mimosa, Gordonia arborea, Fici, Nauclea, Careya, Gmelina arborea,* bamboo and *Dipterocarpus tuberculatus*, which latter bore signs of having been tapped for the oil : but nowhere was *Ficus elastica* to be seen. The fact of the low water level of the Endawgyee lake being below that of the country, south of the mouth of the Nantain *choung*, has given rise to a legend connected with this lake, which I shall here give, as illustrative of how ready an uneducated class are to envelope in mystery any circumstance they cannot easily account for, and what implicit confidence the present generation place in the mythical traditions handed down to them by their forefathers. The fable is this : the *nát* of Endawgyee lake having refused to give in marriage his daughter, to the *nát* of Nantain *choung*, war was proclaimed, but the latter deity being the more powerful, gained the object of his affection. An agreement was now entered into, by the two spirits that, in celebration of the marriage day—which is supposed to have taken place early in July—the *nát* of Nantain *choung* was always to send his father-in-law a gold cup, a bundle of plantain leaves, a bale of silk thread, and some firewood. This stipulation was scrupulously acted up to, until within the last few years, when the *nát* of Nantain *choung*, finding all the valuable articles were stolen *en route*, resolved for the future to commemorate the day, by presenting merely a bundle of faggots. Prior to this war, it is believed, that the Nantain *choung* flowed in the opposite direction, but since the date of this memorable event, the current was changed with a view to facilitate the floating down of the presents. So firm is the belief of the people in this tradition, that towards the tail-end of a spur which extends 700 yards into the water, they have built a rubble wall rising in three tiers to a height of eighteen feet, which is five feet above the flood level; each step or tier is protected from the wash of the waves by a casement of woodden piles driven into the ground close to one another; at the end of this promontory, a pagoda has been erected, guarded at the four corners by leogryphs : here an annual fair is held, attended largely both by Bhuddhists, and the mountaineers who likewise reverence this spirit. This promontory in the month of July, when the water has attained the level of the Nantain *choung*, produces a counter-current, and all the *débris* that accumulates round the base of the pier, the poor people in their igorance believe to be the annual offering of the son-in-law to this great spirit. The lake now continued to rise, and the sticks and rubbish gradually floated away; their disappearance being accounted for by the *nâts'* consumption.

330. *Sunday, 8th March 1874.*—Thermometer, 61° at 6 A.M. Heavy fog, dispersing with the same effect as yesterday. The Endawgyee lake is about thirteen miles long and six broad, and fed by numerous mountain-torrents; it is surrounded on all sides, but to the south south-east, by hills: those to the east being the highest and most heavily wooded. So great is the dread of the mountaineers to the east (which is in the Moohnyin District,) that neither Shans nor Shan-Burmans venture to settle among them. I had hoped from here to be able to penetrate the interior some distance north, but coolies were not obtainable, even at two rupees per diem; subsequently I learnt that they had been prohibited coming to me by my guide. Remainder of the day was spent in an excursion to the head waters of the Nang-poung *choung*, the *Kulwa-boung-toung*, about where I had expected to trace the volcano noted in Yule's map; but I was disappointed; even the people about here did not seem ever to have heard mentioned accounts of the eruptions. The highest altitude reached, was 1,200 feet; the vegetation corresponded with that already noticed to the north-west of Winclone, but was far more luxuriant in growth: I got a shot at a fine smooth-skinned bear (*Ursus malayauns*), but only wounded him. My bag consisted of a horn-bill, *Buceros rhinoceros*, *Falco jugger*, *Phyllornis aurifrons*, *Elanus melanopterus*, a number of large green pigeon *(Carpophaga sylvatica)*, peacock, and some jungle fowl; I also missed a number of birds, some of which were new to me. In two different places, I came on nests of the leaf-cutter-bee (*megachile*), and collected other predaceous beetles, none of which I recognized: I returned to my boats, after a very hard day's tramp, at 9 P.M.

331. *Monday, 9th March 1874.*—Thermometer, 60° at 6 A.M. Heavy due overnight; and dense fog, in the morning. Started my boats at an early hour, but they could not get further than the confluence of the Nan-poung *choung*, for the water was too rough: a strong gale had sprung up from the north-west, and the waves were very high. I joined them by land, collecting shells and plants on the way. The black sand that had hitherto characterized the beach, was now changed to a yellow clay, which discoloured the water for a considerable distance from the shore. Dr. Hungerford, Surgeon-Major H. M.'s 45th Regiment, S.F., who had made conchology a study, informed me that there were two shells among my collection new to him; which I believe he sent to Mr. Theobald, to identify but unfortunately, just then the Regiment left for Bangalore, and subsequently

illhealth necessitated his going home : I have not heard Mr. Theobald's decision on the subject. Here was a large Shan-Burman village named after the *choung*, the inhabitants of which appeared comfortably off and contented. I was surprised to find that both the male and female population of this and Winelone were opium-smokers. They spoke of the frequent raids committed by the highlanders to the east, but expressed themselves sufficiently strong to confine the depredations to cattle-lifting. I was amused at their primitive manner of expressing oil from *til*-seed. Through the stem of a tree about three feet from the ground a large hole was cut for the reception of a lever thirty feet long : at four feet from the trunk was a block of wood three and-a-half feet high, with a slight concavity at the top. Serving as a fulcrum on this was placed a fine open work bamboo basket filled with partially bruised *til*-seed, and at the top rested a slab of wood four inches thick, corresponding in size with the top of the block below, the lever being weighted at the extremity by a huge mass of clay, and the process of expression assisted by the additional weight of the owners who sat at the end singing merrily, and dangling their legs as they watched the oil gradually exude from the preparations of the basket and trickle into the hollow, eventually pouring through, the opening left for the purpose. *Broussonetia Papyrifera*, which is plentiful enough here, is manufactured into paper or, rather, card-board (the *parabeik* of the country) by these people. Raspberry and wild rose continued, and wild *Asparagus* and three different *Ipomœa* were noticed. *Bryophyllum calycinum* grew in the vicinity of this village.

332. *Tuesday, 10th March 1874.*—Thermometer, 59° at 6 A.M. Dew overnight, and fog in the morning. Continued round the lake. Spurs from the main range reached to the water's edge untill little south-east of the Wan-maw *choung*, when the country takes the low swampy character I described on entering this lake. The hills attain a good height, and are densely wooded, the intervening valleys being partially cultivated by the Thainbows with paddy, but *toungya* clearings on the hill slopes are few and far between. When abreast of Nan-pau *choung*, I ascended the highest ridge, and my barometer read 1,600 feet; here I came on extensive forests of two varieties of *pine*, both apparently rich in resin : I did not recognize either, but collected specimens of the wood, leaves, and cones. They were growing among *Dipterocarpus tuberculatus, Diospyros, Nauclea, Melanorhea Usitatissima, Briedelia, Fici* (but no *F. elastica*), *Careya, Lagerstrœmia grandiflora, Guttifera, Cedrela toona* (few) and sprinkling of teak, together with numerous other shrubs and trees, specimens of which have been preserved. I did not deem it prudent to shoot here, for it would only have attracted the mountaineers,

and perhaps brought about disturbance. Water-fowl on this lake are remarkably scarce; indeed, nowhere are they to be seen except hugging the banks, and even there I did not notice many. Reached the Endaw *choung* by 8 P.M.

333. *Wednesday, 11th March 1874.*—Thermometer, 61° at 6 A.M. Slight rain overnight, and a little fog in the morning: I was now on my way back to Kamine, and continued to collect *Ficus elastica* seedlings as we went along. It was noticeable how these trees towered above the others, their grand crowns and shining foliage always rendering them conspicuous objects from great distances. Nantain *choung* was reached by noon, and here were a party of mountaineers spearing fish (Barbel). The harpoon was a simple piece of bamboo cut to a point and barbed, with a long piece of string fastened to the end and attached to the wrist. They use this weapon with great skill. Further down we met two officials from Mandalay on their way up stream, with instruction, from the capital, to order the collection of caoutchouc. Shot some night heron, which my people considered good eating. I met parties from the serpentine mines coming overland to Lawsoon, and proceeding thence, *viâ* the Nantain and Endaw streams, to Mogoung.

334. *Thursday, 12th March 1874.*—Thermometer, 59° at 6 A.M. Passed a cliff on the left bank exposing a strata of pipe-clay. I took specimens, and my boatmen collected a large quantity, which they said was used in pottery. We had an anxious time of it to-day, for the shallowness and rapidity of the stream, which was impeded by blocks of serpentine, some feet above the water, imperilled our boats. In places, it became necessary to tie long ropes to the stern, take a turn round some tree, and let them glide slowly one by one through the gates. The Burmese are naturally of an excitable temperament, and under difficulties, seem to lose all control of themselves, and the only wonder was, that any order was preserved: each man at the top of his voice was either abusing, or countermanding his neighbour's order; while one was shouting "hold fast," another was swearing vengeance if the man with the rope did not "slack away," and so on it went, until the danger was past, when they all had a good laugh at the difficulties encountered. Not many *Ficus elastica* seedlings were added to our number to-day. Made fast at the Mahweine Weir, and found, the whole of the Kakhyens had decamped.

335. *Friday, 13th March 1874.*—Thermometer, 59° at 6 A.M.; heavy fog. Singularly the Kakhyens of Mahweine had heard of our arrival, and came down with fifty-two young *Ficus* seedlings planted in bamboos. I purchased these for Rs. 9-4-0; and presented the Tswabwa and his five followers, with a goung-boung each. The

Kakhyens said that the seeds germinate on the ground, but that they have seldom seen them over six inches high, and that all the fine trees now to be seen are from the droppings of birds either in the forks of trees, or ferns. This leads to the idea that the seedlings are either destroyed by fires or die from excess of shade. From the little I have seen of the habits of these trees, I consider that they delight in an abundance of light; for the finest specimens I met with, had unquestionably established their cradle on some high-growing trees; and that they are naturally of an epiphytical habit, in early growth, is an undisputed fact, I believe.

836. *Saturday, 13th March 1874.*—Thermometer 60°, at 6 A.M.; heavy fog up to 9 A.M. When in search of *Ficus elastica* seedlings to-day, our attention was attracted by the incessant and pitiful cry of a deer; on reaching the place whence the sound came, I found a doe samber jammed in the fork of a tree: evidently she had got locked in endeavouring to escape from the pursuit of some animal, She was very thin, and must have been in this position for the last few days. I put an end to her misery with a bullet from my pistol, but it was with difficulty even then, that she could be disengaged. As we proceeded on, shoals of fish lying under the bank kept jumping some feet out of the water as they were disturbed, and some even sprang into the boats. This afforded great amusement to the crew, who kept striking the water with their poles, and shouting with excitement: it seems necessary that these people must give vent to their ebullition of spirits by boisterous exclamations. The fish were *Cyprinus foliata*, and *Opsarimus gracilus*, I believe. Specimens were preserved for future identification. To-day I shot two black pheasants and three otters. We now reached Kamine, and I was busy until a very late hour planting the seedlings collected, during the last two days, for they had now been separated from the trees on which they grew, longer than I had intended. I used up all the little baskets we had made, and filled every available box; still there were numbers of plants to be provided for. I sent Yan Sing and my guide into the village, to see if they could not purchase some paddy-baskets; they returned however saying that there were plenty to be had, but that the people would not sell. A happy thought now struck me, and I sent Yan Sing back with a number of empty pint hock bottles; the bait was irresistible, and I soon found more brought than were required. Having been thwarted hitherto in my attempt to explore the western interior, to any considerable distance, owing to the determined opposition shown by my guide, I thought perhaps here I should be able to obtain a few coolies, and accomplish the excursion I had intended to make from Winelone. I sent for the head-man of the village, who told me that the journey could easily

be undertaken, and that he would provide me with the necessary escort and coolies, with the consent of my guide, for whom I accordingly sent at once, with the view of confronting them; it was amusing to see how readily the former changed, when the latter expressed his disapprobation; and a decided answer was postponed until the next day.

337. *Sunday, 15th March 1874.*—Thermometer, 63° at 6 A.M. Slight fog. The early part of the morning was spent arranging my young plants in a cool place. My guide, and the head-man of the village, were sent for again. I was quite prepared for disappointment, and was not surprised at the tissue of lies that were told me— not only on this occasion was the disturbed state of the country given as an excuse, but I was actually told there was not a single man in the village available. I felt now, the sooner these men were out of my sight, the better for us both. I despatched Yan Sing with a letter to the Governor at Mogoung, soliciting his assistance, but my last interview with this old *charlatan* did not lead me to hope for any good result from my appeal. My object in wishing to make this excursion, was not alone to see the serpentine mines, but likewise to fix the limit of the *Ficus elastica* in that direction, having already satisfied myself, on this point to the east of Mogoung, the Endawgyee *choung*, and south of the lake bearing the name of the latter.

338. *Monday, 16th March 1874.*—Thermometer, 69° at 6 A.M. Cloudy and muggy this morning. I had hoped that this foretold rain, for the benefit of my plants. The whole day was spent in arranging my botanical, and other specimens. During my ramble this evening, I came on a good deal of poppy cultivation. Cows and bullocks were scarce here, buffaloes of a very fine breed taking their place; goats and sheep, there were none.

339. *Tuesday, 17th March 1874.*—Thermometer, 72° at 6 A.M.; cloudy morning: rain threatened, and a few drops fell overnight.

340. *Wednesday, 18th March 1874.*—Thermometer, 72° at 6 A.M. Rain overnight: morning clear, but close. A boat just in, with jade, reported that they had been fired on, about Nan *choung*: the women in the boat having detected the Kakhyens concealed in the bushes, fired on them, killing one man: the steersman's cloth was shot through, and the bullet-hole was shown me.

341. *Thursday, 19th March 1874.*—Thermometer, 69 at 6 A.M. Slight mist: I found this morning, that twenty of my *Ficus elastica* seedlings had been stolen, and in the afternoon, the same number were, strange to say, brought me for sale. I represented this to my guide, and laid claim to the seedlings, by certain distinguishing marks; fortunately, these were apparent to him, though I must confess they were not to me! The result was, however, that they were

made over to me gratis. Yan Sing returned to-day by land, and reported having met with a good deal of teak on the left bank some distance inland, but that it was small. The boatmen who took him down to Mogoung refused to return, which necessitated his joining me overland. The Governor's reply was civil, but, as I anticipated, not favourable: he said my life was too valuable to warrant his countenancing such a perilous journey. This evening as I was writing, swarms of insects flocked round the light; they were not white-ants though their wings were similar : immediately on settling, they laid a single egg almost the size of their entire body, and died. What they were, I do not know, but they were in myriads and covered the whole sheet of water from bank to bank, and for a considerable distance down stream. Some flowers of the *Michelia* were brought me as presents, the tree growing in the village. I shot two peacock pheasants, and some painted partridge towards sunset.

342. *Friday, 20th March 1874.*—Thermometer, 62° at 6 A.M. Left Kamine to-day, and arranged to stop at *Nanhain*, having been promised some *Ficus elastica* seedlings there. When the plants were produced it struck me that the leaves were unsually large, and on pulling one up, I found they were all fresh cuttings. An endeavour was made to wipe out this attempt at deception, by an excuse that my order was misunderstood. This was hardly likely, however, considering that I had refused to purchase cuttings from these very people on my way up. I saw a large herd of wild pigs to-day ; they were just emerging from the forest to drink, but seeing our boats, turned back before I could get a shot. There was a splendid old boar among them.

343. *Saturday, 21st March 1874.*—Thermometer, 62° at 6 A.M. Just below old Mogoung, I met a number of boats collecting firewood for the rains, when, I was told this article sells at Mogoung for twice the price already quoted. Made fast at a sand-bank, a little above Nanpoung village. We were detained somewhat by my inland excursion.

344. *Sunday, 22nd March 1874.*—Thermometer, 61° at 6 A.M. Heavy fog up to 9 A.M. Reached Mogoung by noon, and called on the Governor at once. He received me in the most gushing manner, and the leave-taking on his part was pathetic in the extreme. I was far too annoyed, however, to be more than civil. I acknowledged his politeness with thanks, but expressed both surprise and regret at the treatment I had received during my stay, in his district, and gave him to understand, that this should be made the subject of special report on my return to the capital ; upon which, he replied, "I received no instructions from the King to help you, but was merely "told, you were at liberty to engage what elephants or coolies you

"required." The opposition I met with, in the Mogoung district must be partly attributed to the foolish jealousy, with which both the amber and serpentine mines are guarded from the eye of intelligent observers, and partly to the mandate from the palace (which I believe had already been noticed in the Political Diary of the Assistant Resident at Bhamo,) prohibiting any assistance being extended to me in the collection of *Ficus elastica* seedlings. As to the truth of the order, there is no doubt, for I had been privately told of it, by two of the royal hpoongyees. In spite of the opposition, however, I trust the Chief Commissioner and the Supreme Government of India will consider I have brought my mission to a successful close, and that, although I have been unable to fix the extreme limit of the *Ficus elastica* south of the Assam Province, where the tree is known to abound, yet I have gained much valuable information regarding the natural habits of this tree, which will ultimately tend to its successful introduction into British Burma. I called on the royal poongyee to say, ";good-bye" and cannot conclude this day's diary without observing what a capital specimen he is of his cloth : the good this man had done by befriending the mountaineers, and converting many to the Buddhistic faith, had already commenced to bear fruit. Left Mogoung at 4 P.M., and made fast for the night a few miles below.

345. *Monday, 23rd March 1874.*—Thermometer, 72° at 6 A.M. Rain overnight, cloudy and drizzly throughout the day. With the exception of a few Kakhyen squatters employed catching fish, there are no villages between Mogoung and Tahoon. The river averages 150 yards in breadth, and is remarkably winding in its course ; the country on either side is flat and uninteresting. There had been a considerable rise since my boats came up, which bespoke heavy rain in the hills. Stopped for a little while beneath a spur, just south of Tahpoon, to examine the system by which teak is felled and extracted here : the trees are first killed by the process of girdling, and making a hole through the stem, in two different directions ; they are then felled, cut into lengths not exceding twenty-five feet, and dragged to the water's edge by buffaloes. This work is entirely in the hands of the Kakhyens. The process of seasoning or killing is conducted when the tree is in flower, and under this system the logs are stated to be dry enough to float in twelve months. The largest girth I measured, was four feet three in circumference, and the timber appeared remarkably free from heart shake. Just here, the river deepens considerably, and the scenery becomes more engaging ; but this does not last for long, the country soon again flattening out on either side, and the shore fringed with tall grasses and *salix* : immediately below the large Kak-

hyen village of Latoung, situated on the right bank, and perhaps ten miles south-east of Tahpoon, the rapids commence, and navigation becomes difficult and dangerous : the bed of the river, which is of serpentine, appeared to be formed into eleven tiers or steps, the channel everywhere being impeded by large boulders, and at about the sixth drop, the passage will not admit of more than one boat passing at a time ; for through this gate, the water rushes with terrific velocity. A little above this gate we made fast, and boat by boat was allowed to shoot the fall, the pace being regulated by the combined efforts of the crew who had hold of a rope attached to the stem ; but barely had the boats entered the opening, than the impetus of the current rendered them uncontrollable, and they shot forward nearly being swamped in the descent by the curling foam on either side. The rapids were now again less fierce until the last drop but one was reached, when the water was so shallow as to have necessiated an artificial channel being formed by a dam of stones, across the river, with a small opening on the right bank, just sufficient to admit of boats passing singly. We were delayed here some time by the numbers of boats returning from the fair recently held at Bhamo. It is customary for boats down stream to assist those coming up, and so difficult is the navigation just here and the gate above, that it is generally arranged for the up-journey to be made in batches, with a view to the crews assisting one another. Eventually, we got through ; the same precaution having been taken as was followed when clearing the last opening : but here we were not so successful, for a hole was knocked through the bottom of one of the boats, which had to be plugged up with some cloth. It is in these rapids, when boats are in difficulty, that they are attacked by bands of mountain bandits ; and now a guard of six Burmans, who have to provide their own arms and ammunition, had been stationed here to protect voyagers, but they would be of little service in case of an attack, for Kakhyen dacoits seldom go about in bands of less than twenty or thirty men. Each drop or step has its own name ; they are as follows :—

(1)—Pha-ha-man-hmaw, (ဖါးဟမန်ချွေ့။) signifying "boat-destroyer."

(2)—Nath-a-mee-hmaw, (နတ်သမီးချွေ့။) " signifying residence of *nát's* daughter."

(3)—Har-lone-sai, (ဟာလွှန်းဆယ်ချွေ့။)

(4)—Yin-but-hmaw, (ရင်ဗုတ်ချွေ့။) dangerous place, where boats must be propelled by the chest.

(5)—Toung-phoung-hmah, (တောင်ဖြောင်းချွေ့မလော့။)

(6)—Toung-phoung-gyee-hmaw (တောင်ဖြောင်းကြီးချွေ့။)

(7)—Thoung-myoung-zee-hmaw, (သုန်ကြောင်းဗိုင်မှော်။) signifying great canal prison.
(8)—Sause-sankine-hmaw (ဝော်ဝိုင်မှော်။)
(9)—Patit-hmaw (ပတစ်မှော်။)
(10)—Phassa-loung-hmaw (ဖဿောလောင်းမှော်။)
(11)—Pha-kotechit-hmaw (ဖါးကုတ်ချစ်မှော်။)

Made fast for the night a mile below the last rapid.

346. *Tuesday, 24th March 1874.*—Thermometer, 68° at 6 A.M. Heavy rain during the night; cloudy this morning. The banks were again rich in vegetation, and festooned with *Thunbergia, Clerodendron* and *Letsomia*, which last is used for cordage. A little further on, and the river is sub-divided by a permanent island, densely wooded, below which the banks are of yellow clay; then comes the Shan and Kakhyen village on the left bank of Areloungboree, where teak timber was being converted. We stopped here a little while to get some saw-dust and *powynet*, to stop the leak in the boat recently damaged. Noticed some Kakhyen women dyeing twist brick-red with pieces of *Butia*, and the root of *Rottlera tinctoria*. From here the hills rapidly recede; and by the time the Shan-Burman village of Kouk-toung is reached, they are in the far distance, and the country on either side one continuous flat, that to the east being sparsely wooded and overgrown with *Saccharum*, and *Arundo* grasses, while that to the west is one vast sea of paddy land. Kouk-toung is of some considerable importance, and carries on an extensive trade in paddy, teak, and *endway* resin. It contains sixty houses enclosed by a treble-walled bamboo stockade; without to the south, is a Kakhyen settlement of twenty houses. It is situated on the right bank, and the soil is of a light red, sandy nature, the river flowing some forty feet below, and rising to within ten feet of the top, during the highest flood; here were exposed for sale a Shan mother and daughter brought from the direction of the serpentine mines; the former was about forty years of age, and valued at thirty ticals of opium; and the latter eight to twelve years old, and priced at four hundred baskets of paddy which is equivalent to about Rs. 40. The father had been killed when the village was plundered and burnt down. I felt inclined to pay the price set on these poor creatures, and release them from bondage; but I questioned, whether I should be bettering their condition, for they seemed exceedingly happy where they were; and once free, no doubt poverty might have driven them to crime.

347. *Wednesday, 25th March 1874.*—Thermometer, 63° at 6 A.M. Two miles lower down, and a small creek on the left bank forms the boundary of the Mogoung and Moohnyin District. Another two hours brought us to the mouth of the Mogoung river, where we

heard a good deal of firing, from the opposite bank of the Irrawaddy. Shortly afterwards, I distinguished a European beckoning to us; this turned out to be the late Mr. Graham, who had been attacked while poling along the opposite shore, by a strong party of Kakhyens: he mentioned having shot three of the gang dead and wounded some of the others. Their first action it appears was to send a number of spears at the boat, when all but a Burman lad who he had brought up from childhood jumped into the river and swam away; seeing, however, that the bandits had retreated, they returned to the boats. This statement was corroborated by the deserters themselves, and one out of the five spears that had been lodged in the roof of the boat, was given to me. I suggested that Mr. Graham had better return to Bhamo, but he declined; so we parted. Reached Tsimbo by 4 P.M., where I remained for the night. The river had risen many feet since I was last here, and the defile was described as being very dangerous. I received here a packet of letters and Rs. 600 from the Assistant Resident of Bhamo, which I had written for from Mogoung, at a time I had hoped to have been able to extend my researches.

348. *Thursday, 26th March 1874.*—Thermometer, 69° at 6 A.M. Left Tsimbo at 7-30 A.M., reaching Bhamo by 6 P.M. The danger of the defile had in no way been exaggerated; indeed, as we shot down the impetuous stream, every moment seemed to be our last. It was with difficulty, the helmsmen kept the boats from being carried round, by the violent eddies and whirlpools, and the boatmen rowed their strongest against stream, to reduce the terrific pace at which we were being borne, by the fierce rapids. Our position was too critical to admit of any accurate observation being made; still I noticed that since my northward journey, a new Kakhyen settlement had sprung up, on the left bank, and an extensive *toungya* clearing been made. When we reached Bhamo, I found the usual landing place so crowded with boats, that it was some little time before we could land.

(208)

CHAPTER VI.
[CONCLUSION.]

General recapitulation of all facts associated with the "Ficus elastica."

NATURAL ORDER, ARTOCARPACEÆ—*(Lind).*

FIG TRIBE.

"*Ficus elastica.*" *Vernacular*—ᏣᎷᎶᏋᎥ "*Borde-bane.*"

DESCRIPTION.—A large tree, with irregular-shaped stem, and spreading branches, from which roots descend to the ground. The leaves are thick, coriaceous, shining, elliptic, mid-rib very prominent, with numberless straight parallel fine lateral veins, nearly at right-angles to the mid-rib, blade 3—6 inches long, on seedlings and root-shoots much larger, stipules long, sheathing rose-coloured. Fruit ovoid, greenish yellow, the size of an olive. *Forest Flora of Western and Central India. D. Brandis.* Natives both of temperate and tropical climates : species 184: *Ill Gen.,*— *Morus, Broussonetia, Maclura, Ficus, Urostigma, Sycomorus, Kaprificus, Dorstenia Trophis.—Balfour,* p. 891.

DISTRIBUTION.—The *Ficus elastica* is found along the foot and in the low tropical valleys of the Himalayas, from the Mechi river on the Nepal boundary at 88° E. long., to the extreme eastern boundary of Assam, 97° East long., as well as along the foot, and in the low valleys of the southern mountains of the Brahmapootra valley, *viz.*, the Patkey mountains, the Naga, Khasi Jynteah, and Garrow Hills. Although found so far west as the Nepal boundary, it is not abundant until east of the Bor Nuddee (the western boundary of the Durrung District), where it is common in the forests at the foot of the hills in the Khaling Booree, Goma, and Kooreeaparah Dooars, between the Bor Nuddee and Moora Dhunseeree Nuddee, and has been exported from the forests which extend over about forty square miles, as well as from the low valleys of the Bhootan hills immediately above them, and especially from the forests in the neighbourhood of the exit of the Noonae Nuddee, in the Khaling Dooar, and adjoining hills, and those between the Deemjany and the Rootah Nuddees.

In the Chardooar forest, between the Moora Dhunseeree or Rootah Nuddee, and the Bhoratee river, they are abundant. The Chardooar forests cover about two hundred and twenty square miles. In these forests, between the Beelseeree and the Gobhoroo

Nuddees, they are found as far as sixteen miles from the hills, but as here the atmosphere is drier than at the hills, the produce is not near so abundant.

In the Noradooar forests, covering about two thousand square miles, the atmosphere is drier, but the *caoutchouc* obtained from trees close to the hills is good.

In the Chydooar forests caoutchouc trees are only found in the forest along and immediately at the foot of the hills. They are also most abundant in the Luckimpore and Naga hill districts, as well as in the low valleys of the mountains immediately adjoining them.—*Report on the caoutchouc of commerce—James Collins, F.B.S., Edin.*

In the Island of Java, however, it seems also to be indigenous; Blume (l. C). in 1825, states that it grows on limestone, gives the vernacular name as *Karet, Karet-tapok,* and describes a variety, *Bengalica* (introduced from *Calcutta*), with acuminate, undulate leaves. In the preface to Rumphia ii. (1836), he states that the Java tree is capable of yielding caoutchouc—*D. Brandis.*

According to Mr. Gustav Mann's map, which I have embodied in mine, we find he has fixed the geographical range of the *Ficus elastica* in Assam between 25° 40' and 28° 15' North lat., and 88° 10' and 97° East long., while in Burma Proper I found it extend to 25° 10', and according to report it reaches to the junction of the Chindwin and Ooree rivers, lat. 24° 45'. But it is not known on the east bank of the Irrawaddy, if any reliance can be placed in the information elicited from the mountaineers and Burmese officials.

PROPERTIES.—The plants of this order supply, in many instances, edible fruits; their milky juice often abounds in *caoutchouc*, and in some instances is bland and nutritious, while their inner bark supplies fibres. Bitter, tonic, as well as acrid and poisonous properties are found in the order.—*Balfour* p. 892.

349. Before proceeding to describe the different methods followed in Burma Proper for the collection and manufacture of *caoutchouc*, I propose to devote a few lines to the early history of this branch of industry—information that has been culled either from works of science or trade reports. *Caoutchouc*, I believe, is a French word, derived from the local name of the milky juice extracted from the *Sephonia elastica*, which was discovered by a French botanist in the last century. Now the word is more generally applied, and refers to the inspissated milk of all gum-elastic yielding plants. It was only in 1736 that the fact of *caoutchouc* being a *bonâ fide* vegetable product was set at rest by a reference to the French Government, and for years subsequent it continued to be a mere cabinet curiosity. The earliest mention of its utility is found in the preface of a work published in 1770 by the Rev. Joseph Priestly, L.LD., wherein he writes: " Since this work was printed off, I have seen a substance excellently adapted to the purpose of wiping from

paper the marks of a black-lead pencil. It must therefore be of singular use to those who practice drawing. It is sold by Mr. Naune, mathematical instrument maker, opposite the Royal Exchange. He sells a cubical piece, of about half an inch square, for three shillings, and he says it will last several years."

350. In 1820 its singular elastic and water-proof properties attracted much attention, and led to various experiments, which resulted in Mr. Mackintosh of Glasgow presenting to the public, in 1823, his well-known *Mackintosh*.

351. Up to this date the raw material was nearly entirely imported from South America, though Dr. George Gladstone, F.C.S., tells us that an article almost identical was known to be procurable in India, having been discovered by Dr. Roxburgh, in Assam, about 1809. But for the exhibition of Dr. Forbes Royle, he goes on to say,—"the cost of Indian *caoutchouc* must have remained much longer in obscurity, for when a gentleman up-country sent some to his agents in Calcutta, they wrote in reply that the article being unknown in this market, we are sorry we can give no idea of its value." This happened in 1828, when it was selling in London for two shillings per lb. By 1840, it had become a regular article of export, and by its competition had considerably reduced the price of the South American *caoutchouc*. The various uses to which this staple is turned, which range from a baby's tooth-ring to a railway carriage buffer, are too generally known to need cataloguing here; but the magnitude and importance of the trade will be best appreciated when I state that the total import of india-rubber into the United Kingdom rose from three hundred and forty thousand odd pounds weight in 1845, to over five millions of pounds in 1855; since then public need and mechanical ingenuity have combined to extend its uses, and fortunately fresh natural stores have been discovered, which alone have equallized demand and supply, and moderated the market value. Her Majesty's Secretary of State for India, now, seeing the probable increasing demand for india-rubber in connection with the requirements of State railways and other operations in which the Government has a direct interest, has thought fit to urge upon the Indian Government the necessity of taking time by the forelock, and establishing plantations of *Ficus elastica* and other india-rubber-yielding trees whenever practicable, and among the foremost to take the field has been the local administration of British Burma.

352. In Burma the trade in *caoutchouc* is but of yesterday's date, as will be gathered from the following quotation, extracted from the Political journal of the agent at Mandalay, dated 22nd January 1873 :—

"The existence of the india-rubber in Upper Burma does "not appear to have been known, or at any rate did not attract "attention until somewhat recently, when three Europeans, Messrs. "Miller, Marshall, and Henri, who were employed at the jade-stone "mines, were forced to look and search about in the forests for a "substance that would effectually repair a mining apparatus that "they used in working for jade-stone. They found india-rubber, "and repaired the apparatus. The existence and value of the "juice was then brought to the notice of the King, and Mr. Henri "is now employed in tapping the trees and preparing the juice. "Some 70,000 *viss* of india-rubber was brought from Mogoung last "year. I myself saw thirty or forty cart-loads of it entering the "palace one day. Upper Burma could produce 200 or 300 tons "of this useful substance per annum."

353. Mr. Brown, the Collector of Customs, kindly informs me that *caoutchouc* was first exported from Rangoon in August 1873, as the produce of Upper Burma. The exports have been as follows:—

	Cwts.
1873-74	... 737½
1874-75	... 2,058
Nine months in 1875-76 ...	... 972

354. The culture of the *Ficus elastica* in British Burma may be said to have commenced from June 1874, the date of my return to Rangoon. Whether the climate is favourable to the undertaking still remains to be proved; for, although our results hitherto have been sufficiently encouraging to hope for success, yet at this early stage of the experiment, it would be unwise to predict what change the future may or may not bring about: for my own part, I am inclined to take a sanguine view of things. From a climatic point of view, it is true, the natural home of the *Ficus elastica* is not identical with that of this province, but the extremes of heat and cold in the two countries do not appear sufficiently marked to affect the question; while the general habit of the tree leads me to suppose that it will accommodate itself to a far wider zone than that to which it is geographically limited. The disadvantages under which it continues to grow at Prome, speaks for the hardiness of the tree. There it is growing in the centre of a densely-populated town, with an atmosphere and soil antipodal to its natural requirements; while the pernicious practice Buddhists have of gilding the leaves in sacred adoration for the tree, cannot be otherwise than ruinous to plant life, considering that these organs perform the same functions in vegetable life that the lungs and stomach do in animal. In the Commissariat gardens at

Rangoon, there is a *Ficus elastica*, that was introduced I am told from Calcutta, in 1859, and is the parent of the stock now met with in different parts of the town and its suburbs. Whether the tree was originally a seedling or cutting cannot be ascertained, nor is there anything on record regarding its height and size when first imported ; at present, it no longer maintains its natural habit of growth, the absence of aërial roots alone depriving it of its most characteristic feature, while the leaves are smaller, the stipules less vigorous, and the *tout ensemble* parched and dry in comparison to the umbrageous, rich, shining foliage it exhibits in its own *habitat*. The unhealthy state of this specimen is not attributable to any climatic cause, but unquestionably to its having been too heavily indented on for cuttings—a fact amply supported by its mutilated condition. In nearly every instance in which the cuttings it has furnished have been judiciously treated, they have grown into fine healthy young trees, differing only from the natural character of the species by an absence of aërial roots ; but whether these will commence to develope themselves, as supports to the wide-spreading lateral branches in later years, will be seen hereafter. I here reproduce, in the shape of questions and answers, certain correspondence that has passed between the Honorary Secretary, Agri-Horticultural Society, Burma, and myself, regarding the cultivation of the *Ficus elastica* in this province, from which it will be seen that my hopes of future success in this branch of arboriculture are not wholly unsupported.

No. 1712-806, dated 11th February 1876, from the Deputy Conservator, to the Honorary Secretary, Agri-Horticultural Society, Burma, and Mr. Honorary Secretary's reply No. 322, dated 24th February 1876.

Question.—How many plants of the *Ficus elastica* have you in the Botanic Gardens at Rangoon ?
Answer.—Two dozen.
Question.—Have they been propagated from seeds, or slips, or otherwise ?
Answer.—Propagated from cuttings.
Question.—Can you trace the origin of the plants, and the date of their introduction ?
Answer.—One received originally from the Botanic Garden, Calcutta.
Question.—If the plants have been cultivated in more than one way, which is, according to your experience, the best way of propagation, and the best time of the year for conducting the operation ?
Answer.—I have grown them from cuttings only ; the easiest was, I think, at the commencement of the rains.
Question.—When do the trees defoliate ?
Answer.—In March and April a few leaves fall, but I never saw the trees denuded of leaves at any time of the year.

Question.—Have they yet produced seeds or flowers?
Answer.—No—although two or three trees in the garden are near ten years old.
Question.—At what period of the year does the tree make most rapid growth?
Answer.—At the commencement and close of the rains.
Question.—Have you observed any difference in the size and colour between the stipules of healthy and weak-growing plants?
Answer.—Yes, when planted in swampy or badly-drained localities, the stipules turn yellow, and the whole plant (or tree) looks sickly.
Question.—Does your experience show that the *Ficus elastica* is a tree that delights in shade, or that it thrives better in the open?
Answer.—In the open, in properly-drained localities.
Question.—Is a moist state of the atmosphere, in your opinion, absolutely necessary for the proper development of the tree or its secretions?
Answer.—Three or four of the larger trees in the garden receive no water at all between November and April (planted out in the open) and do not appear to be much affected (if affected at all) with the intense heat of the sun during March and April. They yield milk very freely in these months.
Question.—Do you consider that the mineral composition of the soil, apart from its physical properties—such as humidity, depth, compactness, &c.—has any material influence on the growth of the *Ficus elastica*?
Answer.—The surface soil of the garden is of a reddish, sandy nature, poor, and unproductive. Several pits and thanks, sunk in different parts of the garden, have shown that after a depth of six, seven, or eight feet of this reddish sand and a little clay, the lower strata to a depth of ten or twelve feet is more like laterite in course of formation (I have used it for the garden walks); after sinking below that again, clear yellowish sand is met with, with water. The trees grow very well in this soil; but, as stated before, the only thing that appears to have affected their growth, was when the drainage was bad.
I may mention that I heard the other day from the Rev. Mr. A. Bunker, Toungoo, that a box of cuttings which I gave him, when he was here in December last, have all struck and have been planted out among the Karen hills with coffee, tea, and cinchona, and were thriving vigorously.

355. In *Mason's Burma*, published in 1860, we also find the following encouraging mention of the *Ficus elastica*: "Within a "dozen years the true *caoutchouc* tree of Assam has been introduced "into the Tenasserim provinces, and appears to grow as well as an "indigenous plant."

356. The number of plants I brought from the Laymyo and Mogoung Districts between lat. 24° 16′ and 25° 30′, were 178. With the exception of a few seedlings of a season's growth that were found growing on a rubbish heap (the *débris* of a deserted Kakhyen settlement) in the open on the banks of a river, my collection consisted of epiphytic plants that had either germinated in the forks of trees, or in the cup-like receptacles formed by the peculiar

habit of growth of the *Platycerum wallicii* fern, which is generally situated on high trees, and full of rich humus. Nowhere did I come across a solitary instance of natural reproduction on the ground in the forests, which is attributable, I conceive, to the two following causes, both of which militate against the perpetuation of this tree:—(1) fire ; (2) excessive density of canopy, the latter proving injurious, either from want of light, or by depriving them of meteoric precipitates, *e. g.*, rain, dew, &c. The matured specimens of the *Ficus elastica* met with, were of a solitary habit; groups of over twos and threes seldom occurring, and these without exception had originated in one of the above ways. The difference in habit of growth between the aërial roots and branches were sufficiently marked to admit of the exact height from the ground being fixed, at which the descent of the former commenced; and among the numerous measurements taken, the maximum distance was ascertained to be forty-seven feet, and the minimum sixteen. Ultimately, the tree is killed that has served as a cradle in infancy and a support in later years to this epiphyte, and, by a process of inosculation, the aërial roots unite, forming into one massive furrowed trunk, for which these trees are conspicuous. The lateral branches, however, continue to develop numerous abnormal roots, which ultimately reach the ground and become subterranean, when they serve the double office of props to the wide-spreading limbs,—which appear too heavy to support their own weight,—and organs of absorption. This is the natural habit of the *Ficus elastica* as is met with in its natural home. The plantation at Magayee, which forms part of the *quasi*-evergreen belt that marks the change in vegetation between the plains and hills, situated within three miles of the railway, and sixty miles from Rangoon, is the locality that has been selected as the site to start this new branch of arboriculture. Here the humidity of the atmosphere and physical conditions of the soil, including light, shade, humidity, and drainage correspond nearest to the *habitat* of the tree, while the difference in the chemical composition of the soils is, I am inclined to think, of secondary importance in tree growth, provided a good loamy soil of sufficient depth can be substituted—one in which the admixture of clay and sand are, in such proportions, as to ensure the loose and porous qualities of the one being corrected by the plastic and retentive qualities of the other : a preponderance of sand or gravel, however, should be avoided, and drainage carefully attended to. Men who have devoted time and thought to this subject, do not attach the same importance to the chemical properties of a soil for arboriculture, as they do for agriculture, on the score that the leaves of trees return to the earth, the mineral food absorbed by them.

(215)

It has also been stated that all soils contain the required mineral constituents necessary for the growth of trees, and, further, that even the meteorological matter contains a sufficient supply.

357. Elsewhere, I have spoken of the *Ficus elastica* in Upper Burma, growing in carbonate of lime, but I must explain myself for fear of being misunderstood. The tree was not found in pure carbonate of lime, but in a calcareous form ; *i. e.*, one in which the proportions of lime, clay, humus, and sand gave to it a peculiar physical character ; and may be described according to Schübler's (taken from Fischbach) classification of soils tabulated below, as, *clayey calcareous, loamy calcareous, sandy calcareous,* and *loamy sandy calcareous.*

Description of soil.	Clay.	Carbonate of lime.	Humus.	Sand.
Clayey calcareous	Over 50 per cent.	Over 20 per cent.	5 to 1 per cent.	Remainder.
Loamy ditto	30 to 50 per cent.	Ditto	Ditto	Ditto.
Sandy loamy ditto	20 to 30 per cent.	Ditto	Ditto	Ditto.
Loamy sandy ditto	10 to 20 per cent.	Ditto	Ditto	Ditto.

358. The following will be found a useful and simple rule for determining the quantity of lime in a soil :—Take a hundred grains of the soil (which has been previously heated to redness, to destroy the vegetable matter) and diffuse it through about half a pint of distilled water ; add about one ounce of hydrochloric acid, and allow the mixture to stand for a few hours, observing to stir it from time to time. Bubbles of carbonic acid are given off. After the action has ceased, pour off the clear liquid, dry, and then heat the residue to a redness, and weigh it : the loss is nearly the weight of lime and carbonate of lime in the soil.

359. The method of planting has been the following :—Rides in the forest thirty feet wide and a hundred feet apart were deforested, and the plants established at thirty feet by a hundred and thirty. When the rains set in, however, it was found in places that the trees commenced to close in over-head, and that the young *Ficus* suffered from excess of shade or drip, or both combined. The plants thus affected were either removed to more open places, or the evil remedied by lopping the crowns of the trees when practicable. It must not, however, be gathered from this that I advo-

cate the exposure of young plants to the direct rays of the sun; on the contrary, they require to be carefully shaded throughout the day during the scorching droughts that prevail from March to May; but the plant should not be deprived of the night dews.

360. With us at present this branch of forest industry is entirely empirical, and we can only hope for success by careful observation, and the noting of facts; being careful, however, not to mistake *cause* for *effect*, and *vice versâ*. Experience thus far has proved that light is not injurious to the *Ficus elastica*; but, on the other hand, I have met with a few trees, which were growing vigorously in a shade, which might almost be called dense. Shade over-head, especially from "high" trees, seems to be injurious, but whether this is on account of the actual want of light, or from drip, or because little dew is condensed on the leaves of the plant beneath, I will not at present hazard an opinion.

361. Hitherto, as a rule, those trees have been found to succeed best when shaded only on the south and west, by low trees, and exposed to light on the north and east sides. The leaves of such trees are in most cases loaded with dew. I would suggest that over-hanging trees are injurious, perhaps less on account of the shade they give, than because they prevent the formation of dew on the leaves of the plant beneath. This formation of dew seems peculiarly grateful to the *Ficus elastica*.

362. The one hundred and seventy-eight plants imported varied in age from seedlings of a season's growth to plants of two years old, the minimum height being four inches and the maximum three feet two inches: of these, up to 1st February 1876, two have died: one of which was browsed down by cattle owing to the Overseer having failed to fence it in substantially according to orders; but there is no direct evidence to show what caused the death of the other. Exclusive of these trees, I despatched from Bhamo and Katcho to Rangoon two large consignments of cuttings made in the months of January and February; but these, the Conservator subsequently informed me, had all died in transit. Besides the above stock, six young *Ficus elastica* plants from Bhamo (supposed to have been seedlings) were introduced into the Magayee plantation in June 1872, when they were nine to eighteen inches high. Ever since, they have continued to grow vigorously, and now average a height of ten feet four and-a-half inches, with a proportionate developement of luxuriant foliage. They have not, however, yet commenced to throw down aërial roots, and I am inclined to think that, unless these trees start as epiphytes, they do not obtain this habit until the lateral branches have reached a certain stage of

growth that require support. From this stock forty-four cuttings have been taken under the following processes :—

Propagation.—Reproduction has either been brought about by layers or cuttings. I give a preference to the former practice, as being less hurtful to the parent, surer of success, and admitting of larger and more vigorous plants being obtained ; there are cases, however, where the branches are not conveniently situated for layering ; in that case, the same end can be accomplished either by being *struck* in a basket, suspended to a tree, or by the ingenious method of *gootee,* to be described presently.

Layering—has always been conducted before the ascent of the sap, or postponed until the process is completed; in other words, between the 15th March to 15th April, or the 15th June and 15th July, are the seasons at which this operation has been carried out; when the former part of the year has been chosen, the layers have had to be constantly kept moist and sheltered from the sun during the heat of the day and exposed to the dews at night.

363. The branch operated on has been selected from wood of the previous year's growth ; a notch being cut to half the thickness of the layer just under a leaf bud, with a slit of an inch or so up the stem, which is kept apart by a splinter. These precautions prevent the return of the sap to the main channel, and result in the surplus fluid being employed in the formation of roots to the new plant.

364. The ground was well worked up, and the layer buried to a depth proportionate to its size, but care had to be taken that the future plant was held firm in its place by hooked pegs, and that the top of the layer was preserved in an upright position.

365. Beyond seeing that the layers do not spring, and that shade, and a uniformity of moisture is preserved, no further precaution is required until the time arrives for severing it from the parent tree, which is generally about the end of September. GOOTEE is another method of propagation practiced with success; it corresponds nearly to the Chinese system of layering. I prefer it to the first process, for the branches of the *Ficus elastica* are not always conveniently situated for layering in the ordinary way.

366. The following description · is taken from *Firminger on Indian Gardening,*—a work I am indebted to for the system :—

" The mode of propagation by Gootee is thus described by Mr.
" Masters, formerly head-gardener in the Calcutta Botanical Gar-
" dens : Select a firm, healthy branch, the wood of which is well
" ripened, and immediately under a leaf-bud take off a small ring
" of bark, about one inch wide. Scrape the woody part well, so
" that none remains. Apply a ball of well-tempered clay ; bind it

"on securely with tow or other soft bandage; make it fast to a stake,
"if necessary; hang a small pot, having a hole in the bottom, just
"over the *gootee*, and supply it with water daily. In a few months
"you will obtain a fine, well-rooted plant. As the fibres are emit-
"ted from the buds that are above the wound, they will descend into
"the ball of earth and form roots. As soon as they are seen pro-
"truding themselves through the bandage, the branch may be cut
"off from the parent tree, and planted where it is intended that it
"should remain. This appears to be the most expeditious method
"of obtaining strong, well-rooted plants, and, at the same time, is
"a sure method of procuring duplicates of any desirable variety.
"Of sixty-five *gootees* made in June, of the *Jonesia Asoca*, the whole
"were well-rooted in October; while of forty-five layers made at the
"same time, and on the same individual tree, none were well-rooted,
"and some only just beginning to form. The *leechee* requires four
"months to form good roots.

"Unless some precaution be taken, the water in the pot above
"the *gootee* will flow out too fast, and very often not fall upon the
"*gootee* at all. To obviate this, therefore, the following contri-
"vance is commonly resorted to:—

"A piece of rope has a knot tied at one end of it; the other
"end is passed within the pot and drawn through the hole at its
"bottom till the knot is brought down to fall upon and close up
"the hole. The rope thus secured by its knotted end within the
"pot is carried on at full stretch, and coiled round the *gootee*.
"By this means the water, when poured into the pot, oozes slowly
"out, trickles down the rope and along the coil, and so distributes
"itself over the whole *gootee*."

367. Propagation by cuttings in the case of the *Ficus elastica* is one of the most simple methods of continuing the species, and may be conducted at nearly all seasons of the year, though, of course, the best time to take cuttings is when the sap is in full motion, cuttings taken between the middle of March and end of April also do well, but more caution is necessary at this season.

368. The cuttings should be selected from wood somewhat ripened, rather than from that still in a stage of formation; and a preference given to the branches nearest the ground, those having always the greatest tendency to throw out roots. Amputation has to be performed with a clean cross cut below an eye or bud, the formation of roots most readily developing there. A loamy soil is, perhaps, the best for striking cuttings, which should be inserted in a slanting direction with not more than two buds exposed above ground; and the leaves allowed to drop off, of their own accord. Excess of moisture must be avoided, which points to the necessity

of eschewing sites tenacious of wet. It must be borne in mind that in this instance, as in all others where vitality is exhausted, excesses have an injurious effect; external appliances must therefore be resorted to in moderation. I extract from the *Magazine of Botany*, volume VIII., page 205, Sir J. Paxton's views regarding the character of plants produced from cuttings. Certainly he refers to shrubs and garden-plants, but his views are equally applicable to tree life in general :—

"In plants where there are two kinds of branches, one sort
" ascending and another branching along the ground like runners
" of strawberries, the difference is much the same as that between
" common shoots and suckers in ordinary shrubs and trees.

" The lower trailing shoots employed for propagation, form
" plants very like those from suckers, healthy, vigorous, and dis-
" posed to occupy a large space, without blooming.

" Cuttings of the upper shoots produce flowering laterals in a
" very short time; and a fine blooming specimen may even be
" raised in one season, by taking off the extremities of the longest
" shoots as cuttings. Indeed, the dimensions and early blooming
" of the plant may be regulated by the distance at which the cut-
" ting is taken from the main stem.

" Cuttings from the extremity flower speedily, and in a dwarf
" condition.

" Cuttings from a shoot in an early stage of its growth will
" constitute larger specimens, and be longer in bearing flowers."

369. I have had no experience in propagating by seed, and therefore give, in an epitomised form, the system advocated by Mr. Officiating Deputy Conservator Mann, in his interesting report on the *caoutchouc* plantation in Assam from where seed might be obtained, and cultivated in this province. Seeds are sown in nursery beds prepared with either broken brick, broken charcoal, or with earth only; although those on the broken brick germinated most freely, those on the charcoal succeeded best in the end ; the plants which germinated on the earth all died, but as this was the result of excess of shade, it cannot be said that the seed if sown on earth only would not produce good plants. The fruit was sown with the same results, except that the young plants came up much thicker. The seedlings form thick tuberous roots which probably enable them to stand the drought better than cuttings.

370. Nursery beds four feet wide and one foot high were made and covered with broken charcoal (about one hundred and ninety maunds to the acre). The germination was satisfactory.

371. At Darjeeling the same modes of sowing were adopted, but the seeds germinated best on the garden soil and worst on the charcoal.

372. Further on, Mr. Mann recommends on the grounds of economy *alone* that seedlings in cane baskets be started in the forks of trees. This would reduce the cost of the plantation, he says (including surveys, formation, conservation, roads, buildings, and salaries), from Rs. 10 to Rs. 5 per acre. He holds, however, that seedlings would succeed just as well if sown on the ground.

373. I would here suggest that the *Platycerum fern*, which abounds throughout our forests, be substituted for the cane baskets, or, rather, that a little seed be sown in the cavity formed between this plant and the tree to which it is attached. Beds of rich vegetable mould might also be tried.

Process of extracting and preparing " caoutchouc" in Burma Proper.

374. *Caoutchouc* is obtained from the *Ficus elastica* either by making incisions through the bark into the wood of the trunk, branches, aërial roots, or roots, and the juice collected in hollow pen-shaped bamboos driven into the lower end of the cut; or the milk is allowed to coalesce round the wound, and subsequently wound off into a ball. The fluid that has been collected in bamboos, is treated in two different ways. The inspissated milk is either reduced to a solid mass by being poured in a thin layer on mats (round which has been raised a clay moulding of about an inch high) which, by exposure to the sun, soon dries, and becomes coherent and elastic; the desired thickness being subsequently obtained by repeated additions of the liquid; or consolidation is brought about by boiling the fresh juice in an iron pan over a slow fire, with its own bulk of water; this prevents the coagulated *caoutchouc* sticking to the sides or bottom of the vessel and becoming burnt. In all three of the above methods, the coagulum on parting with its aqueous portion gradually, by exposure to light and heat, changes to a deep brown colour, and eventually becomes black, although the fluid as first drawn is of the consistency of cream, and of a yellowish white tint.

375. No system is observed in the process of tapping; but vertical, horizontal, and oblique cuts indiscriminately are made with the *dah* of the country all over the tree, varying in distance from one foot to eighteen inches apart. This wasteful practice is not altogether the result of ignorance on the part of the people, for they have a very good idea of the season and age at which different parts of the tree yield the most prolific flow of sap; but since 1872, when Mr. Henri and his party made the discovery already alluded to, the

value of India-rubber has so steadily continued to increase, that the desire for gain, and an improvident spirit has induced the mountaineers to carry on this occupation throughout the year; and it is now by no means an uncommon thing to meet with trees perishing from sheer mutilation. Prior to 1872, when *caoutchouc* was simply used by the highlanders for torches, and water-proof covering to baskets, the *Ficus elastica* was only tapped between the months of December and March, and the operation confined to the higher portions of the trunk and woody branches of mature trees. This system appears correct enough, so far as it goes, and is one that would naturally suggest itself to all familiar with vegetable life; for the season chosen is when the tree is richest in *caoutchouc*; neither does the operation then interfere with, or obstruct the vigorous vegetation of the tree in the hot months, as it would, were the sap withdrawn during the period of rapid growth. No doubt there is ample room for improvement in the method of tapping, *i. e.*, in respect to the position and direction of the incisions, which should be regulated with regard to a *copious flow*, and cicatrization. However, we have still a long time to wait before our trees will be fit for tapping, and as I have not sufficient knowledge from personal experience in this branch of the business, I cannot offer better advice than, that we be guided by the opinion of Mr. Gustav Mann, who has already submitted most valuable reports to the Government of India on the *Ficus elastica* plantations in Assam, of which he has been in charge for some years past.

376. The age of the tree and other circumstances all have their influence in regulating the proportion of *caoutchouc* in the sap, but no reliable information could be obtained as to the yield per annum of mature trees; by some it was computed at fifty-six *viss*, though I am inclined to think fifty pounds would be nearer the mark.

377. Before concluding I will say a few words regarding the preparation of *caoutchouc*, for it often happens that, for want of care in the manufacture of the article, its price falls in the home market, and gains a bad name for the province whence it is exported, although the inferiority is wholly attributable to carelessness on the part of the collectors, who, in this instance, are likewise the manufacturers of the raw material. For *caoutchouc* to realize its highest value, it is not only necessary that it should be free from adulterations and all impurities, but it is of still greater importance that the aqueous portions of the emulsion should be entirely expelled. From what I have, however, seen of the rubber produced in Burma Proper, this last precaution is seldom attended to; the consequence is that, on cutting open the lumps

of *caoutchouc*, they are found either to give off a rank sickening scent, which reduces the value, for the fœtor adheres even to articles manufactured from it; or to present a honey-combed appearance, each cell containing a viscid substance which when brought in contact with the air, decomposes the whole mass, and renders it perfectly useless. Of course, under the present system of collecting *caoutchouc* in Upper Burma, no better results can be looked for; but the fact I wish to establish is, that the inferiority of the article sometimes produced must not be attributed to the unfitness of the climate to the growth of the *Ficus elastica*, but solely to an absence of care in the preparation of *caoutchouc*.

INDEXES.

INDEX.

CHAPTER I.—*Introduction.*

	Para.	Page.
Explanation of delay in publication of report	1	1
Jottings on subjects foreign to object of Mission	2	2
Origin and object of Mission to Upper Burma	3	ib.
Time occupied in voyage from Rangoon to Mandalay	5	3
Particulars of visit to Donabyoo	6	4
Description of scenery, and observations made, between Rangoon and Zaloon	7	ib.
Properties of *Rhizophora mangle* briefly discussed	8	5
Visitation of insects by candlelight	9	ib.
Description of country from north of Myanoung to Prome	10	6
Extensive *toungya* clearings observed. Brief notice of evil effects	11	ib.
Charming views and extensive orchards	12	7
Trees and grasses noted	13	ib.
Rocks first observed	14	8
The town of Prome; review of its population and manufactures	15	ib.
Examination of *Ficus elastica* at Prome	17	9
Station of Thayetmyo	18	12
Visit to Thayetmyo jail, in connection with sericulture	19	ib.
Jail manufacture of ropes and gunny from roselle fibre	20	15
Suitability of roselle and other fibrous plants growing in abundance in the province for this purpose	21	ib.
Reputed medicinal virtues of *Calotropis Hamiltonii*	22	ib.
Data on experimental cultivation of tobacco, cotton, Carolina rice, and sorghum, obtained from Mr. Parrott	23	ib.
Brief notice of Allanmyo	24	16
Meaday to Joungyah	25	17
Agencies of Chinese and Indian firms at Joungyah, and progress to Minhla	26	ib.
Minhla, head-quarters of Governor of Maloon, and fuel station for steamers	27	18
Town of Minhla described	28	ib.
Description of Governor's house	29	19
South end of town allotted to certain class	30	ib.
Success of tamarind cultivation	31	ib.
Description of market and wares	32	ib.
Interpreter "chaffed" by Burmese maidens	33	20
Visit of the "Woon," or Governor	34	ib.
Badge of authority	35	ib.
The "Woon" described	36	ib.
Secretary taking notes	37	21
The Woon purchases a diamond ring. Profit made by broker	38	ib.
Further progress up to the river to Nyoungoo	39	ib.
Mengoon	ib.	ib.
Nyoungoo, and its manufacture of boxes	40	22
Box manufacture described	41	ib.
Plants, scandent shrubs, and epiphytic orchids between Zaloon and Thayetmyo	42	23

	Para.	Page.
Fruit trees	43	23
List of trees	ib.	ib.
Wood fuel *versus* coal discussed	44	24
List of birds	45	ib.

CHAPTER II.

My stay at Mandalay from 4th to 18th December 1873.

	Para.	Page.
Arrival at Mandalay	46	26
Illustration of the unsatisfactory nature of dealing with Mandalay officials, and malpractices of Mint Authorities	47	ib.
Failure to elicit information from a resident of Mandalay	48	27
Incidents of the night, and character of escort	49	ib.
Preparations for landing and attendant circumstances described	50	28
Costume and toilet of Burmese described, and contrasted with that of British Burma	51	ib.
Invitation to put up with the Resident	52	30
What transpired during ride from landing-place to the Residency	53	ib.
Royal granary and summer-house	54	31
Sundry observations on vendors and conversion of timber	55	32
Low price of teak as compared with British Burma	56	ib.
Condition of public works, roads, bridges, &c.	57	ib.
Conservancy arrangements, and Buddhist scruples	58	33
Arrival at the Residency; description of the building, and Burmese system of espionage	59	ib.
Detention of fire-arms by Burmese Customs Authorities	60	ib.
The Rev. J. E. Marks's S. P. G. Mission School	61	34
Introduction to His Majesty the King of Burma, and what transpired on the ride to the palace	62	ib.
Mandalay city briefly described. Also public reception-room in the palace	63	35
The unbooting process	64	ib.
Introduction to the Ministers of State, and attendant circumstances	65	36
The Italian Consul	66	37
Hall of Audience	67	ib.
Ceremony of His Majesty's entrance and exit, and what occurred at the audience	68	38
Cursory description of principal buildings in the enclosure	69	39
Failure to scrutinize the palace grounds	70	40
Return to Residency from the palace	71	ib.
Arts and manufacture in the City	72	41
Weaving	73	ib.
Brass-foundry	74	ib.
Carving and carpentry	75	42
Glass-blowers	76	ib.
The City Market	77	ib.
The hairy family of Burma	78	43
Convicts and their treatment	79	44
Encamping-ground of Shans and Paloungs: their system of trade	80	ib.
Trip to Mengoon in search of *Ficus elastica*	81	45
His Majesty's State Barge, and neglected Steam Saw-mills	82	ib.
Failure to find *Ficus elastica* at Mengoon	83	ib.
Vegetation and ornithology of Mengoon	84	ib.
The Great Pagoda, Mengoon	85	ib.
The Great Bell of Mengoon	86	48
Unusual style of a Pagoda in the neighbourhood of Mengoon	87	ib.
Future plans discussed with Resident for attaining object of Mission	88	49
Receipt of Royal orders to the Governor of Mogoung	89	ib.
Visit to City of Amarapoora	90	50
Population of Amarapoora	91	ib.

	Para.	Page.
Chinese Temple	92	51
Smoking and refreshment parlours in the Temple	93	52
Palo-daugyee pagoda	94	ib.
Temple of Mah-myat-mini	95	ib.
Inability to traverse the eastern road to Amarapoora	96	53
Remains of an indigo factory	97	54
Belt of tamarind	98	ib.
Vegetation observed	99	ib.
Birds and insects	100	ib.

CHAPTER III.

Journey between Mandalay and Bhamo, including return voyage.

	Para.	Page.
Information embodied not of a novel type	101	55
Departure from Mandalay	102	ib.
Objectionable habit of opium-smoking on board	103	ib.
Burmese game of chess described	104	56
Village of Singoo, and navigation of the river	105	58
Intricate navigation on this river	106	59
Entrance to third defile	107	ib.
Rock near Thingadaw the most romantic place in this defile	108	60
Visit to see the tame fish at Thingadaw village	109	ib.
Trees, shrubs, and grasses	110	61
Coal-fields	111	ib.
Natural character of the river	112	ib.
Village of Malee	113	ib.
Shallow state of river	114	ib.
Other trees noticed	115	62
Fuel for steamers	116	ib.
Woman a marketable commodity	ib.	ib.
Teak timber	117	63
Towns of Pagan and Tagoung	118	ib.
Villages of Thingyain and Myalloung	119	64
Burmese crucifix	120	ib.
Shweley river	121	ib.
Town of Katha	122	65
Vegetation	123	ib.
Village of Moda	124	66
Birds observed on banks of river	125	ib.
Arrival at Shwegoo	126	ib.
Funeral obsequies of a hpoongyee at Shwegoo	127	67
First acquaintance with Kakhyens	128	ib.
Intuitive knowledge of Burmese pomology	129	68
Island of Shwegoo entrance to second defile	130	69
Animals seen in second defile	131	70
Manner in which fish are here caught	132	ib.
Scarcity of birds	133	71
Vegetation	134	ib.
Brief history of Tsenkan	135	ib.
Vegetation	136	ib.
Indications of thermometer on the way from Mandalay to Bhamo	137	ib.
Return trip, and change in the weather	138	72

CHAPTER IV.

Bhamo, including a trip to the Kakhyen hills, viâ the Taping river.

	Para.	Page.
Delay in landing	139	73
Mr. Cooper notices certain irregularities of procedure	140	ib.

	Para.	Page.
Bhamo, situation and description of	141	74
The palisade—a protection against raids of wild mountaineers, and its subsequent disrepair	142	ib.
Former elaborate buildings and construction of *khyoungs* and pagodas	143	ib.
Observance of sanitary rules; description of houses, and roads avenued by fruit and ornamental trees	144	75
Means of livelihood among men, and mode of living	145	76
Legal amount of alloy in silver	146	ib.
Industry of women, and system of mattrass-making, detailed	147	ib.
Description and occupation of immigrants from Hotha and Latha valleys	148	77
Detailed account of the Chinese quarters	149	ib.
Governor's private residence and court-house	150	78
Specimen of Burmese ecclesiastical architecture described	151	ib.
Ficus elastica trees	152	79
Detailed description of the Bhamo Residency	153	80
Excursions with Mr. Cooper, and account of the sights	154	81
Conversation of certain Chinese visitors on Christmas day	155	82
Pagoda intended as memorial of Governor's good deeds	156	83
Official visit of the Woon	157	84
National sports of Burma described	158	85
Royal mandate prohibiting collection of *Ficus elastica* sucklings	159	ib.
Mission of Rev. Dr. Mason and his wife	160	86
Arrival of Roman Catholic Priest at Bhamo	161	ib.
Private interview with the Governor	162	87
Subject of my approaching departure	163	88
Governor's visit	164	89
Misconduct of two Peons	165	ib.
Observations on the Kachyens found encamped under a *Ficus elastica* tree	166	ib.
Description of the Kachyens, with their dress and ornaments	167	90
The Tsawbwa of the Latoung hill	168	91
Country surrounding the town	169	92
Account of the Dragon-festival	170	ib.
Account of the Water-festival	171	94
Succession of Captain Cooke to post held by Mr. Cooper	172	ib.
Vegetation—indigenous and cultivated		ib.
Birds		95

SECTION II.

	Para.	Page.
Robbery of cotton	173	ib.
Excursions at Bhamo	174	96
Further examination of the country	175	97
Village of Tamine	176	ib.
Two *Ficus elastica*	177	ib.
Shan village of Sinekau	178	98
Instance of Shans' affection	179	99
Further observations during the excursion	180	ib.
Manloung stream	181	100
Town of Tsain-pin-ago	182	ib.
Return to Tseekaw	183	ib.
Country between Bhamo and Tseekaw	184	111
Village of Tseekaw	185	102
Process of manufacturing *shamshoo*	186	103
Lake of Manloung	187	ib.
Excursion from Tseekaw up the Taping	188	104
Return by land to Tseekaw, and observations during journey	189	105
Catalogue of plants collected during adventures	190	106
Preparations for another excursion	191	107
Start in the direction of old Bhamo, and stay at village Seitket	192	109
Obstructions during the ascent in a north-easterly direction until arrival at Ronclein	193	110

	Para.	Page.
Stay at the picket	194	112
Intimation to the Tsawbwa at Ronelein of my intended visit	195	ib.
Commencement of second ascent and arrival at Ronelein	196	114
Collections of things in the Tswabwa's house	197	116
Interview with the Tswabwa, and description of him	198	117
Manners and customs of these people to be subject of next chapter	199	118
Observations during breakfast	200	ib.
Different growths round the homesteads	201	120
Return to Tseekaw, and ultimate arrival at Bhamo	202	ib.

CHAPTER V.

A DIARY FROM BHAMO TO MUN-TSOUNG (LATITUDE 26°) AND BACK, VIA MOGOUNG ... 121

CHAPTER VI.

GENERAL RECAPTULATION OF ALL FACTS ASSOCIATED WITH THE "FICUS ELASTICA" ... 208

Description : Distribution : Properties.

ERRATA.

CHAPTER I.

Page 5, foot-note *read* "*Geosoriscæ.*"
,, 7, line 12 from the top, *for* "but the" *read* "but that the."
,, 7, line 18 from the bottom, *for* "carica, papaya" *read* "carica papaya."
,, 9, line 7 from the top, *for* "are" *read* "is."
,, 12, line 21 from the top, *for* "detracts and leads," *read* "detract and lead."
,, 12, line 4 from the bottom, *for* "accompanied by" *read* "and."
,, 13, line 14 from the top, *for* "all having" *read* "having."
,, 14, line 9 from the top of foot-note, *for* "from" *read* "frame."
,, 15, line 10 from the top, *for* "would otherwise be" *read* "would otherwise have been."
,, 17, line 6 from the top, *for* "is" *read* "are."
,, 18, line 11 from the bottom, *for* "who" *read* "which."
,, 19, line 6 from the top, *for* "all having" *read* "have."
,, 19, line 11 from the top *for* "depend" *read* "depends."
,, 20, line 7 from the top, *for* "was" *read* "were."
,, 20, line 9 from the top, *for* "grows" *read* "grow."

CHAPTER II.

Page 27, line 9 from bottom, *for* "indifferent" *read* "in different."
,, 29, line 1 from the bottom, *for* "is" *read* "are."
,, 29, line 5 from the top of the foot-note, *for* "contended" *read* "contented."
,, 29, line 3 from the bottom of the foot-note, *for* "black" *read* "slack."
,, 29, line 2 from the bottom of the foot-note, *for* "srought" *read* "brought."
,, 31, lines 12 and 13 from the bottom, *for* "Buettneria" *read* "Büttneria."
,, 32, line 3 from the bottom, *for* "loose" *read* "lose."
,, 49, line 2 from the bottom *for* "governor" *read* "governors."
,, 50, line 8 from the bottom, *for* "ordinance" *read* "ordnance."
,, 50, line 16 from the top, *for* "has" *read* "had."
,, 52, line 25 from the top, *for* "capital" *read* "capitally."

CHAPTER III.

Page 57, line 14 from the top, *for* "squares" *read* "squares noted."
,, 61, line 10 from the top, *for* "Mimosia" *read* "Mimosa."
,, 62, line 10 from the top, *for* "dellenia" *read* "dillenia."
,, 62, line 5 from the top, *for* "depterocarpus" *read* "dipterocarpus."
,, 62, line 14 from the bottom, *for* "partys" *read* "party's."
,, 68, line 1 from the top, *for* "perhaps over" *read* "perhaps not over."
,, 68, line 7 from the top, *for* "was suspended" *read* "were suspended."
,, 68, line 1 from the bottom, *for* "fructiferous for reproductive" *read* "fructiferous reproductive."
,, 71, line 10 from the bottom, place colon after "bamboo."
,, 71, line 6 from the bottom, *for* "has blown steadily" *read* "blew steadily."

CHAPTER IV.

Page 73, line 15 from the bottom, *for* "provided by" *read* "from."
,, 74, line 15 from the bottom, *for* "the defence" *read* "it."
,, 83, line 7 from the bottom, *for* "cost" *read* "coat."
,, 88, line 13 from the top, *for* "Residency's boat" *read* "Residency boat."
,, 88, line 24 from the top, *for* "Day-myo" *read* "Lay-myo."
,, 88, line 1 from the bottom, *for* "was" *read* "were."

ERRATA.

Page 92, line 2 from the bottom, *for* "prevails" *read* "prevail."
„ 94, line 11 from the bottom, *for* "for that officer" *read* "the latter officer."
„ 96, line 6 from the bottom, *for* "was" *read* "were."
„ 99, line 2 from the top, *for* "notice" *read* "noticed."
„ 100, line 18 from the top, *for* "found we" *read* "we found."
„ 101, line 8 from the top, *for* "circumstances" *read* "circumstance."
„ 102, line 7 from the top, *for* "are" *read* "is."
„ 103, line 17 from the bottom, place — after "country."
„ 109, line 20 from the top, *for* "tap" *read* "tape."
„ 109, line 9 from the bottom, *for* "at base" *read* "at the base."
„ 110, line 7 from the bottom, *for* "steps" *read* "step."
„ 114, line 18 from the top, *for* "hill" *read* "hills."
„ 117, line 14 from the bottom, *for* "over the" *read* "our."
„ 117, line 13 from the bottom, *for* "questions" *read* "matters."
„ 117, line 9 from the bottom, *for* "view" *read* "views."
„ 118, line 17 from the bottom, *for* "*våritas*" *read* "*veritas*."
„ 119, line 1 from the top, *for* "spitting" *read* "splitting."
„ 119, line 7 from the top, *for* "which are used as necklets" *read* ("which are used as necklets").
„ 120, line 15 from the bottom, *for* "from when" *read* "whence."

CHAPTER V.

Page 140, line 9 from the top, *for* "who" *read* "which latter."
„ 142, line 5 from the bottom of the foot-note, *for* "criminal" *read* "animal."
„ 147, line 3 from the top of the foot-note, *for* "quantities" *read* "quantity."
„ 152, line 5 from the top, *for* "evidently" *read* "evident."
„ 156, line 2 from the top, *for* "who" *read* "which."
„ 163, line 5 from the bottom, *for* "to-day" *read* "day."
„ 165, line 2 from the top, *for* "is" *read* "are."
„ 186, line 10 from the top, *for* "cubit" *read* "cubic."
„ 197, line 4 from the top, *for* "or" *read* "and."

www.ingramcontent.com/pod-product-compliance
Lightning Source LLC
Chambersburg PA
CBHW031743230426
43669CB00007B/455